EARLY
INTERVENTION

EARLY INTERVENTION

HOW CANADA'S SOCIAL PROGRAMS CAN WORK BETTER, SAVE LIVES, AND OFTEN SAVE MONEY

JAMES HUGHES

JAMES LORIMER & COMPANY LTD., PUBLISHERS
TORONTO

Copyright © 2015 by James Hughes

Notice to educators

This book is available for purchase in print and ebook form. Copies can be purchased from our website at www.lorimer.ca. Copies of individual chapters or portions of the full text in print or digital form are also available for sale at reasonable prices. Contact us for details at rights@lorimer.ca.

The publisher and the author of this work expect that portions of this work will be useful for education, and expect reasonable compensation for this use. This can be readily achieved by arranging to purchase these portions from the publisher. Contrary to the view of university administrators and their legal advisors, it is unlikely that use of a chapter or 10% of this work for educational purposes with no payment to the publisher or author would be found to be fair dealing under the Canadian Copyright Act.

James Lorimer & Company Ltd., Publishers acknowledges the support of the Ontario Arts Council. We acknowledge the financial support of the Government of Canada through the Canada Book Fund for our publishing activities. We acknowledge the support of the Canada Council for the Arts which last year invested $24.3 million in writing and publishing throughout Canada. We acknowledge the Government of Ontario through the Ontario Media Development Corporation's Ontario Book Initiative.

Cover design: Meredith Bangay
Cover image: Shutterstock

Library and Archives Canada Cataloguing in Publication

Hughes, James, 1965-, author
        Early intervention : how Canada's social programs can
work better, save lives, and often save money / James Hughes.

Includes bibliographical references and index.
Issued in print and electronic formats.
ISBN 978-1-4594-0877-7 (pbk.).--ISBN 978-1-4594-0878-4 (epub)

        1. Canada--Social policy--Case studies. 2. Human services--
Canada--Case studies. 3. Social problems--Canada--Case
studies. I. Title.

HN107.H76 2015   361.6'10971   C2015-901404-2
C2015-901405-0

James Lorimer & Company Ltd., Publishers
317 Adelaide Street West, Suite 1002
Toronto, ON, Canada
M5V 1P9
www.lorimer.ca

Printed and bound in Canada.

To the love of my life, Jane Wheeler,
my amazing wife and my partner in all things

CONTENTS

CHAPTER 1

Canada's Social Safety Net: A Snapshot

SIGNS OF THE TIMES

Canada's social safety net is showing its age. Not a day goes by that the media doesn't highlight some problem or other facing the country's health and social services. Reports about Canadians having problems accessing critical services are commonplace. The following, which concerns autism services in Nova Scotia, is only one such example:

> Referrals to a Halifax treatment program for children with autism jumped by 14 per cent this year — forcing some parents to wait nearly a year for treatment. As of Wednesday, the IWK [Health Centre] was treating about 44 kids in its Early Intensive Behaviour Intervention program, while another 90 were on a wait list to get into the program. The intensive therapy is one of the only known effective treatments for autism — and it's time-sensitive — working best on children before they hit school age. Jen Morris has a four-year-old daughter who's waiting to get into EIBI [early intensive behavioural

*intervention] therapy at the IWK. "It's really difficult,
knowing there's something out there for your child and
having to wait," said Morris. Sadie was diagnosed in
November 2013, but Morris was told there wouldn't be
space for her daughter in the program until September
2014.[1]*

Affordable housing is another part of the safety net that is deeply challenged. Here's a September 2014 media report on housing for low-income Ontarians:

*The waiting list for affordable housing in Ontario is now
at a record high, according to a report released today by
the Ontario Non-Profit Housing Association (ONHPA).
According to the report, 165,069 households in the
province are currently waiting for subsidized housing —
the highest since the ONHPA started collecting data in
2003. Sharad Kerur, ONPHA's executive director, says
the number of households on the list started rising during
the recession — and it just keeps going up. "This is one of
the first times we've seen it in a number of years actually
skyrocket," Kerur said. "People's incomes aren't keeping
up with the pace of overall housing costs." Additionally,
Kerur says tenants already in social housing are staying
there longer and the number of new units being built falls
dramatically short of demand.[2]*

Lineups and wait times for services have become common features of the system. Many Canadians have learned to expect them. In the health-care field, a consortium of fourteen medical groups called the Wait Time Alliance had this to say in the introduction to its 2013 annual report: "Despite many good intentions and efforts, Canadians are still waiting too long to access health care. In many regions, medical specialties and practices, no substantial or sustained progress in reducing waits has been achieved in recent years."[3] One group facing the challenge of wait times is seniors with physical or mental impairments. These conditions prevent them from staying at home, so they end up in hospital. André Picard of *The Globe and Mail* wrote a column on this topic in 2011. Here's part:

> *In New Brunswick alone, there are 700 patients living in hospital beds awaiting placement in cheaper, more appropriate care. That is fully one-third of all hospital beds being misused. Why do we tolerate such systemic inefficiency? Why do we tolerate such casual callousness? "It not only costs us all in dollars and cents, it runs counter to our values as Canadians," says Dr. (Jeff) Turnbull [president of the Canadian Medical Association].*[4]

The impact of large numbers of Canadians waiting in hospitals, often for months and years, for alternative-care placement is well-known and documented. It reduces the capacity of the hospital to perform its core emergency, intensive, and acute-care functions. It contributes to perpetually overcrowded hospital emergency rooms, which have become symbolic of a system that is not adapting to the needs of patients. In his blog, *Personal Health Navigator,* Dr. Paul Taylor of Sunnybrook Health Sciences Centre in Toronto, Ontario, explained that overcrowding in the emergency department (ED) is a system-design problem.[5] He cited a recent study of the member countries of the Organisation for Economic Co-operation and Development (OECD), published in the *Canadian Journal of Emergency Medicine,* that placed Canada second-to-last among thirty-four developed nations in terms of the availability of acute-care beds in 2009. "The inability for admitted patients to access in-patient beds from the ED is the most significant factor causing emergency department overcrowding in most busy Canadian hospitals,"[6] the OECD paper concluded.

EDs and hospitals are not the only social institutions facing overcrowding. Homeless shelters are another. In 2013, Toronto city councillor Joe Mihevc called for more emergency shelter capacity in his city. The local Toronto *Metro* filed the following report on the subject:

> *"We have a problem. We don't have enough beds to meet demand," said Councillor Joe Mihevc, the committee's vice-chair. The 172 emergency beds — located in 18 existing shelters — are normally activated to accommodate increased demand during cold weather alerts but can be activated for other purposes, the [City of Toronto Community Development] committee was told. The 3,800-bed, 57-site shelter system is running at 96 per cent of capacity, but Mihevc believes it should be at about 90 per cent to conform to longstanding city policy. The city needs to open an additional 300-bed shelter rather than continue to overcrowd the existing facilities, said John Clarke, of the Ontario Coalition Against Poverty.[7]*

Canadian jails are another milieu where overcrowding occurs. The Auditor General of Canada gave a press conference on the issue in 2014, reported on by the *National Post*:

> *Canada's prisons are so jam-packed with inmates that many are forced to "double-bunk" in shared cells — even though corrections officials recognize this breeds violence and poses a risk to offenders and staff at the facilities. Moreover, although recent construction will resolve the over-crowding in the "short-term," Correctional*

> *Service Canada (CSC) has failed to develop expansion*
> *plans for its penitentiaries to properly take into account*
> *the growing number of inmates, according to a report*
> *released Tuesday by Auditor General Michael Ferguson.*[8]

Some prisons are forced to release prisoners prematurely without having properly prepared them for reintegration into society, especially those with mental illness. A CBC report on the annual meeting of the Canadian Association of Chiefs of Police in August 2013 drew this conclusion: "Too many people who live with mental illness are being released from provincial [correctional] institutions before they're ready, then going on to commit crimes."[9]

The social safety net is challenged to address other problems as well. For example, our country has fared poorly in addressing complex social issues like bullying in schools. A 2012 Harris/Decima poll found that half of all adults in Canada were bullied when they were young and that the problem continues to be widespread.[10] A UNICEF study confirmed that Canada is struggling when it comes to bullying, finding we have the ninth-highest rate of bullying among twenty-nine developed countries.[11]

Mental illness is the same. While it will touch between 10 and 20 per cent of Canadian youth aged twelve to twenty-five, only one in five of these young people will receive any services at all.[12] Canada's youth suicide rate is thus, not surprisingly, the third highest of all industrialized countries.[13]

Even in the poverty file, where Canada has seen tremendous improvements over the last fifty years, the statistics are troubling. A 2013 report on poverty in British Columbia portrays a typical picture: "Child poverty in British Columbia has increased 4.3 per cent since last year's numbers. But the increase is much larger for single mothers, whose poverty rates increased almost 30 per cent in one year to 49.8 per cent, the highest poverty rate for any persons or family type in B.C."[14]

Long wait times for many services, overcrowding in our major social institutions, and a range of troubling social trends are key features of today's social safety net in Canada. These features are not identical across Canada, as some provinces fare better in some areas, while others may have higher track records in other dimensions. However, few places where health and social services not stretched to the breaking point.

THE SOCIAL SAFETY NET

The social safety net has been defined in various ways. The following is an apt description:

> *The social safety net refers to a range of benefits, programs and supports that protect citizens during various life changes that can affect their health. These changes include normal life transitions such as having and raising children, attaining education or employment training, seeking housing, entering the labour force, and reaching retirement. There are also unexpected life events such as having an accident, experiencing family break-ups, becoming unemployed and developing a physical or mental illness or disability that can affect health. The primary way these events threaten health is that they increase economic insecurity and provoke psychological stress, all important determinants of health.[15]*

The net is vast. It encompasses the entire health-care system, the remedial parts of primary, secondary, and post-secondary education, employment insurance, programs for people with disabilities, housing, seniors' pensions, and criminal justice and corrections. It includes child protection, daycares, income security, and homelessness programming.

In Canada, managing and maintaining the social safety net is a governmental responsibility, sometimes federal, sometimes provincial, sometimes both. The social safety net is implemented directly by government (e.g., hospitals are uniformly state-run in Canada) as well as indirectly through governmental funding, regulation, and oversight of independent for-profit or not-for-profit bodies like homeless shelters, nursing homes, and children's aid societies. Programs can be universal in nature (generally where all people are eligible without reference to a specific vulnerability) or targeted (where only specific classes of vulnerable people, e.g., those with low incomes, are entitled to a benefit). The social safety net also comprises government regulations and standards to control activity in the private sector to prevent such odious practices as child labour, employment discrimination, and unfair housing eviction.

Canadian governments are at the centre of and have control over the social safety net. They work with and through myriad partners, professionals, unions, and agents to fulfill their responsibilities, but it is clear and accepted that the federal, provincial, and territorial governments bear the weight of managing the "welfare state," a term first used by Archbishop William Temple in England in 1941[16] and synonymous with the notion of the social safety net.

LATE INTERVENTION

The social safety net has not been adequately adapted to address today's greatest health and social challenges, including chronic illness, dementia, autism, chronic poverty, and homelessness, among others. The queues, overcrowding, wait times, and worrying statistics demonstrate this. These problems result largely from the fact that the existing social safety net operates on a late-intervention principle. This means, as a general rule, that the individual facing difficulties will only get access to state or state-sponsored support after all other recourses and resources to deal with the issue have been exhausted. As the individual or family tries to work through a problem in isolation, the situation (e.g., health condition, addiction, job trouble, family trouble) often deteriorates. When the deterioration reaches a critical stage, the state is usually able to step in and provide support. Sometimes it doesn't step in, even then. The point is that a Canadian or a Canadian family has to fall a long way to be caught by the existing social safety net.

The intention of this book is to make the case that we need a different approach to addressing the health and social challenges Canada is facing. It looks in detail at six different parts of the social safety net and contrasts the status quo approach to each, namely late intervention, against research that shows how a different approach, namely early intervention, holds the promise of producing better results.

The term "early intervention" has been defined many different ways. It is commonly used to describe programs for children up to six years of age. This is not how it will be used in this book. Instead, it will be used more expansively to describe any measure designed to address a potential or emerging problem at the earliest opportunity before it is able to escalate into a graver challenge. As such, early interventions can be designed for any point in the course of a person's life. They can also be deployed across all aspects of the social safety net. Prevention efforts designed to benefit the entire population, such as vaccination programs, are included in this definition as much as interventions of a more targeted nature, such as income supplements for seniors with low incomes.

Early intervention is not an original idea or a new concept. It is an extension of the adage that "an ounce of prevention is worth a pound of cure." What is new in this book is the proposal that early intervention methods be applied across the entire network of health and social services as the system's prime directive. In doing so, I hope this work adds to the important debate about how to reform and reconstruct Canada's care systems in ways that are truly world-class.

STRUCTURE

This book is composed of nine chapters. This first chapter discusses the purpose of the book, namely to articulate an alternative vision for Canada's social safety net, and describes the professional experiences that have led me to research and write the book. Chapter 2 contains a brief history of Canada's social safety net and my view on how it came to be developed as a late-intervention system.

Chapters 3 to 8 are each about one particular component of the social safety net. These components are child protection, autism, schools and bullying, health, poverty, and homelessness. In each chapter, a representative individual or family is described in some detail to put a human face and a real-life experience at the centre of the challenge being addressed. Each chapter, too, presents an important researcher who has explored and implemented a new approach to addressing the challenge and whose work is now widely recognized. The six areas have been selected from my direct experience or interest in those fields. However, any number of other areas could have just as easily been chosen, given how widely the field of early intervention research has started to extend. The six selected areas should, therefore, be read as only a few examples of the applicability of early intervention concepts.

Finally, Chapter 9 concludes the work with an analysis of the implications of the research for the system as a whole. It also discusses the range of methods that might be deployed to commence a wholesale redesign of the social safety net along the lines of early intervention.

ORIGINS

I've spent my adult life around the social services, but it was while running Montreal's Old Brewery Mission that the ideas in this book started to ferment. The Old Brewery Mission, the largest organization in Quebec serving homeless men and women, was founded in 1889 by a pair of well-to-do Methodist women, fired-up by the Social Gospel movement, who wanted to provide shelter to the city's homeless alcoholic men. This aging and largely forgotten group, having nowhere else to rest their heads, congregated at an abandoned brewery that the men nicknamed the "old brewery." The name stuck.

Fast forward to the twenty-first century, and the Old Brewery, now a large not-for-profit organization managing a multi-million-dollar budget, numerous buildings, and a unionized staff, continues to provide support to the lonely and the sick. The difference in 120 years is the stunning increase in the number and variety of people needing a bed, a hot shower, and a meal. The number of clients the Old Brewery serves has been increasing steadily since the mid-1990s; the figure now stands at more than 4,000.[17] Most are living with mental-health challenges, a great many are addicted to alcohol and drugs, and all are living in poverty.

Interestingly, the state provides significant funding to the Old Brewery, though it remains mostly privately funded through individual, corporate, and philanthropic donations. It is, therefore, to some extent, the government's agent in terms of dealing with Montreal's most distraught. When I think of the kind of people the Old Brewery Mission serves, I think of André. When I was working at the Old Brewery, André, a middle-aged man with schizophrenia, did a daily afternoon walk around the organization's main building on Saint-Laurent Boulevard. These walks were characterized, unfortunately, by André's psychotic symptoms, namely angry rants and screaming obscenities at pedestrians. When not at the Old Brewery, André spent most of his time wandering the streets or resting in the emergency room of the nearby Saint-Luc Hospital. I also think of another resident of the Old Brewery, a woman named Rosemarie, who smoked outside the organization's women's pavilion on de Maisonneuve Boulevard, wondering if she'd ever get to see her young children again. She called the social worker every day, filed extensive legal proceedings to regain access to her kids, and roamed the streets roiling in equal parts anger and shame.

CROSSROADS

The Old Brewery, like most homeless shelters in Canada, the United States, and Europe, is a veritable crossroads of people who have fallen way off the wire of their lives, and the only net that detered the plummet was a partially state-funded private charitable organization doing its best to help them get through the day. How did it come to this?

The roads to homelessness are many, and each person who sleeps on the street or in a shelter has a different story. However, homelessness does not usually happen overnight. The deterioration of a person's status, relationships, well-being, and opportunities is usually a gradual process, though the occasional sudden drop in fortune is common. As well, each journey includes encounters, usually very frequent, with government agencies created to support those in need, in trouble, or at risk. To work at a homeless shelter is to see and hear, upfront and regularly, how these other agencies were unable to assist and, ultimately, prevent the often-ugly descent into total loss.

Homeless people have usually lost everything, including money, jobs, families and friends, and health. To be homeless is, therefore, to have fallen through the cracks in the state infrastructure responsible for preventing poverty, educating and training the workforce, assisting families to overcome challenges, and delivering timely and pertinent health-care services. All of these failures of the organs of state to intervene and help are on display at the shelter.

The emergency homeless shelter is, ultimately, akin to the ocean fed by these rivers of system breakdown. We place such reliance on shelters because the systems that met, touched, and attempted to address the individual's or family's needs in the first place are porous. Too many clients slip through because the services are not designed to catch all the people they come into contact with. Their mandates and skill sets are too limited to manage the need. So clients fall, further and further, from the dreams and hopes they set for themselves. And the state, in failing to provide its agents with the mandate and means to assist people in the early stages of distress, wastes vast amounts of resources inadequately addressing the problem when it escalates.

It must be said that these are system failures, not failures of individuals; in general, Canada's helping class is nothing less than heroic, given the limitations placed on its functions. It is, therefore, the responsibility of the government to help pay for the services of homeless shelters like the Old Brewery, as it is the very ineffectiveness of its other agents that, to a large extent, has produced a homeless clientele in the first place.

While the Old Brewery has implemented an array of wildly successful, award-winning programs to help its clientele get out of homelessness permanently, the state system within shelters operate has been deadly slow in arming itself to prevent homelessness from occurring in the first place. And when clients do fall through the cracks, they are failed again by a homelessness service sector not adequately equipped to help its clients quickly into permanent housing.

While I could see so many of the problems during my time at the Old Brewery, systemic solutions were elusive.

NEW DIRECTIONS

My stay in New Brunswick's civil service gave me the opportunity to see the operation of the social safety net from on high. From this vantage point, I was offered the chance to see and participate in the fundamental renewal of one important component of the safety net, child protection.

Until the 2008-09 child-protection reform in New Brunswick, the system emphasized intervention in families and households where there was clear evidence of child abuse, neglect, or a serious risk of one or the other. Its main tools were removing the child(ren) from the home, court proceedings, and group homes or foster care. The province's Department of Social Development staff and resources were mostly focused on identifying these "code red" situations and intervening to avoid disaster.

The reform measures, collectively called New Directions in Child Welfare, changed the existing legislation in order to invest in social workers hired and trained in early intervention. Instead of waiting until a family's situation was dire, the new cadre of social workers, called family enhancement workers, would begin working with families at the first sign of trouble in order to reduce the number of code red cases. They use a variety of techniques (described in Chapter 3) to identify the problems, offer options to address them, and act as proactive partners in keeping the family together to the extent it's possible.

Within a year of implementing the New Directions, the department started to see results. The number of families from whom children were removed went down by 20 per cent, and with it came a drop in the government costs to litigate the removal of the children and to provide care for them in a group home or foster setting Theses cost savings exceeded the investments in new family enhancement workers and other early intervention measures. The parents were better off, the children were better off, and the government saved money. Early intervention in child protection turned out to be both morally right and financially smart.

New Directions was particularly innovative and even risky because it was based on the idea that code red families were not the only priority clientele the department needed to deal with. Families in the early stages of conflict were not left to sort out their emerging problems alone.

Was early intervention potentially applicable with the same results across the entire social safety net? The basic intent of this book is to discuss and answer this very question.

CHAPTER 2

The Development of Canada's Social Safety Net

RELUCTANT WELFARISM

In pre-industrial Canada, the extended family was largely responsible for ensuring life and limb of family members in need. Following Confederation, Canada was essentially an agrarian country, with only 25 per cent of its population of four and a half million living in cities as of 1881.[1] The new country was based on a very strong sense of individualism and private charity. Calls for the state to do more for the poor and the wayward were few. This value set dominated the character of governments for decades and impacts it still to this day. On the topic of the prevailing view of the individual at that time, Canadian health policy expert Professor Dennis Raphael of York University had this to say:

> With the rise of 19th century liberalism, poverty was seen
> as a failure of the individual to cope with the economic
> and social system. Providing relief to the "able bodied"
> would lead to undesirable behaviours of laziness and sloth
> in those who received it.[2]

Even so, the forces of industrialization and urbanization began to have an impact. As the Canadian population began to move increasingly into cities in the late 1800s and into mechanized work, class consciousness and the Canadian union movement were born. Highly publicized workplace accidents and loss of life led union representatives to call for better monitoring of workplaces and protection of workers. These calls, in turn, led to the establishment of workers' compensation legislation in many provinces in the 1890s, representing among the very first of the state's modern powers to relieve suffering. However, it was employers and employees who paid the tab, not the government.

These early expressions of state concern for vulnerable citizens were what one Canadian social historian called "reluctant welfarism."[3] The state continued to rely mainly on families and the private sector to manage the plight of the young, poor, sick, and unemployable through private charitable undertakings like schools, hospitals, settlement houses, training agencies, and homeless shelters (e.g., the Old Brewery, the Fred Victor Mission in Toronto, and the Salvation Army scattered throughout the country, all of which received no governmental funding at the time). In the laissez faire days of economic industrialization, the state maintained what Professor Dennis Guest called a "residual" role in providing social security to Canadian citizens, leaving the primary role to the private sector.[4]

Even the progressive-minded Old Age Pension scheme enacted by the Mackenzie King government in 1927, a means-tested program implemented as a federal transfer to the provinces, enshrined these values of residualism by allowing provinces to deny financial assistance to the elderly who had working adult children, presuming they were providing direct support to their aging parents even if such was not, in fact, the case.[5]

Politicians were reluctant to be proactive on the social front, for moral and financial reasons. Morally, they felt individuals and families should be the first responders when problems arose. Financially, they had other priorities (roads, bridges, dams, canals, railroads, and sewage)[6] and wanted to keeps their books balanced. So when they did act to support the needy, it was only for those facing tragedy with no other place to turn. This response satisfied both their moral reluctance and limited their financial exposure as assistance was reserved for only those in the most dire straits. This pattern would repeat itself over and over throughout the decades ahead.

THE DEPRESSION AND SECOND WORLD WAR

The Great Depression firmly cemented in the minds and hearts of Canadians the need for a stronger set of protections to prevent misery, hunger, and even death due to changing economic cycles. Professor Dennis Raphael has said, "It was only when recessions and depressions swelled the ranks of the unemployed that higher levels of government stepped in."[7] They stepped in cautiously, providing relief only to those in greatest need. In *The Great Depression: 1929–1939*, Pierre Berton pilloried the presiding Conservative government in this way: "Balancing the budget was more important than feeding the hungry. The bogey of the deficit was enlisted to tighten the purse strings."[8]

If the Depression created the moral foundation for a more activist, though cautious, political role in protecting the poor and vulnerable, the Second World War created the economic circumstances for change.[9] The requirements of the war in terms of manpower and resources had a massive impact on employment, which was managed somewhat wage and price controls. These developments dealt the working population, in general, and the labour movement, specifically, strong hands to push for reform. The Cooperative Commonwealth Federation (CCF) became the Official Opposition in Ontario in 1943 and, under the leadership of Tommy Douglas, was elected to govern Saskatchewan in 1944. Liberal Prime Minister Mackenzie King saw the ascension of the Labour Party in the United Kingdom and the successes of the CCF in Canada and knew he had to give an answer to the bourgeoning calls for better protections and programs for the lower and middle classes.

King had successfully brought the country's first unemployment insurance scheme into effect in 1940, following a Supreme Court reference and an agreement with all ten provinces. However, the *Unemployment Insurance Act* was a legislative framework creating benefits largely funded by employers and employees (though the federal government did assume the risk of making the federally managed fund whole in the event it was underfunded). The initial legislation was very narrow, covering only 42 per cent of the Canadian working population and conferring no benefits on employees leaving work due to illness, injury, or pregnancy. Interestingly, a contributing employee was disqualified from receiving benefits if he or she had participated in a work stoppage.[10]

As he himself had done on Old Age Pensions in the 1920s and Conservative Prime Minister Bennett had enacted on relief payments in the 1930s, King was careful in going too far. Leonard Marsh, Director of Social Research at McGill University, was appointed to lead the research efforts of a federal government advisory committee on post-war social reconstruction. Marsh, who emigrated to Canada in 1930, was a British-born graduate of the London School of Economics and had worked for several years under Sir William Beveridge, the left-leaning architect of the British welfare state programs aggressively introduced by the Labour government after the Second World War. In his *Report on Social Security for Canada*, released to the Canadian Parliament in February 1943, Marsh proposed the aggressive rollout of a centralized system of social programs. In *Policy Options* in 2004, Antonia Maioni described what has come to be called the Marsh Report in the following way:

> *Drafted in less than one month in January 1943, this extraordinary document mapped out a dense and detailed plan for comprehensive social programs, constructed around the ideal of a social minimum and the eradication of poverty. The realization of*

*this ideal, according to Marsh, meant the recognition
that individual risks were part of modern industrial
society, and that they could be met by collective benefits
throughout the lifecycle. Full employment at a living
wage would be the engine for this vision, supplemented
by occupational readjustment programs. "Employment
risks" were to be met through income-maintenance
programs, such as unemployment insurance and
assistance, accident and disability benefits, plus paid
maternity leave (a proposal definitely ahead of its time).
"Universal risks" were addressed through national health
insurance, children's allowances, and pensions for old age,
permanent disability, and widows and orphans.[11]*

Marsh had previously done extensive research on the impacts of the
Depression and was convinced a dramatically different approach was
necessary to prevent its recurrence. However, it wasn't to be. Maioni said
this of the denouement of the committee's work:

*Despite its "intellectual and symbolic" weight, historians
Bothwell, Drummond and English remind us that the
content and provenance of Marsh's report were enough
to generate a great deal of hostility, not to mention
embarrassment, on the part of Mackenzie King and his
Liberal cabinet.[12]*

Against the recommendations of the committee, King enacted only
one significant social welfare program, namely the 1945 universal Family
Allowance (the "baby bonus") for all Canadian parents, regardless of
income. Caution had prevailed.

GOLDEN AGE

Some positive social reforms were enacted in the 1950s, including eliminating the means test on Old Age Pensions (making it a universally accessible benefit for Canadians at the age of seventy), introducing provincial hospital insurance schemes, and improving federal funding to the provinces for hospital services. However, it wasn't until the 1960s that determined expansion of the social safety net took place.

The NDP government's introduction of universal medical coverage in Saskatchewan on July 1, 1962, which followed a decade of hostile debate with the province's physicians (including a doctor's strike) signalled the beginning of an era of reform.

The Pearson Liberals, in vulnerable minority governments from 1963 to 1968 and facing pressure from Quebec's "revolution tranquille" with its "Maîtres Chez Nous" agenda, acted with purpose to enact a number of seismic changes to the Canada's social safety net. It created the Guaranteed Income Supplement for poor Canadian seniors; launched the Canada Pension Plan; lowered the minimum age for eligibility for old-age assistance from 70 to 65; passed the *National Housing Act,* providing low-interest loans to provinces for constructing public housing; began funding universities through federal-provincial transfer agreements; and created the Canada Assistance Plan to cost-share provincial social and health services.

Most notably, it put into place a national medical insurance program modelled on the Saskatchewan regime. The contentious medicare legislation introduced by Liberal Health and Welfare minister Allan MacEachan was supported by the NDP, and the historic legislation came into force on July 1, 1968, providing coverage for primary care and hospital services for all Canadians. However, the legislation didn't go as far as the recommendations of the Royal Commission on Health Services under Justice Emmett Hall, which had urged the federal government to include home care, pharmacare, and dental care as insured services.[13]

Despite these omissions, medicare signalled the golden age in terms of the country's social development, and to an extent, it fulfilled the Marsh Report recommendations. Social policy historian Allan Moscovitch described this muscular period in the development of Canada's social safety net as follows:

> By the end of the Pearson years, therefore, the essentials
> of the Canadian welfare state were in place. The total
> package, coupled with Unemployment Insurance
> amendments in 1971 and Family Allowances in 1972, led
> to rapidly increasing social expenditure. Including social
> welfare, health and education, they grew from 4% of
> GNP in 1946 to 15% by the mid-1970s.[14]

It would be the only time in Canadian history when deep reform trumped caution.[15] The Pearson Liberals enacted universal programs that covered entire classes of people instead of just those in the greatest need. This same progressiveness infected the provinces. Legislation and resources for child protection, social assistance, residential care for seniors, and public housing for people on low income were all put in place across the ten jurisdictions in more or less similar forms, in large part due to the generosity of federal transfers that funded these provincial health and social services.

DEFICIT FIGHTING

While the Trudeau Liberals made improvements to unemployment insurance and family allowances in the early 1970s, the economic recession from 1974 to 1978 caused the government to curtail further expansion of the social safety net. Caution had returned. Progress stopped in the 1980s as the deficit-fighting Mulroney government clawed back Old Age Security. Social security went into decline in the early 1990s when the Liberal Party returned to power. Facing difficult recessionary times and a significant annual deficit, the Chretien government eliminated the *Affordable Housing Act* that had helped provinces fund low-cost housing for almost forty years, slashed transfers to provinces for both post-secondary education and welfare, and decreased employment insurance benefits. One outcome was the surge in homelessness across the country.[16]

The economic expansion from the mid-1990s to 2008 altered the governing Liberals' approach. The much-improved economic conditions in first decade of the twenty-first, combined with strong and vociferous calls by the provinces for reinvestment in social programs, gave spending impetus to the Chretien and Martin Liberal governments. They proceeded to significantly increase transfer payments to the provinces for health services in 2004; reenacted the federal *Affordable Housing Act*; offered marginal improvements to provincial transfers; and introduced a national daycare program, the Millennium Scholarship Fund, and an anti-homelessness initiative. These combined measures largely returned the level of federal social spending as a percentage of GDP to what it had been in 1993, when the first Chretien government came to power.[17] They succeeded, somewhat, in rebuilding the safety net they had tattered in the '90s.

Though often criticized for a disinterest in all things social, the Harper Conservatives, elected with a minority government in 2006, have been disinclined to repeat the slash-and-burn practices of the governing Liberals in the 1990s, despite the economic downturn in 2008.[18] Nor did the take any determined measures to significantly improve federal social programs or provincial transfers once the economy turned around in approximately 2010–11. Indeed, in true Bennett–Mackenzie King form, the Conservative government stipulated in 2011 that any growth in the Canadian Health Transfer would be limited by growth of the economy.[19]

These policies and practices have not trickled but poured down to provincial capitals dependent on the federal treasury. Provincial governments, from the mid-1970s to today, have limited the growth of social programs in general (except for hospital-based health care and, more recently, residential services for seniors with low incomes) by becoming adept at modulating eligibility requirements and benefits with an eye on controlling spending and promoting economic attachment to the workforce by employment or self-employment. Quebec's welfare laws, for example, were amended early in the first decade of the twenty-first century to create a new category for youth in order to make training requirements a condition of receiving benefits.[20]

CAUTION

Throughout the development of the social safety net in Canada, politicians have been generally careful and cautious about going too far and too fast. According to Professor Moscovitch, the process by which it was knitted together was a "disjointed one" and invented "piece by piece."[21] New programs and announcements have been generally tailored to balance the needs of the economy against the needs of people at risk.[22] Politicians have consistently had an eye to at least two constituencies in moving the safety net forward or backward: one that advocates for improvements to the safety net and another that fears overspending and overextending. Spending on reinforcing the safety net, while potentially generating a political advantage, may concurrently create an image of the government as profligate and irresponsible. It's an ongoing political trade-off. Caution is the by-product.

Caution means most social safety net programs get targeted to those in greatest need to the exclusion of those having less-urgent needs. Resources get directed to those areas where there is a chance of saving people from death or serious injury, like hospitals and high-risk child-protection programs, and not into areas where the risks are lower. By allocating limited resources to high-needs clients, the system's overseers are able to confirm their commitment to needy Canadians, limit the risk of being blamed in the media should a catastrophic event occur, and keep the cost of managing the safety net to a minimum.

This approach to shaping social programs has the added benefit of appearing to avoid waste in public finances. Over the long years of developing our social programs, governments of both stripes have shared a deep-seated fear of being perceived as spending tax revenue unjustifiably and inappropriately. A general approach of spending on those in the greatest need minimizes the risk of such a perception.

This minimalist approach has ultimately led to the practice of late intervention across the social safety net. Manifestly needy, vulnerable, or sick people generally don't start out that way. In the early stages of a difficulty, there is usually little threat that serious harm will occur. The state has largely closed its eyes to individuals and families facing low-risk or non-emergency situations. It is only when the threat rises to a crescendo that the state has felt compelled to act. A late-intervention signature across the social safety net emerged from this political reality and administrative logic.

Additionally, I believe this model of intervening only as a last resort has been preserved in part by a set of values that lies deep in our country's history and that continues to unconsciously guide many holding the reins of political power; namely, that the individual and the family primarily are responsible for dealing with problems when they arise. Engrained in Canadian social policy is the expectation that an individual or family facing financial difficulty will rely on its own assets to try to turn the corner until those assets are exhausted. It is expected that parents, grandparents, siblings, and other family members will intervene to help resolve problems. As we've seen, since pre-Confederation days, the idea of self-reliance has been factored into the architecture of Canadian social programs, and that continues to this day. Though it often goes unstated, social policy-making to this day embeds the sometimes-perverse ethic that the state should not intervene too early and thereby deny the individual or the family the restorative benefits of resolving problems for themselves. It is only when the individual and family are clearly unable to deal with the prevailing issue, whether it be money, housing, a disability, or an aging relative, that it becomes appropriate for the state to begin considering a role for itself.

In sum, with certain exceptions, notably the golden age of the 1960s, the social safety net in Canada was built to minimize political risk, limit financial exposure, avoid waste, and rely on the individual and family first to manage the problem in question. The result is a welfare state that prioritizes those with the greatest need, who, by definition, are usually those in crisis or requiring emergency services. Consequently, the state prioritizes spending resources on, for example, rescuing children from child abuse, assisting persons who have depleted all their worldly wealth, and expanding the capacity of ERs and homeless shelters. The state has largely refrained from considering the alternative approach to the development of the social safety net, namely that of early intervention.

THE CHALLENGE

The challenge I face is to show that early intervention can produce better outcomes for Canadians in need, while at the same time limiting the political and financial risk governments may face in changing the prime directive for the design and implementation of health and social programs. In other words, I must show that the deep-seated caution that animates the development of Canadian social policy can be set aside because early intervention approaches across the social safety net can improve the well-being of vulnerable Canadians and, over time, improve, not undermine, state finances.

While this challenge is policy-based in nature, it is not intended to be theoretical by any means. This is why in every chapter, I make sure the ideas encapsulated in the book are grounded tangibly in the lives of real Canadians. André and Rosemarie, introduced in Chapter 1, are real people. A system of late intervention put them and thousands of others like them in the Old Brewery Mission homeless facilities. Could a system of early intervention have averted their descent into homelessness with its attendant financial costs?

You're also about to read the Bilerman family's story and their journey through the health system; about Juanita Black's travels into and out of poverty; Reena Virk's tragic encounter with bullying; Pete Montour's multiple visits with a plethora of social systems; and others. They have primary, not secondary, roles in this book. Their lives are the settings in which the central question of this book is asked, namely whether early intervention is a more effective operating principle for Canada's social safety net, in both moral and financial terms, than the existing late-intervention system.

CHAPTER 3

Safer Child Protection

THE LANDSCAPE

Child abuse and neglect in Canada has a long and undistinguished record. As of 1998, the Public Health Agency of Canada started to systematically gather and publish statistics on child protection, including cases investigated, substantiated cases, and cases in which the child or children in question were removed from the household. Here's the landscape Public Health paints.

In 2008, 235,842 cases of child maltreatment were investigated across Canada. This means that about forty children out of every thousand are deemed by child-protection services to be at risk.[1] Three-quarters of these investigations concerned possible incidents of abuse or neglect that may have already occurred, while a quarter related to the risk of future harm. Here's the most important statistic. Thirty-six per cent of the investigations turned out to be substantiated (85,440 cases). In other words, in 2008, fourteen kids out of a thousand were actually in danger or at risk. This is an underestimate of the actual number of children needing protection because many cases go unreported.[2]

In 1998, only 135,261 investigations were conducted by Canadian provinces and territories, which have responsibility for child protection.[3] This represents almost a doubling of investigations over the ten-year period from 1998 to 2008. The authors of the Public Health Agency report suggest a number of reasons for this increase, including changes in public and professional awareness of the problem, changes in legislation, and an increase in actual cases of maltreatment. Whatever the reason, provinces and territories have increased their capacity to respond to incidents of actual or potential risk by significantly boosting their spending. Spending in Canada's most populous province, Ontario, is indicative of what is happening across the country. Ontario government allocations in child protection went up more than 100 per cent over this period, and the number of staff serving children needing protection increased by 77 per cent.[4]

It's interesting to look more specifically at how all these new tax dollars were spent. Again, in Ontario, in addition to the big increase in investigations, the number of children removed from their families went up by almost 50 per cent, and the average number of days these kids spent in some form of foster care was up by a third.[5]

The same trends are taking place in the United States. There, more than three million children were investigated in 2012 (more than ten times the number in Canada). In approximately one-fifth of these cases, the children were found to have been abused.[6] Twenty per cent of those children who were found to have been abused were placed in foster care, where they stayed an average of two years. About 60 per cent of children in care eventually return home, while 15 per cent are adopted and the rest linger in the system until they age-out at eighteen years old.[7]

This data is telling us that governments, though spending more money on child protection, are not spending it any differently than they have in the last few decades. Provinces and territories seem generally content to keep a close eye on families, through their increased investigative capacity, when they receive reports of actual or potential neglect or abuse. And, in the event that the case is substantiated, they will intervene aggressively, often by removing the child from the home environment.

CHILD PROTECTION OVER THE YEARS

Once seen and treated as property in the nineteenth century, children are now considered persons with rights to whom society owes a debt of care and nurturing. Canada's original children's aid society was created in 1893 in Toronto, and Ontario enacted the first-ever child-protection legislation in the country soon after, in 1888.[8] This seminal legislation made the abuse of a child a criminal offence for the first time in Canada. Child-protection services have also progressed enormously from these early days. Beginning in the 1960s and early 1970s, professional social work began replacing volunteer, charitable, and religious control of orphaned, abused, or neglected children. Like all parts of the welfare state that have emerged over the last seventy years, child-protection services have become largely the responsibility of the government, often through the children's aid societies it funds and regulates.

Today, Canadian child-protection law emphasizes and prioritizes the protection of the child's "best interest." This concept has received a massive amount of attention in academia and the courts.[9] The legal responsibility to protect children's best interests, combined with many highly mediatized, mind-numbing stories of child abuse or neglect, have considerably reduced the provincial governments' tolerance for permitting children to endure risk.[10] This political sensitivity and risk aversion are key factors that have led governments to raise provincial and territorial child-protection budgets and establish increasingly precise standards regulating what its social workers must do under any given circumstance.

The rules governing when and how someone may enter a family's private home and private life to protect a child have become increasingly sophisticated over the decades. Safety and risk-assessment tools and techniques have been developed within the last twenty-five or so years to help social workers judge not only the intensity of the threat to the child under investigation, but also the course of action that should be taken. According to Linda Graff, risk management involves "identifying and assessing all potential sources of harm, and taking steps to decrease the likelihood that harm will occur."[11]

Social workers consider a wide number of factors in their assessment and include everything from dress, cleanliness of the house, punctuality for school, appointments (including with child protection), health, substance use and misuse by parents and children, eating patterns, financial matters, and many others. In our present-day model of child protection, we defer to the professional social workers to assess the risk. And they are trained to ratchet up their presence the greater and more frequent the problems.

The higher the present and future risk in relation to the assessment factors, the greater the likelihood the child will be removed from the family. The lower the risk, the greater the probability the family will be allowed to retain the child in its care (often with conditions).

Although safety and risk-assessment approaches vary, from ones that give wide decision-making discretion to social workers to ones that severely limit their authority (often through the use of computer algorithms), they all share the characteristic: the intervention is intensified as the risk of immediate harm to the child increases.

The logic of this objective and systemic approach would appear to be sound and defensible. Indeed, it is this same logic that drives the entire social safety net. The principle that animates this distribution of resources is proportionality. Proportionality is a category of fairness that is deeply ingrained within us and crosses all fields of public services. Not surprisingly, proportionality has justified the spending of the highest proportion of public resources in on situations presenting the highest risk to a child. Conversely, proportionality has limited the availability of spending, training, staffing, and tools in child-protection cases assessed as low risk. Proportionality is the basis for weighting the system in such a way that the social workers who maintain it have many more resources, training, and tools to intervene in dangerous situations than in situations that are not overly dangerous at present but may become dangerous in the future. It is balanced entirely on intervening late in a family's breakdown, not early when its challenges are developing.

Removing a child from the care of a parent is the capital punishment of the child-protection system. It occurs only in situations of high risk. This is when the full array of government power comes to bear on a family with the intent of protecting the child. If the child is in immediate danger, the social worker alone (with a supervisor's agreement) can remove the child from the home. A court order is generally required to confirm the decision. Depending on the local rules and regulations, the child may then be placed in a group home, a foster home, or in the care of a relative of the child (called "kinship care" or just "kin care"). Placement in any of these situations is always a temporary measure until such time as the child is either reunited with one or both of the parents or legally adopted through the province's adoption program (which is a component of the child welfare system). A child can be moved from one temporary placement to another, and placements can often last for years.

PHOENIX SINCLAIR AND THE DANGERS OF PROPORTIONALITY

The case of young Phoenix Sinclair of Fisher River Cree Nation in Manitoba is an example of why a child-protection system based on proportionality can have the perverse effect of increasing the danger a child may face as opposed to diminishing it. This was a highly publicized child-protection case that was the subject of a provincial commission of inquiry. As such, the record is in the public domain and includes a detailed description of the facts of the case, as well as how the existing system functions. It, therefore, provides a setting to explore both the weaknesses of the existing system and the merits of one based instead on early intervention techniques.

Phoenix was born on April 23, 2000, to parents who immediately acknowledged themselves unready financially or emotionally for parenthood and gave the child over to the province of Manitoba for care. Phoenix's mother, Samantha Kematch, had an exceptionally challenging childhood herself, having grown up in an abusive household. She had her first child at age sixteen and committed a number of violent acts warranting criminal charges. In fact, in her youth, Kematch was taken away from her parents and placed in foster care by the Manitoba government, as was Phoenix's father, Steve Sinclair. When Phoenix was born, hospital staff noted that her parents had done nothing to prepare for the baby's arrival, had taken no prenatal training, and "confessed to having no plan for what to do about the child."[12]

Thus, like her mother and father before her and her half-brother born two years previously, Phoenix was removed temporarily from the parents' care, at less than one week old.

While Kematch always appeared ambivalent toward being a mother, Phoenix's father seemed to be capable of providing some level of parental care, according to the attending social workers. Because he acted in a determined way to care for his daughter, Manitoba Child Protection Services agreed to give Phoenix back to the parents under a three-month temporary order of guardianship. To prepare for this renewal of contact, Sinclair enrolled in parenting classes and asked for, but did not receive, help searching for a job, setting up daycare for Phoenix, and finding a pediatrician. These latter requests were not part of the basket of services available to parents in the Manitoba child protection system.

In September 2000, Phoenix was, in fact, returned to her parents, and a follow-up visit by the social worker determined the baby to be in good health. However, several months later, the parents split up, and full custody of Phoenix and her newborn sister, Echo, were given, with the mother's consent, to the father, Steve Sinclair.[13] In March 2002, following its own standard procedure, the government closed its child-protection file on Phoenix due to the absence of reported incidents. A year later, social services reopened the case after Phoenix was hospitalized with Styrofoam stuck in her nose. Phoenix was then removed from the father's care with his voluntary consent and put under the supervision of foster parents when it became clear he had a drug and alcohol problem.

The foster parents were friends of Steve Sinclair. The placement of Phoenix in their care was seen favourably by the child-protection authorities because they had already been heavily involved in helping her father with her care. Phoenix's birth mother, Samantha Kematch, who was now back in the picture, agreed with this arrangement. However, in May 2004, Kematch took Phoenix back into her own care, as was her right as the mother of a child being fostered in a voluntary care arrangement. After a successful site visit by a social worker a month later, child-protection services closed its file for the second time.

In December of that same year, social workers were advised that Kematch and her boyfriend, Karl McKay, had had a child together. The department made no follow-up on Phoenix, failed to do a background check on McKay, and the file remained closed until March of 2005, when the case was mysteriously reopened, then reclosed, in the space of about forty-eight hours. Tragically, Phoenix Sinclair died in June 2005; however, child-protection services only discovered she was missing in March 2006. Criminal investigations, public inquiries, and internal investigations were launched. Samantha Kematch and Karl McKay were convicted of first-degree murder in 2008.

In April 2013, CBC reported that a public inquiry into Phoenix's death revealed that "social workers sometimes lost track of who had care of the girl, failed to monitor the family and closed Phoenix's file without seeing her."[14] They also failed to investigate the violent background of Karl McKay in 2014, when they learned he was living with Kematch. When asked why he thought it took so long for anyone to realize Phoenix was missing, the RCMP investigator said it was because McKay and Kematch were very deceptive and they moved around a lot, which created jurisdictional issues for authorities.

Writing about the case in the *National Post* in 2012, Christie Blatchford said this: "As the complete documents aren't yet exhibits, it isn't known what the rationale was for the 'open/close' [in March 2005] or what happened to what appears to have been the final opportunity for Phoenix to have been rescued from the basement pen where Kematch and McKay kept her."[15] The public inquiry was finally told the rationale in early 2013, and it is instructive of what the government's perspective and practices were at the time of the incident.

The department did, indeed, receive a call on March 9, 2005, reporting that the child was being abused and locked in her room. Two social workers were sent to appraise the situation. At the public inquiry, one testified that a "shy" Kematch met them at the door, but refused them entry, claiming to have a visitor. In the hallway, Kematch explained away the suspected abuse by confessing that she had shouted at Phoenix, then four years old. Kematch admitted she had a lock on the bedroom door. The workers warned Kematch that it was not safe to lock her in the room in the case of a fire and testified that "Samantha agreed." The social worker conceded there was no record in his case notes that he even asked to see Phoenix, despite his belief he would have. He did say, "It would have been in my practice to ask to see Phoenix." The worker added that the rationale for closing the case included that Kematch offered a "possible" explanation for what led to the abuse call and that she was "loving" toward her baby. (Kematch had given birth to another baby, fathered by McKay.) "I believed at that time that (Phoenix) was safe," he concluded.[16]

A NARROW MANDATE

The social worker was only concerned about the immediate safety of the child. Because he erroneously determined that Phoenix was safe, he actually "closed the file." He and his colleague had a slew of tools to protect her if she was unsafe, including removing her from the premises. What he didn't have were the tools to help the family work on the profound underlying and long-term issues that were manifestly before them. The mandate of the relevant Manitoba department at that time did not extend to inquiring about the health and welfare of both the child and the parents early on. Nor were resources made available to the social workers to assist the family to guide their child on a stable and fruitful path to adulthood. A limited mandate to protect children from harm and tools to increase the intensity of the state intervention as danger increases are the parameters of the existing child-protection system.

The province of Manitoba has acknowledged that is wasn't equipped to help Samantha Kematch and Steve Sinclair prevent their problems from spiralling out of total control. It was predictable that both mother and father would have serious parenting challenges. It was predictable that they would not be able to address these challenges alone. Phoenix's father actually asked for the kinds of help that might have allowed him to be a more adequate caregiver (e.g., job-search assistance and daycare), but to no avail. It was foreseeable that a cohabiting boyfriend with a violent past would likely create an unsafe situation.

It was obvious that more could have and should have been done to protect Phoenix from the beginning of her short life. Unfortunately, the Manitoba child-protection system, designed as it was on the basis of proportional response to protect the best interests of the child, did not have a toolbox of interventions that might have helped Phoenix's parents provide her with a safer environment from birth.

High-risk family situations almost always start as low-risk situations, just as in most oncology cases, a big tumour starts as a small one. The question isn't if the health system will have to address the cancer, it's when it will have to devote resources to the problem. The same is true in child protection. The system checked in on Phoenix's safety, but was not equipped with a set of appropriate tools to prevent the obvious dangers from actually occurring.

EARLY INTERVENTION IN CHILD PROTECTION: THE NEW ZEALAND EXPERIENCE

In early 2008, the province of New Brunswick was staring at the same criticism and outrage the Manitoba government faced over the Phoenix Sinclair case in 2006. In New Brunswick, it was the Juli-Anna case that caused the eruption. Eerily similar to Phoenix Sinclair's story, baby Juli-Anna lost her life at the hands of her mother and her mother's boyfriend in 2002.[17] By 2008, the province's Department of Social Development had already begun to consider early-intervene options, to prevent cases like Juli-Anna's from becoming high risk with all the attendant problems and costs. In search of an inspiring model and not restricting themselves to Canada, department officials landed on the groundbreaking work of Mike Doolan, a New Zealand social worker who had a hand in the significant reforms that took place there in the 1980s and 1990s. He was also in demand from several European countries wanting to reform their own child welfare systems.

As the New Zealand government's former chief social worker, Doolan was responsible for child protection for much the 1980s. What was obvious to him and others at the time was the statistically disproportionate number of Maori children coming into contact with the country's child-welfare and correctional services. Dominant white governments failing aboriginal children was not new trend, and, of course, was not restricted to New Zealand. Assimilationist and discriminatory policies put in place by the national government in the early and mid-twentieth century took no account of Maori cultural norms and practices. Canada and the United States had a similar approach to aboriginal people. Now, Maori leadership was calling on the New Zealand government to effect reform.

After the Second World War, Maori families moved in large numbers from traditional and farming communities into urban settings. Following a similar narrative to aboriginal North Americans, Maori children became a prominent feature in state programs, particularly youth justice. Mike Doolan aptly describes this type of child protection as the "child-rescue model of practice."[18] Child rescue was the approach taken in the Phoenix Sinclair and Juli-Anna cases. It is the model that uses professional standards implemented by professional social workers who are legally mandated to protect a child from a harmful environment. It is the emergency-based, late-intervention approach of the existing child-protection system. Though child rescue remains the dominant model of practice in Canada, it was abandoned in New Zealand because, quite simply, it wasn't working.

Doolan notes the following:

> *A system of professional practice that had been designed to respond to the needs of settler families and their children — a system based on what were regarded as the progressive systems operating in the United Kingdom and the United States from the early years of the 20th century — was applied to this new intake of families. There was no adjustment of method that recognized the change in clientele. As a consequence, professionals doing their duty presided over the alienation of thousands of Maori children from their families, communities, and hereditary rights, "in their interests and for their own good." New Zealand still bears the scars of that practice today.*[19]

Maori children were hugely overrepresented in the cohort of children removed from their families in New Zealand; the cultural impact of this was substantial. In his senior governmental role, Doolan was a part of the conversation about this issue, and he was convinced a better way could be found to produce improved outcomes for New Zealand's Maori children.[20] Doolan also wondered if this better way might also be applicable to the general population. In partnership with Maori leaders, he and his colleagues in the child-welfare branch began an extensive review of Maori practice in restorative family health and justice. They ended up focusing on three specific aspects of traditional Maori methodology to bring harmony and balance back to the family.

First, as the nuclear family unit is the source of the problem, the family has to be stretched beyond parents and children to correct the problem. Aunts, uncles, grandparents, cousins, neighbours, and friends, all with a concern for and interest in the well-being of the family and children, are summoned together to work with the nuclear family to develop a plan to solve the issues. Everyone has an equal voice in seeking a new path to health and prosperity. Second, there is no time limit on discussing the issues and agreeing on a plan. Many voices all need to be heard to yield the best plan possible. The goal of the discussion is not to ascribe blame or pass judgment, but to figure out the best way forward. Last, the gathering works toward a consensus that everyone can live with and that everyone takes ownership of. The extended family becomes jointly responsible for improving how the nuclear family functions. In sharing the load with others, the weight of the world is somewhat lifted from the parents' shoulders, but they have a new accountability for their behaviour inasmuch as the eyes and ears of family and friends, not those of the welfare state, are watching and listening.

In 1989, the Maori traditional practice became the new model for the New Zealand child-protection system. The new Family Group Conference (FGC) displaced both social workers and the courts as the primary arbiter of planning and decision making regarding children in danger, for both Maori and non-Maori children alike. A Family Group Conference Plan has legal status, and the child-welfare agency has the legal obligation to provide the resources necessary to put the plan into action.[21]

In effect, Doolan and his team oversaw the dissolution of the child-rescue model. Instead, the extended family was placed at the centre of the efforts to work out and implement a plan of action to improve family functioning and child outcomes. As Doolan has written,

The Family Group Conference interrupts orthodox pathways in child welfare — pathways that had catapulted large numbers of children and young persons into the custody of state agencies or the courts — and seeks to keep children and young persons in their communities and in their families, with family groups taking the lead in how this can occur."[22] Under the new model, legal action is a last resort, and the courts are not allowed to decide upon the fate of a child until the Family Group Conference has determined that it cannot resolve the matter.

This new way forward in child protection ensured that problems in the family were attacked early on. Social workers were trained to work with the family, not against it, to solve problems when they could be solved. Professionals had a new role: to explain to troubled families the opportunity that the Family Group Conference presented as soon as a substantiated reference to child-protection services was made. Even families finding themselves in high-risk situations benefited from FGC, which helps to de-escalate conflict and spread responsibility for the care and well-being of the child. Social workers work with the family to identify and bring together other family members and friends to officially participate in the decision-making process. Social workers then assist the process as coordinators and facilitators. FGC didn't work for all families for a variety of reasons, and the program is still fraught with resource and implementation challenges.[23] However, FGC, which is now practised in more than seventeen countries across the globe, is a gold standard in child protection when done correctly because child outcomes are improved and overall costs to government are reduced.[24] An example of how FGC typically achieves these two results is below. Though the surname of the family in question is withheld, it is a true story from Barnardos, one of the largest child welfare charities in the United Kingdom,[25] and it speaks to the promise of protecting a child through the use of FGC, without resorting to the punitive and confrontational practices of the child-rescue model.

FAMILY GROUP CONFERENCE IN ACTION

Michael, a fifteen-year-old boy living with his father in England, faced a difficult future.[26] After his father's heart attack, Michael, who had no siblings and was estranged from his mother, took on much of the housework. John, Michael's father, fell into a serious depression, which led Michael to experience constant anxiety. Michael would often wake up in the night to check on his father. The boy's emotional stability was threatened, and he began acting out at school. The father was also deeply concerned about his son's fate if he should have a second heart attack. The situation was unsustainable. Social services was alerted to the family's dangerous status and sent social workers to investigate. The lead worker invited the family to consider convening a FGC. Michael and his father agreed that a wide circle of family and friends was necessary to address their challenges. In short order, Michael's mother, aunt, uncle, several friends, and neighbours were brought together to determine a plan of action. At the conference, it was agreed that Michael would begin staying with his mother twice a week during the evenings and overnight. This would start the process of rebuilding this fractured relationship. Michael's aunt and uncle agreed to do regular housework every couple of weeks and be available to support John and Michael emotionally whenever necessary.

They all established a contingency plan to be implemented if John's health took a turn for the worse, including identifying a first point of contact for Michael if a medical emergency occurred. Michael agreed to go to a counselling agency for emotional support and participate in local club activities.

At a follow-up meeting several weeks later, Michael was continuing to see his mother and he seemed to be getting some benefit from the counselling service.

Social services did a formal review of the family's situation two years later. John's health continued to be poor, so the plan that was put in place through the initial FGC was renewed. Michael continued to do some housework, but was generally faring well. He saw his friends regularly, continued to have consistent contact with his mother, in whom he became able to confide, and was even around the youth club frequently. Family and friends were generally available to help out. John continued to worry about his health and Michael's future, but was greatly comforted by the contingency plan that was developed for him. John said that without the FGC, they would have been lost.

Michael stayed with his dad, reconnected with his mom, and got on with his life within the family. The social workers supported the efforts of the FGC and succeeded in avoiding both court proceedings and foster care.

Michael's story ends up not being a story of crisis, confusion, punishment, and loss. It's the opposite — one of problems avoided because of early intervention. The story, thankfully, does not devolve into material for headlines, and Michael does not become an expensive ward of the state. Court costs are avoided. Foster care expenses are avoided. Michael becomes a normal kid with some difficult though manageable challenges that he doesn't have to take on alone.

THE RESULTS

In New Zealand, the results of this new approach based on proactive early intervention were quite startling.[27] A decade after the new model was introduced, the number of child-protection cases going to court went from 650 per 10,000 in 1987 to 250 per 10,000 in 2001. Cases resulting in incarceration dropped from more than 300 in 1987 to under 100 in 2001. The Family Group Conference succeeded in more than 80 per cent of cases in coming up with a plan to keep kids at or near home without any court intervention.[28]

Although there were costs to implementing this new regime, with the Family Group Conference at the centre, tremendous savings were achieved in the form of reduced court proceedings and the huge decline in the number of children coming into the care of the state. Generating accurate data on these savings is difficult, and the available research is thin. However, in the United Kingdom, where the Family Group Conference has been put into practice for the benefit of Michael and thousands of other children, we have the following information. In hearings before the House of Commons Justice Committee in 2011, a director of a local child-protection agency testified that "FGCs cost between £1,000–2,000 per family. A typical court case would cost the local authority £4,825 in court fees alone."[29] As well, the same committee was advised that FGC in Liverpool "cost £88,000 to run but saved the local authority approximately ten times that amount in care fees."[30] One study confimred that FGC "generated considerable savings in foster care; that when costs of lawyers and the court system are considered savings will be even greater; and that the program is probably cost-neutral with regard to staff time."[31]

These savings do not take into count the decrease in school dropouts and youth incarceration that are predictable outcomes of family breakdown. Nor do they account for the increase in due course of both employment and tax revenue from children who might otherwise become users of welfare, social housing, and other government programs.

Mike Doolan's work shows that doing the right thing, namely intervening early to help families stay together to the extent possible, can pay off handsomely. In 2008–09, New Brunswick introduced a whole suite of new early intervention measures based on New Zealand's experience. Family Group Conference was the signature part of the reform. Mike Doolan himself came to Fredericton to introduce the concept to government social workers as part of an ambitious training program. The New Brunswick government's investments in early intervention did not take long to bear fruit. A review of child services by the province's Child and Youth Advocate in 2011 had this to say about the reforms:

> *In its first year of application, the FGC model has met with great success in New Brunswick, leading to an 18% reduction in the number of children placed in care within the first year alone. This translates into millions of dollars in savings which, in our view, should be reinvested in improved mental health services for children in need. International experts in this field have pointed to New Brunswick's success with this family-centric program as a leading best practice in social work worldwide.[32]*

Savings generated by reduced caseloads were, indeed, reinvested in other early intervention measures, including for following: family enhancement services for families at low risk, where social workers help to identify problems, open doors to new resources, and provide ongoing advice; kinship care, where children can be temporarily fostered with family members other than parents without extensive court proceedings; and child mediation to direct families away from the judicial system towards a lighter and faster process.

Ironically, New Brunswick families who are today benefiting from these measures can, in part, thank the Juli-Anna tragedy for bringing to bear the intense political pressure that is often necessary to provoke reform. To its credit, when the tragedy did strike, the New Brunswick government did not react by simply tightening its standards and increasing its child-rescue capacity. While it did, indeed, take these measures, it also introduced its early intervention measures, which simultaneously empowered its social work staff and New Brunswick families to work much earlier on to solve problems.

KEEPING FAMILIES TOGETHER

FGC and other methods of early intervention are based on the premise that children are better off growing up in the care of their parents as opposed to fostering or group-home environments, which Mike Doolan calls "stranger care." The research bears out this presumption. In a 2007 report entitled "Child Protection and Child Outcomes: Measuring the Effects of Foster Care," Joseph J. Doyle, Jr. asked whether children presenting similar risks are better served staying at home or being placed in foster care. Using a 15,000-person data set from Illinois, Doyle reported that, in terms of likelihood of becoming a juvenile delinquent or teen mother, children in foster care fared worse than those who remained at home. Kids were also more likely to obtain and retain employment as young adults if they had stayed at home than if they had been removed.[33] In 2008, the same author found convincing evidence that children coming through foster care were two to three times more likely to become adult offenders than children who, though facing similar challenges, remained in the custody of their parents.[34]

As well, a 2007 study of Romanian children in the state's care showed markedly superior cognitive development for children who were never in institutional care versus those who were taken into group-like residential settings.[35]

As far back as 1988, studies began showing that providing training to challenged parents paid off in terms of reduced risk of abuse and better management of the household.[36]

In effect, this research is telling us that, in most cases, the best way to protect a child's long-term interest is to intervene early enough so that the family can be helped to stay together. This does not mean allowing the child to remain in the care of the parents under any circumstances, as they must always be shielded from immediate danger. However, an approach that gives the family the best chance of staying united is also the child's best chance to flourish over his or her lifetime.

CHILDHOOD TRAUMA

Another key reason to consider an early-intervention-based child-protection system is to avoid or reduce childhood trauma. One of the United States' largest providers of health-care services, California-based

Kaiser Permanente, has a formidable research capacity largely because of its size. It serves approximately nine million Americans through a vast array of hospitals, clinics, and almost 200,000 employees and physicians.[37] Thus, it can reach into a set of vast health records to conduct research and testing to improve the quality of its services. In 1985, one of Kaiser Permanente's clinician-researchers, Dr. Vincent Felitti, an obesity specialist, observed that those patients who were most successful in losing weight were also those most likely to drop out of the program. This observation led Dr. Felitti to dig into the medical records of almost 300 such patients at Kaiser to see if it was a coincidence or a pattern. He ascertained that a significant proportion of these patients had experienced physical or sexual abuse as children. Dr. Felitti found that these patients were unconsciously using their obesity as a protective shield against unwanted attention. This explained why successful patients were dropping out of the weight-loss program. They needed their weight to prevent the repeat of the crisis they experienced as children.

This observation led to the Adverse Childhood Experiences (ACE) Study, a large, decade-long and ongoing collaboration between Kaiser Permanente's Department of Preventive Medicine in San Diego and the American government's Centers for Disease Control and Prevention (CDC). Dr. Felitti and his colleagues tapped into the massive Kaiser Permanente database, tabulating more than 17,000 medical records. This research confirmed that childhood trauma is a predictor of future health concerns. The study revealed that an inordinate number of adult patients coming to the Department of Preventive Medicine for comprehensive medical screening the experienced family crisis in their childhoods. The crisis could have involved experiencing physical or sexual abuse, but also included dealing with emotional or physical neglect; living with alcoholic, drug-using, mentally ill, or imprisoned parents; witnessing an abusive spousal relationship, or having parent commit suicide. These are the same criteria used for intervention in child-protection cases.

From the ACE study, a scorecard was developed. In simplified terms, the greater the number of traumatic events a child has experienced, the greater the ACE score. And the greater the ACE score, the more likely the person is to experience health challenges as an adult. For example, those with an ACE score of four or more "are twice as likely to be smokers, 12 times more likely to have attempted suicide, 7 times more likely to be alcoholic, and 10 times more likely to have injected street drugs."[38] It also predicts greater chances of liver disease, depression, teen pregnancy, and chronic obstructive pulmonary disease (COPD).[39]

The ACE study tells us that if we want to reduce the chances that a person needs future health services, we need to reduce the incidence of childhood trauma. Intervening early with a robust set of tools to help the family stay together in safety is a powerful and proven way to achieve this objective.

A traditional late-intervention child-rescue system increasingly inclined to remove children from the care of parents (as reported in the 2008 by Public Health Agency) is a form of trauma in and of itself, is ill equipped to address the dangers and long-term cost implications of childhood trauma.

PHOENIX SINCLAIR AND DISPROPORTIONALITY

Like the Juli-Anna case in New Brunswick, the Phoenix Sinclair tragedy also had a silver lining.

As of the writing of this chapter, the public inquiry into her death is ongoing. However, the Manitoba government's response resembled that of New Brunswick. New investments in training, work-load relief (to reduce the number of cases, especially high risk, per social worker), critical incident stress management, peer support, and information technology were announced. The measures to protect children in high-risk cases were complemented by significant new investments in early intervention. A new initiative called Differential Response was developed, piloted, and implemented. Speaking at the Sinclair Public Inquiry on May 14, 2013, John Rodgers said this about Differential Response:

The idea of differential response, as recommended in the reports, was based on the research that the reviewers had done in other jurisdictions and the research they had done into some of the statistical trends in Canada and the United States and predominantly those trends were indicating that very often when the child welfare system has to become involved in a family in an intrusive way, like taking their kids into care, in a high number of cases those families had come to the attention of the child welfare system earlier and had been closed and they came back at a later date. So the idea of differential response is to identify those families early, who are most likely to come back later on and require a more intrusive response, to identify those families and then to provide them with supports then, as opposed to later, and by doing so keep those kids from having to come into care later on.[40]

Differential Response is simply another way of expressing the importance of early intervention in child protection.

New Brunswick and Manitoba, as well several other provinces, are now laying the foundation to intervene much earlier with more sophisticated tools and teams in their child-protection services.[41] Outside Canada, a 2011–12 report on Australian child protection indicated that "out-of-home care" is now an intervention of last resort.[42] The United Kingdom and the United States both deploy Family Group Conference in a significant way in their respective countries. Early intervention is starting to take hold and, as the ACE study tells us, preventing childhood trauma saves and improves lives, and also reduces future expenditures in the health sector.

In the emerging era of early intervention in child protection, responsible governments don't abandon their capacity to deal with children in immediate danger. They must retain the power to pull children out of harm's away. However, over time, these situations are supposed to lessen in number, as early intervention successes reduce the need for them, as was the case in New Zealand. However, it is only by investing in a broad set of early intervention measures that costs will fall. In a political firestorm over the death of a child, putting investments into early intervention is not easy to do. Systems, generally speaking, err on the side of precaution. They tend to go overboard to reinforce the policies that pull kids out of trouble. It takes a great deal of political courage and far-sightedness to spend limited political and financial capital on early intervention that never has an immediate payback.

To spend some of this capital on measures like Family Group Conference is to violate the rule of proportionality, which calls for spending less early on and more as risk rises. However, the evidence calls for disproportionate attention on early intervention approaches so that both children and state finances are better off.

CHAPTER 4

Addressing Autism

Autism Canada produces the *Autism Physician Handbook* to assist general practitioners in identifying children with symptoms that may point to an autism diagnosis. The handbook is free and available to download.[1] Its first pages are directed at concerned parents, asking them to answer three simple questions about their child at eighteen months:

1. Does your child look at you and point when he/she wants to show you something?

2. Does your child look when you point at something?

3. Does your child use imagination to pretend play? If the child does not make eye contact, does not look at something pointed to, and does not use imagination, the handbook warns the parents: "Your child may be at risk for AUTISM. Please alert your physician today."

This chapter describes the disability known as Autism Spectrum Disorder (ASD) and details what researchers and parents say can be done about it. It also tells the story of how the policy-makers are neither reading the research nor listening to parents, because, if they did, they would know that intervening early is the best way to address autism. It can help many children and save the government a great deal of money in the process.

PERVASIVE

Autism is not a mental illness that can be treated with medication.[2] Nor is it a short-term or episodic condition that will simply go away with time. Rather, it's a lifelong neurodevelopmental disability. It is also pervasive, meaning that its symptoms involve the entire range of the person's functioning from social interaction to cognition. Its causes are unknown; however, research is focusing presently on genetics, pollutants, viruses, and chromosome abnormalities.[3] There was a time when it was thought that autism derived from a mother's aloofness and disengagement from her child. Dr. Leo Kanner was arguably the first scientist to identify autism back in the 1940s, and although at first he viewed the condition as biological in origin, he later shifted to a psychological source, namely the "refrigerator mother," essentially blaming autism on a mother's aloofness.[4] Today, there is consensus in the research field that children are born with the disorder. To immediately alleviate any sense of parental responsibility, the Ontario government states in its Autism Parenting Kit that "we do know that autism is not caused by the way a child is raised."[5]

The *Diagnostic and Statistical Manual of Mental Disorders* is published by the American Psychiatric Association. Though controversial and often criticized, it is nonetheless generally considered the standard diagnostic tool for brain disorders. The section relating to autism and autism-like conditions was greatly simplified in the May 2013 fifth edition. In the past, separate diagnoses were offered for Asperger's Disorder,

Childhood Disintegrative Disorder, and the generic Pervasive Developmental Disorder Not Otherwise Specified. In the latest edition, there is simply one condition, Autism Spectrum Disorder (ASD), which contains a range of different symptoms. The authors say the following about these symptoms:

> People with ASD tend to have communication deficits,
> such as responding inappropriately in conversations,
> misreading nonverbal interactions, or having difficulty
> building friendships appropriate to their age. In addition,
> people with ASD may be overly dependent on routines,
> highly sensitive to changes in their environment, or
> intensely focused on inappropriate items. Again, the
> symptoms of people with ASD will fall on a continuum,
> with some individuals showing mild symptoms and others
> having much more severe symptoms. This spectrum will
> allow clinicians to account for the variations in symptoms
> and behaviors from person to person.[6]

These are the general traits we commonly associate with people on the spectrum: communications challenges, social challenges, fixations, and cognitive difficulties. Self-harm is also common. While these more negatively viewed characteristics are most common, there are often incredibly positive traits associated with autism: savant-like abilities (like Dustin Hoffman's character in *Rain Man*) and genius (Sir Isaac Newton, Albert Einstein, Bill Gates, and Steve Jobs are among many people claimed to be high-functioning individuals with ASD). While most people with ASD are neither savants nor geniuses, they very often do have excellent focus and show a great deal of competency in their fields of interest.

In the 1960s, autistic people were seen as untreatable pariahs. A *Life* magazine article in 1965 described children with autism as "far-gone mental cripples" and "utterly withdrawn . . . whose minds are sealed against all human contact and whose uncontrolled madness had turned their homes into hells."[7] *The New Yorker* was, if it possible, less generous. In a 1968 article, one of its authors said that those who work with autistic people are saintly as they "encounter beings so badly scarred, so remote that it must be hard for a psychoanalyst to even acknowledge them as fellow creatures."[8] Even into the 1990s, one autism activist encouraged desperate parents to think of their autistic child as stranger. As one parent put it, "This is an alien child who landed in my life by accident. I don't know who this child is or what it will become. But I know it's a child, stranded in an alien world, without parents of its own kind to care for it."[9]

Arguably, the most famous person living with autism in the English-speaking world is Dr. Temple Grandin. In many ways, through her speaking tours, her books, and her appearances in film and on TV, she has opened the door to understanding autism from the first-person perspective. In *Thinking in Pictures*, she describes in detail her oversensitivity to touch, her difficulty interpreting social cues, and a variety of other challenges she faced as a child, including the "auditory scrambling" that initially impeded her language development.[10] Grandin acted out in frustration and sometimes with physical violence when she couldn't understand what was going on around her or could not be understood herself.

Physical violence, both to self and others, can be almost intolerable. In 2003, Scott Sea wrote about his autistic daughter in *Salon.com*:

> *When you see the balled up pants and diaper on the floor,*
> *you know you are too late. A bright red smear across*
> *the door, the moulding, the wall. Turn the corner and*
> *the bedroom is a crime scene. An axe murder? In fact, it*
> *is only your daughter at her worst . . . Shit everywhere.*
> *Splashes of blood glistening like paint, black clots, yellow-*

brown feces and a three-foot-in-diameter pond of vomit
that your daughter stands in the middle of, a dog-eared
copy of Family Circle in one hand, reaching for the TV
with the other. She is naked except for stockinged feet,
blood soaked up to her ankles. Hands dripping, face
marked like a cannibal, she wears an expression of utter
bewilderment.[11]

This is the experience of so many families who can't access, understand, and support their autistic children. In "Welcome to Beirut," the mother of an autistic boy shares her view of some of the parenting challenges she faces:

Your child regresses for no apparent reason, and it feels like
a kick in the stomach. Some bully makes fun of your kid
and your heart aches. You're excluded from activities and
functions because of your child and you cry. Your other
children are embarrassed to be around your disabled child
and you sigh. Your insurance company refuses to provide
therapies for "chronic, life-long conditions" and your blood
pressure goes up. Your arm aches from holding onto the
phone with yet another bureaucrat or doctor or therapist
who holds the power to improve or destroy the quality of
your child's life with the stroke of a pen. You're exhausted
because your child doesn't sleep.[12]

And the number of people with the diagnosis appears to be on the rise.

PREVALENCE

In 1960, the autism rate was 1 in 2,500 births. In 2014, the American Centers for Disease Control and Prevention published a revised prevalence rate of 1 in 68 children, or 1.47 per cent of all births. This is up from 1 in 88 births in 2012. These are American rates. The average prevalence across North America, Europe, and Asia is closer to 1 in 100 children; however, rates will be higher or lower on a country-by-country basis. For example, South Korea has a rate of 2.6 per cent or 1 in every 38 children. Boys are about 5 times as likely to receive the diagnosis as girls. Thus, in the United States, ASD will be found in 1 in 42 boys and 1 in 189 girls.[13]

With this massive increase — due, no doubt, to increased awareness and changes in diagnostic regime — has come an equivalent increase in media and political attention. In his book *Far From the Tree*, Andrew Solomon notes that "the number of books and articles published per year about autism increased more than six fold."[14] The Director of the American National Institute of Mental Health, Dr. Tom Insel, once observed: "We get more calls from the White House about autism than about everything else combined."[15]

American Congress passed the *Combating Autism Act* in 2006, and the Canadian government announced its first publicly funded research chair in autism treatment and care in 2012.[16] These initiatives and investments directed largely at finding the cause of ASD are laudable. However, more important than laws and chairs is the need to make effective therapy available to autistic children as early as possible. In fact, the therapeutic benefits of structured early intervention have been known for almost thirty years.

DR. IVAR LOVAAS

When one reads the vast literature on autism and what can be done about it, the name of Ivar Lovaas figures prominently. Norwegian-born and educated in the United States, Lovaas landed in the Psychology Department of UCLA in the 1950s. A behavioural scientist following in the footsteps Ivan Pavlov and B. F. Skinner, Lovaas once said, "If I had gotten Hitler here at U.C.L.A. at the age of 4 or 5, I could have raised him to be a nice person."[17]

Lovaas applied his behavioural techniques to autistic children. In 1981, he published the seminal text on intensive behavioural therapy for autistic children entitled *Teaching Developmentally Disabled Children: The ME Book*. The book immediately brought hope into the lives of families touched by autism. It must be remembered that until the 1980s, the medical community had largely given up on autistic children and adults, and had relegated those with the condition to short lives in secure state-run facilities. As I'll discuss later in the chapter, Lovaas has turned out to be a scientist of some controversy, but his great gift was that he did not give up on this client group. Where there had previously been literally no clinical or therapeutic options, Lovaas found a way, in many cases, to improve children's communication and interaction skills and reduce self-harm.

The American National Library of Medicine describes Lovaas's work in this way:

> *O. Ivar Lovaas (1927–2010) devoted nearly half a century to ground-breaking research and practice aimed at improving the lives of children with autism and their families. In the 1960s, he pioneered applied behavior analytic (ABA) interventions to decrease severe challenging behaviors and establish communicative language. Later, he sought to improve outcomes by emphasizing early intervention for preschoolers with autism, provided in family homes with active parental participation. His studies indicated that many children who received early intensive ABA made dramatic gains in development. Lovaas also disseminated ABA widely through intervention manuals, educational films, and public speaking. Moreover, as an enthusiastic teacher and devoted mentor, he inspired many students and colleagues to enter the field of ABA and autism intervention.*[18]

In 1987, Lovaas published "Behavioural Treatment and Normal Education and Intellectual Functioning in Young Autistic Children."[19] The article summarized a behavioural intervention project he'd begun in 1970, the objective of which was to maximize "behavioural treatment gains by treating autistic children during most of their waking hours for many years."[20] He had decided to focus on children under the age of four, on the theory that they would be better able to generalize their lessons than older children, thus paving the way to ultimately mainstreaming them. In effect, Lovaas was trying to equip the children in the study with the social and cognitive tools to function in environments typical for children of their age.

Lovaas divided the test group into two sub-groups. Group 1 children would receive full intensive treatment of at least forty one-on-one treatment hours per week. Group 2 children received minimal treatment of ten one-on-one treatment hours per week. Treatment for both sub-groups would last at least two years. Parents of the children in group 1 were trained to support student therapists from Lovaas's UCLA classes. Together, they provided the children with therapy based on positive and negative reinforcement of desirable and undesirable behaviour. Positive reinforcement consisted of enthusiastic feedback and rewards, while an inappropriate behaviour was negatively reinforced primarily by simply ignoring it. Lovaas describes the treatment program for group 1 children this way:

> During the first year, treatment goals consisted of
> reducing self-stimulatory and aggressive behaviours,
> building compliance to elementary verbal requests,
> teaching imitation, establishing the beginning of
> appropriate toy play and promoting the extension of the
> treatment into the family. The second year of treatment
> emphasized teaching expressive and early abstract
> language and interactive play with peers . . . The third

year emphasized the teaching of appropriate and varied
expression of emotions; pre-academic tasks like reading,
writing and arithmetic and observational learning
(learning by observing other children learn).[21]

A classic example of the method is matching. To teach a child to match one identical object with another, the therapist places an object, say a ball, in front of the child, then hands him or her an identical ball and asks the child to place the second ball beside its identical mate. The therapist (or teacher or parent) may have to physically assist the child to complete the requested task initially. In time, with positive reinforcement, physical assistance is replaced and only a verbal prompt is used. Cups or candles eventually replace the ball as the child is encouraged to generalize the matching skill he or she has developed. Later on, randomized objects are placed about and the child is prompted to match the pairs to demonstrate the new learned capacity to discriminate. Later still, multiple sets of the same object differentiated by characteristic are presented to the child, who is asked to match, for example, the blue pencils, or the short pencils, or thin pencils, to further hone discrimination skills. The Lovaas method teaches skills such as matching (pattern recognition) across twelve different programs, including receptive and expressive language, non-verbal imitation, social language, play, and self-help skills.

The Lovaas teams relentlessly went about their work. There were no summer recesses or holiday breaks. The therapy was a 365-days-a-year effort. No week contained less than forty hours of lessons, unless the child was successfully integrated into kindergarten at five years old.

The results of this determined and tenacious intervention were startling. Although there was no difference between participants in group 1 and group 2 at the beginning of the research program, by the end, 47 per cent of group 1 children achieved normal intellectual and educational functioning in contrast to only 2% of the control group subjects (Group 2).[22]

What is meant by "normal functioning" is that the child has registered and successfully completed kindergarten and achieved an average IQ score. Almost half of the children in group 1 were able to fully integrate into a mainstream environment. Lovaas concluded his summary of the experiment by stating that "these data promise a major reduction in the emotional hardships of families with autistic children."[23] It's an exhausting, incredibly time-consuming process, but in many cases, the gruelling commitment works not to "cure" autism, but rather to equip autistic children with the tools to function unassisted in a social and interactive world.

In *The Autistic Brain*, Temple Grandin explains that although she was born prior to the development of applied behavioural analysis, the approach her mother decided upon to bring her into the larger world around her was the same one used by behavioural therapists today. Writing about her mother, Grandin says,

> She made sure that every game the three of us [Temple and her siblings] played was a turn-taking game. During meals, I was taught table manners and I was not allowed to twirl my fork around my head. The only time I could revert back to my autism was for one hour after lunch. I had to live in a non-rocking, non-twirling world. Mother did heroic work. In fact, she discovered on her own the standard treatment that therapists use today."[24]

Not all participating children in the Lovaas study achieved normal function, despite the almost 3,000 hours a year the teams of parents and student therapists put in. However, even for those who did not become fully functional, the benefits were nonetheless significant. Many were able to join a special needs class and meet its required standards in a local elementary school. Even the small minority, about 10 per cent, who achieved little improvement might have been given the potential to become verbal as opposed to remaining non-verbal for the rest of their lives.[25] All to say, it was a start.

EARLY START DENVER MODEL

A tidal wave of work on autism began in the 1990s with the development of new and different techniques, some modelled on the Lovaas method and some inspired by it. For example, the Early Start Denver Model (ESDM) employed the pivotal response training method to guide the development of autistic children's skills as a function of the child's interests (as opposed to the more adult-driven structured approach developed by Lovaas). In 2010, the ESDM was subjected to a randomized control trial in which forty-eight children with ASD were put into one of two groups, the first receiving twenty-five hours per week of applied behaviour analysis, following the ESDM model, from trained therapists and parents for two years, and a control group that received the kind of support commonly available in the community.

The results were reported in 2012, and children in the experimental ESDM group showed "significant improvements in IQ, adaptive behavior, and autism diagnosis . . . The ESDM group maintained its rate of growth in adaptive behavior compared with a normative sample of typically developing children. In contrast, over the 2-year span, the comparison group showed greater delays in adaptive behavior."[26] The authors concluded that the study emphasized "the importance of early detection of and intervention in autism."[27]

In a 2011 article entitled "A Systematic Review of Early Intensive Intervention for Autism Spectrum Disorders," the authors conducted a full review of the existing literature and noted that, though more research is necessary, the only existing therapy that has produced significant gains for children with ASD is the type of treatment originally conceived by Ivar Lovaas and further developed and adapted by clinicians in the thirty years following.[28] As one commentator put it, "Those findings touched off a flurry of interest in the Lovaas method, now often referred to as applied behavior analysis, and spurred the development of variations on his method as well as a variety of other forms of intensive intervention."[29] The biggest challenge in the sector now is trying to understand which type of early intervention behavioural therapy is best suited for which type of child. Research is now attempting to ascertain which suite of interventions is best adapted for particular child characteristics and challenges. Without Lovaas, one must question whether autism treatment would have reached this next stage.

CATHERINE MAURICE

In 1993, Catherine Maurice published the story of her experience as a parent of two autistic children.[30] Her book, *Let Me Hear Your Voice*, encapsulates her family's experience with behavioural therapy. One commentator described the book as "the catalyst for a new wave of excitement, hope and controversy surrounding the application of behaviour modification techniques to young children with autism."[31] It's the story of how one family battled autism using behavioural techniques developed by Ivar Lovaas, and it is somewhat emblematic of the challenges all families face; however, not always with the same happy results.

On Anne Marie Maurice's first birthday, her parents, Catherine and Michel, noted with concern their daughter's general disinterest in all the party activities going on around her. Anne Marie appeared to be so much more serious than the other children at the party as well as her older brother, Daniel. She didn't interact with the other children and was intensely shy around them.

The Maurices went on two family holidays during Anne Marie's infancy. During their trip to Spain, Catherine became intensely worried about her daughter's panicky reaction to change of any kind. Anne Marie's apparent refusal to talk was another indication that she was facing different developmental issues than most children her age.

Catherine reached out to her network for advice on what to do. One friend told her not to worry, as Anne Marie was probably just reacting to Catherine's pregnancy. Even the family's pediatrician initially thought the issue was a physical problem, such as a hearing deficiency. When Anne Marie was found to have no hearing problem, the pediatrician sent them to a neurologist. After ninety minutes with Anne Marie, the neurologist diagnosed her with infantile autism.

Catherine then began to read extensively about the condition and learned that autism was a lifelong disability. Though deeply saddened, Catherine decided to do everything humanly possible for her daughter. She began to observe Anne Marie's behaviours for what they were, namely the manifestations of an autistic brain, and not lack of love for or antagonism to her. Anne Marie increasingly ran her hands over radiators, stared at inanimate objects for long periods of time, showed absolutely no interest in people, and demonstrated no verbal or social skills whatsoever. Catherine commenced looking for options to deal with these symptoms. One doctor told her nothing could be done and advised her to watch the show *St. Elsewhere*, in which there is an autistic character, to prepare herself for the future.

Catherine noticed further deterioration in Anne Marie, including an increase in behaviours like toe walking (a typical behaviour for autistic children) and teeth grinding. More worrisome was the increase in Anne Marie's capacity for self-harm, including face hitting.

One day, a friend called to tell Catherine about a new technique developed by Dr. Ivar Lovaas at UCLA called behaviour therapy. After reviewing books and tapes from the UCLA autism unit on this novel method, Catherine and her husband decided to enroll their daughter into the treatment program. They hired a trained behavioural therapist, Bridget Taylor, and began working assiduously with Anne Marie to increase positive behaviours and reduce negative ones. A remarkable moment occurred many months later when the neurologist who originally diagnosed Anne Marie with autism retested her and found the little girl to be in the "normal range" for her age. Catherine had specialists from the UCLA Lovaas clinic visit her, and they also noted Anne Marie's stellar improvements.

At five years of age, Anne Maire began preschool on time. Her mom attended classes with her daily for the first two months, but by November, it was clear she no longer needed to shadow her daughter. Anne Marie's success in integrating into a mainstream environment ran parallel to the family's efforts to work with their son, Michel, who was also diagnosed with autism. In time, again with the help of Bridget Taylor, Michel also developed the skills and aptitudes to join a kindergarten class at five years of age.

The dedication and tenacity of any family with autistic children cannot generally be overestimated. Luckily for the Maurice family, their efforts translated into two fully functional children. Many families are not so lucky for a variety of reasons, including access to behavioural therapists in a timely way and the resources to pay the sizeable cost.

THE ECONOMICS OF BEHAVIOURAL THERAPY

Ivar Lovaas actually concluded his seminal 1987 paper by speaking to the economics of ABA. At that time, the assignment of one full-time special education teacher for two years would cost an estimated $40,000, he said. He then suggested that the lifelong cost to the state of institutionalizing an autistic client was $2 million in direct costs alone.[32]

This rather crude analysis was the beginning of a chain of study into the cost-benefit of ABA investments. Any such investments have to be measured against the price of doing nothing. As we saw in child protecting, the failure to intervene or to intervene early enough is often very costly. Autism is the same. In the Supreme Court of Canada case of *Auton v. British Colombia,* in which the parents of Cameron Auton sought to compel the province to fund ABA-type therapy for their autistic child, the court accepted evidence that without such therapy, 90 per cent of children "end up in group homes or other residential facilities."[33] These are generally very costly methods of serving and supporting people with autism. There is a great deal of literature on the economic burden of autism, especially in the United States.[34] One report calculated the average cost to be at least $17,000 more per year to provide services and support to a child with ASD versus one without the disability (including health care, special education, ASD-related therapy, family coordinated services, and caregiver time). The cost differential for a child with a more severe form of ASD escalates to $21,000 per annum.[35] The cumulative expense between federal and state governments for autistic children in the United States has been put at approximately $11.5 billion annually.[36] What would the overall economic implications be if all these autistic children were offered Lovaas-type or Lovaas-inspired therapy, like Anne Marie, at an annual average cost of say $50,000? We know such investments produce functional improvements for the child, but do they also produce economic returns for the state?

One of the first professional economic analyses on this topic was published in 1997, entitled "Cost-Benefit Estimates for Early Intensive Behavioural Intervention for Young Children with Autism" by John Jacobson and colleagues.[37]

The authors studied the projected lifetime costs to the state of Pennsylvania of three separate groups: 1) autistic children provided with early intensive behavioural intervention (EIBI), meaning any one of a range of Lovaas-styled ABA therapies; 2) autistic children who received treatment as usual in the community; and 3) children without any disability at all. Based on the literature relating to the general effectiveness of EIBI, the authors made the assumption that children from group 1 who received three years of therapy prior to kindergarten would themselves fall into one of three categories: normal functioning; moderate functioning (needing some state support); and little improved (but more functional after therapy than before).

An elaborate economic model was developed that ultimately asked the following key question: Given the differing levels of effectiveness of EIBI, what would the overall cost or contribution picture be for a group of 100 children diagnosed with autism? They found that even if only 20 per cent of the group achieved full functionality (with the 70 per cent achieving partial gains and 10 per cent minimal gains), there would, nonetheless, be a net cumulative contribution to the state of over $168.5 million over the course of subjects' lives. If the effectiveness rate ran up to 50 per cent (40 per cent partial gains and 10 per cent minimal), the state could expect a total inflation-adjusted contribution to its coffers in the amount of over $281.5 million over the subjects' lifetimes, more than a quarter of a billion dollars.

Jacobson and colleagues made the case that Lovaas-styled intensive early intervention programs don't just pay for themselves; they make tremendously strong financial contributions to a given jurisdiction's revenues, even at low levels of effectiveness. Another way to put it is that intervening early to help even a modest number of autistic children achieve full functionality contributes enough to the workforce and tax-paying cadre of society to easily cover the lifetime costs of all those who do not achieve full functionality, but who nonetheless see functional improvements.

A more recent Canadian study (2006) looked at the lifetime costs and benefits of extending IBI (intensive behavioural intervention) programming to all Ontario children with autism.[38] At the time of the report, 485 autistic children were receiving behavioural therapy in the province. The authors designed their research around the cost benefit of three scenarios: 1) maintaining the status quo (485 kids receiving three years of state-funded treatment); 2) providing therapy to all 1,309 children in the province having or likely to have ASD; and 3) offering no programming whatsoever. Unlike the Jacobson study, this paper compared an expansion of ABA services to the cost of doing nothing. As well, the authors were more conservative in their estimates of the efficacy of treatment than in the Jacobson report.

Their sophisticated mathematical analysis led them to a conclusion that similar to that of the Jacobson report. Extending therapy to all 1,309 Ontario children with ASD was the least costly of the three options, if lifetime costs were all factored in. The authors said this: "Expansion of the current program to fund IBI (Intensive Behavioural Intervention) for all autistic children in Ontario younger than six years of age results in net cost savings of $45,133,011 for the government."[39] These numbers improve considerably as the efficacy of the behavioural therapy increases and when productivity measures are included. The researchers make explicit in their report that investing early pays off later on. The caveat was added, quite rightly, that the therapy had to work; if treatment did not produce the increased functionality the model was predicated on, the numbers wouldn't hold. The early interventions had to meet a minimum level of professional quality to produce both the clinical and economic results.

WAIT TIMES

What do we know? We know Lovaas-style or Lovaas-inspired behavioural therapy is recognized as the prevailing evidence-based treatment for children with autism. We also know it is most effective when administered to children very early in their lives. For many children, it can help them develop the skills, aptitudes, and behaviours to function independently by school age. For children with more severe autism, it can also produce marginal to significant increases in functionality. EIBI can make the difference between a solitary, disengaged life and one that is more socially engaging and vital. The Canadian Institutes of Health Research makes the following observations:

> *While there is no demonstrated single best treatment regime package for all children with ASD, it appears that they respond well to highly structured, specialized programs. It is generally agreed that early intervention is important.*[40]

We also know that even at modest levels of clinical efficacy, the economics of ABA show it is cost- effective to government.

Thus, headlines like this one from *Global News* in October 2013 are admittedly surprising:

*Autism treatment means months on wait lists, relocation
for some Canadian families. Lack of funding and
long wait times for autism treatment can mean many
Canadian children don't get the early intervention that
one mother believes makes all the difference.*[41]

The mother interviewed in the news report, Brigitte Forget, moved from Ottawa to Alberta to get state-funded behavioural therapy for her son. According to the report, she felt she had no choice at the time. As a single mother, she couldn't afford private therapists, but she also knew the literature clearly said she had to get help for McKeigan as early as possible. Alberta had the shortest wait times to get therapy, so she headed west. "When you see what my son has accomplished in seven months — it's amazing," said Forget in the interview. She added that "her friends back home are taking out second mortgages just to fund private care."[42]

Most Canadian provinces have instituted programming for children diagnosed with ASD that directs government funding at some form of Lovaas-type behavioural therapy. However, it appears only Alberta has decided to make it universally available to very young children, within only a few weeks of the parents registering their children for the program. In other provinces, the wait times for services range from seven months in Saskatchewan to up to four years in Ontario.[43] Quebec has two-year wait times (longer in Montreal), and Nova Scotia has eighteen-month wait times. Another problem appears to be that children are not getting services early enough. For example, the average age for a child in Ontario to begin publicly funded behavioural treatment is seven.[44] The cross-Canada data on this topic is sketchy, but there is enough anecdotal information from parents and autism organizations to conclude that, with the exception of Alberta, no province appears to be practising the kind of proactive early intervention in autism that would produce not only the functional gains we've seen for children, but also economic returns to government.

In response to a recent Quebec controversy over operating permits for a private centre devoted to engaging mid- to high-functioning autistic children, a *Montreal Gazette* editorial had this to say: "Of all groups let down by the inflexibility — and let's face it — frequent mediocrity of Quebec's financially strapped public health system, children with autism and their families might top the list."[45]

CONTROVERSIES

Notwithstanding the strong clinical and economic evidence supporting the expansion of behavioural therapy as an effective early intervention approach in autism, it is a controversial approach because of its very objectives and because of its founder, Dr. Ivar Lovaas.

People with autism often have to live with exclusion and antipathy because of neurodevelopmental delays and barriers along with their attendant symptoms. However, the very therapy that can, in many cases, address these delays and barriers carries the risks of dismantling or even destroying the individual's unique skills and capacities. For example, over time, ABA wires children to be attentive and involved in their social surroundings. Children are programmed to engage when being engaged by others and not remain in their own world, seemingly devoid of interest in the activities, conversation, and play occurring around them. They are taught to allow themselves to be interrupted and distracted. Yet, isn't it possible that it is a gift to be able to focus without distraction or interruption, even at risk of rudeness, on one topic or challenge for hours and hours on end? And might it not only be a gift that gives the autistic person pleasure, but also a gift to society insofar as their limitless and intense capacity to concentrate on one task can produce amazing results?

The unique talents of autistic people are a potential economic asset whose value is only beginning to be realized. At least that's the theory behind Specialisterne, a headhunting firm that matches employers with autistic job seekers.[46] Software firms like SAP are beginning to seek autistic hires for jobs like software testing and debugging — tasks where they believe autistic people perform better than neurotypical employees because they are better at repetition and attention to detail.[47] Other jobs for which autistic people may be uniquely suited include writing detailed instruction manuals, managing supply chains, and even simply providing a different point of view on creative tasks.

This idea that we need to "normalize" autistic persons through ABA or otherwise was challenged by Michelle Dawson, a Canadian woman living with autism who intervened in the *Auton v. British Columbia* case at the Supreme Court of Canada.[48] Ms. Dawson disagreed with the parents of Cameron Auton, who were asking the court to force the British Columbia government to pay for ABA for their autistic son on the grounds that it was "medically necessary." Ms. Dawson contested the claim on various grounds, including the characterization of autism treatment as medically necessary. She said this in her factum:

> *No allowance is made by the parties or the Courts below that untreated autistic traits which result in atypical learning and intelligence have great benefit both to autistics and society. The inherent strength of autisitics based on measurable differences in cognition (perception, attention, memory; and kind, not level, of intelligence) are unavailable to non autistics and, according to the principles of ABA and its practice, are unavailable to treated autistics.[49]*

In *Far From the Tree*, Andrew Solomon gives a lot of attention to this issue and refers to the decision of one family, the Lehrs, not to "fix" their autistic son, Ben. Solomon describes a conversation between the boy's mother and sister wherein the sister asks: "Do you ever wonder what it would be like if Ben were normal?" Ben's mother responds, "Well, I think he's normal for himself."[50]

There is a personal and ethical question to be asked and answered in every family facing autism; namely, the extent to which a child's autistic symptoms should be "treated." Is it for the child to adapt in all cases to the world around him or her, or for the world to adapt to the child?

Another significant controversy concerns Dr. Lovaas himself. First, the results of his ground-smashing study on treating autism through behavioural intervention have never been successfully replicated by later studies attempting to confirm his results. The Lovaas study has been criticized for a methodology that excluded autistic children with low IQ scores from treatment groups, assigning them instead in a self-serving way to control groups. While Lovaas appears to have stacked the deck in his own research study, it is clear that he was right in his general view that behavioural therapy could make a sizeable difference for many children. Many studies, including the Early Start Denver Model study, and thousands of families, like the Maurices, have confirmed the general conclusions of Lovaas's original research paper (though not its specific results).

Second, at the time the study was conducted in the 1970s, the treatment protocols he used for the research included what he called "aversives." Aversives, such as the "delivery of a loud 'No' or a slap on the thigh," were recommended by Lovaas as a last resort in the treatment of a child repeating unacceptable aggressive or self-stimulatory behaviour. According to Neurodiversity.com, "Lovaas actually used electric shock (as well as yelling and hitting) as aversive stimuli with children on the spectrum. As late as 1981, he advised parents to 'practice hitting on your friends, to see how hard you hit.'"[53] Catherine Maurice refused to allow the professional therapist she'd hired to administer any aversives to Anne Marie.

Thirdly, Lovaas used his behavioural techniques in the 1960s and 1970s in an effort to treat what he called "deviant sex-role behaviors in a male child."[52] Part of the treatment regime was to teach mothers to promote masculine behaviours in their sons and extinguish feminine behaviours (including clothing choices, use of cosmetics, and voice inflection). The family of a participant who later committed suicide blamed these procedures for causing him to abhor his own homosexual identity.[53]

However, with respect to these latter two controversies, Lovaas was a man of his times. Using aversives and trying to "treat" feminine behaviours in boys is seen as repugnant from the lens of 2015, but not from a 1970s perspective. Caution should be used against too harshly judging these methods from a twenty-first-century perch.

Lastly, the methods employed by Lovaas and his therapeutic progeny are limited to behavioural symptoms and have no way of getting at such characteristics as empathy and compassion. Behaviouralism does have its limits. That it has no module for love or sympathy should not be surprising as the objective of behavioural therapy is to effect functionality, not emotional aptitude or range. Perhaps it's not a wholly bad thing that behaviouralism is, indeed, limited, remembering Michelle Dawson's assertion that society needs to take measures to preserve the sometimes-uncanny abilities of autistic people.

FINAL THOUGHTS

Like so many other areas of the social services, the autism dossier could be greatly improved. While most provinces are offering publicly funded early intervention services based on the behavioural model, severe wait times for diagnosis and behavioural treatment are denying a very large number of children the opportunity to benefit from functional gains that can only be made in the early years. By following Alberta's lead and funding early behavioural intervention in an expeditious way for all children whose parents who wish it, all provinces can capture the opportunity to save taxpayer money over the long term. It is clearly a part of the social safety net where everyone gains by eliminating wait times.

CHAPTER 5

More Peaceful Schools

THE DANGERS OF BULLYING

A 2007 survey of Canadian adults undertaken by the Canadian Council on Learning asked participants whether they were bullied while attending school. The survey found that 38 per cent of men and 30 per cent of women "reported having experienced occasional or frequent bullying during their school years."[1] These same adults were asked about their own children's exposure to bullying and 47 per cent of participants who were parents reported that their child was subjected to some form of bullying.[2]

In 2010, the Public Health Agency of Canada reported that "22% of Canadian students between the ages of 11 and 15 reported being bullied, 12% reported having bullied others, and 41% reported both having been bullied and having bullied others."[3]

Canada has more than five million elementary and high-school students,[4] thus the universe of children that is exposed to bullying is immense.

The impact of bullying is as significant as its frequency. In a 2005 study of more than 120,000 students from twenty-eight different nations, it was found that bullied students, namely ones subjected to unwanted attention, teasing, intimidation, or violence twice a week or more, had twice the probability of experiencing headaches, stomach aches, backaches, or dizziness as non-victims. They were also up to seven-and-a-half times more likely to experience loneliness, nervousness, and depressive symptoms, among others.[5] Unsurprisingly, a bullied student is also at a higher risk of avoiding school, dropping out of school, and lower academic achievement.[6]

What about the bullies? Outcome studies have revealed that those victimizing others are at risk of higher substance abuse than their peers, aggressive behaviour with its attendant problems, and lower scholastic success.[7]

The provincial governments have jurisdiction for education, and many have introduced legislation or amended their education legislation to address school bullying. Ontario, for example, introduced the *Accepting Schools Act* in 2011.[8] The new law sets out a series of objectives that include increasing awareness about bullying, improving teacher training on its causes and effects, developing prevention and early intervention strategies, and creating a new regime of penalties for bullying behaviour. The law empowers schools and school boards to get organized to prevent bullying where possible and to discipline when it does occur. Other jurisdictions have also adopted similar measures, including Quebec and Manitoba.

While our education system in general is more of a springboard for young people than a safety net[9], components of it, like remedial and special education programs, breakfast and lunch programs, dropout-prevention projects, and anti-bullying measures, operate as a safety net for them.

Despite many legislative, awareness, and training initiatives regarding bullying and its dangers introduced by Canadian provinces and territories, the most recent UNICEF report on child well-being (2013) ranked Canada near the bottom on bullying. Canada placed twenty-first out of twenty-nine developed countries on the issue.[10] While the report adds that Canada has, in fact, improved on the bullying front since UNICEF's previous report in 2007, 35 per cent of school-aged children are still reported to be exposed to the phenomenon. This compares to an 11 per cent incidence rate in Italy, the first-ranked country.[11]

THE REENA VIRK STORY

In order to understand the driving forces behind these numbers, a specific example may be helpful. The Reena Virk story from British Columbia is a well-documented case of severe bullying, offered here to show the four-sided reality of most bullying incidents. These four sides are the victim, the bully, the school system, and the parents. The collection of incidents leading up to Reena Virk's death in 1997 is unusually well-documented, having been the subject of several books, one of which was written by Reena's father, Manjit, as well as extensive criminal court proceedings. We are able to see from this public record the manner in which the school system viewed and acted (as well as failed to act) in the circumstances.

Reena was born in March 1983, the first child of Manjit and Suman Virk. Her father had emigrated from India to Canada in the late 1970s, while her mother, also of Indian descent, was Canadian-born. There would be two other children, Simren and Aman, born after Reena. The family appeared to enjoy a happy and loving life in Saanich, British Columbia. The parents brought the children to the Punjab to meet Manjit's family. They holidayed in Hawaii and were thrilled by Disneyland. Manjit helped his wife with child care, cleaning, and shopping. Like any family, there was conflict. According to her father's memoir, Reena, from early on, "had an insatiable desire for attention."[12] On one occasion, out of anger or jealousy or both, she bit her baby sister Simren's finger. Despite such incidents, "teaching moments" according to Manjit Virk, the family appeared to be stable and happy. The Virks lived, in short, a typical middle-class Canadian existence.

The changes started in 1994 when Reena turned eleven. She began talking back and picking fights with her parents. She became regularly agitated and aggressive. Reena began to withdraw to her room and refused to attend worship services with the rest of the family on Sundays (the family were Jehovah's Witnesses). Manjit describes Reena as not being comfortable with herself. She refused to do homework and was careless in her dress and hygiene. The tension between Reena and Suman was palpable, and Manjit felt he had to play referee between them.

The problems with Reena festered and grew to the point that her parents considered either sending her away to India to stay with her paternal relatives or picking up and moving the whole family to their native country to start over. In the end, they decided to stay together in Canada and try to work through the issues, which Manjit and Suman attributed to the normal patterns of puberty. Manjit writes in his memoir that, in retrospect, he should have trusted his instincts and moved away.

No one will ever know the full causes of Reena's malaise, but it wasn't hormones alone. It was also bullying. Reena was a "big girl," as described by her father (the tallest in her class), from a minority community and had a deep need for attention and approbation. She was an ideal candidate to become a victim of bullying. From the beginning of middle school in 1994, Reena was teased, excluded, and taunted by classmates. She'd come home sad and cranky. Not surprisingly, she stopped wanting to go to school altogether. When her parents raised these problems with Reena's teachers, the advice given was simply "to avoid those kids." Reena made excuses to try to stay home. She was constantly feigning illness. Reena was easily agitated, taking out her frustration on her parents and siblings.

Manjit admitted that he and his wife did not take the bullying seriously enough. Clearly, Reena's teachers didn't, either. Neither parents nor teachers realized the stress and mental anguish Reena was increasingly experiencing. The Virks moved houses, and Reena moved schools, which helped temporarily. She managed to graduate from middle school in 1996.

Entering high school later that year, Reena hooked up with a tough crowd, which concurrently accepted her and victimized her. In effect, she put up with the abuse, including the theft of her money, clothes, and belongings, in exchange for their acceptance. Reena started smoking and doing drugs to keep up with this crowd. It appeared she'd do anything to be included by her peers. Her parents, fighting to disconnect her from what they saw as a dangerous gang and reconnect her with the family, became increasingly judgmental. In reaction, Reena told the police her father had sexually abused her.

After a summary investigation, child protection and the police placed Reena in the care of her grandparents. Manjit was charged with sexual assault and spent a night in jail before bail was posted. Reena was in and out of her grandparents' and foster homes over the course of the next year. She attempted suicide on one occasion by cutting her wrists. Confused and increasingly alone, Reena recanted her rape story in the early fall of 1997, moved back into the family home, and started attending a new school. But the reunion would not last long. Manjit felt little trust for his daughter and little respect for the way she dressed or her smoking habit. He refused to talk to her for fear of being re-accused of an offence. In November 1997, Reena abandoned the home and went to stay at the Kiwanis Emergency Youth Shelter, where she met Sally and Norah.

Sally and Norah befriended Reena, then bullied her. They included her in conversation, then excluded her. They took her makeup. When Reena's parents were away one weekend, Reena brought them home with her, where they proceeded to burglarize the house, taking jewellery and cash. One of them took Reena's Club Monaco sweater and, while Reena wanted it back, according to her father she preferred their "friendship" to the sweater.

On November 14, 1997, these new friends invited her to an outdoor party. Reena was staying at home that night, and her parents strongly recommended she not go. Reena went to the party anyway. What happened next has been reported widely in the press. Here's one version:

> *Reena was a mixed-up teenager who had drifted into*
> *a friendship with young people routinely described as*
> *"at risk." On the night of Nov. 14, the Grade 9 student*
> *at Colquitz Junior High was invited to party near the*

Gorge waterway. When she got there, she was surrounded by seven girls and one boy and beaten. Someone put a cigarette out on her forehead. The toughest girl in the pack eventually declared a stop to the assault. Reena walked away. But two people in the group returned to Craigflower Bridge, beat Reena again and dragged her to the water, where her head was held under. No one reported the incident to the police. Her body washed ashore eight days later. Police attention soon turned to a group of teenagers . . . Within weeks, police arrested six girls for the original assault on Reena. All of them were eventually convicted, receiving sentences ranging from 60 days to one year. Two other teens, Warren Glowatski, then 16, and Kelly Ellard, then 15, were charged with second-degree murder. Police investigators concluded that Glowatski and Ellard had returned to Craigflower Bridge to resume Reena's beating. Together, they dragged her into the water, and Ellard held her head under.[13]

Warren Glowatski was tried and convicted of second-degree murder in 1999. He received a life sentence with no eligibility for parole for seven years. Kelly Ellard was also tried and convicted, but the ruling was overturned on appeal and the case reheard. The second trial resulted in a hung jury, leading to yet another legal showdown. The third trial ended in a conviction that, though overturned in appeal, was confirmed on further appeal by the Supreme Court of Canada.[14] Glowatski served his time and was released on conditional parole in 2007; Kelly Ellard remained in prison as of the writing of this book in late 2014.

Manjit Virk summarized Reena's adolescent life in a few sentences in his autobiography: "Bullies put gum in her hair, teased her about her appearance and threatened to beat her up. This continued even in high school. Finally, bullies killed her."[15]

The Virks were participants in and witnesses to the distressing deterioration of their daughter. They talked to teachers, moved Reena from one school to another, and even considered moving away from Canada to protect their daughter from the bullying she was regularly and increasingly facing. Did the Virks do enough? Did they make the right decisions? Were they too tough and too strict? From the outcome of the case, it is easy to conclude the Virks mishandled their daughter and the situation in general. So did the school system, which had information and specific knowledge not only about Reena's ongoing troubles, but also about Warren Glowatski and Kelly Ellard. These latter were known by their teachers and administrators to be problematic, but nothing significant was done to discourage their dangerous behaviour. It is interesting that the only specific proactive intervention by a teacher and school social worker was to accompany Reena to the police station where she could make a formal report about being abused by her father. In other words, the sensitivity the system demonstrated to abuse by an adult was demonstrably more intense than that of abuse by peers. The teachers' only advice to Reena (and her parents) was to avoid the bullies.

The Reena Virk case is exemplary of the profound difficulties the school system has in assessing whether conflict between students is an opportunity for personal growth or dangerous to the mental and physical health of the participants. Too often, the system does nothing due to the mythology regarding childhood development, which emphasizes standing up for oneself and building character through conflict resolution.[16]

WAITING TOO LONG TO INTERVENE

These myths, along with the age-old adage that "kids will be kids," have contributed to a system-design problem in the educational sphere. The existing scholastic model continues in general to concentrate on delivering a set curriculum to groups of children in a classroom setting. Schools and teachers are evaluated largely on their capacity to deliver the core curriculum to approximately twenty-five to thirty children at a time. The social and emotional well-being of all students is not core to the scholastic mandate as a rule. This creates significant tension as teachers must try to deal with difficult and often-disruptive students and situations without falling behind in delivering the syllabus to the rest of the class. Managing these situations is one of the leading causes of teacher burnout[17] and explains why socially charged situations are often dealt with not by the teachers themselves, but by the school social work staff or the administration. These challenging children and situations are dealt with mostly through punitive measures, after the behaviour has become too disruptive for the teacher to manage alone. Suspensions and transfers are among the most common interventions when dealing with young people who don't conform to school rules and expectations.

In Reena's case, the system waited too long to make a difference. Multiple opportunities to address the issues were missed, including the first time Manjit and Suman raised the problem. The school did not have a structured and deliberate method of handling such a case as Reena's at the time. It is an example of a system locked in a pedagogical mindset, leaving the resolution of social conflict to the corner of the desk.

The problem is not one of personal fault or bad faith on the part of administrators or teachers. It is a system-design and capacity problem. Canadian educational leadership is awakening to the need to begin setting objectives that include the social and emotional well-being of students. For example, the Canadian Safe School Network, which includes a plethora of school board partners, envisions a society in which all children and youth can

- learn and grow in a caring, tolerant and violence-free environment;
- become empowered, self-advocate and apply strategies to respond in socially acceptable ways to personal safety issues, especially those that are potentially violent;
- trust adults to believe, respect and protect them from harm; and

- behave responsibly and accept the natural consequences of their own behaviour.[18]

However, the international bullying statistics and other figures cited at the top of this chapter suggest Canada is, at best, at the beginning of a process to include a focus on dealing with social conflict as a primary component of its model.

CYBERBULLYING

Reena Virk's tragic story from the late 1990s was a profound challenge for the school system. It took place prior to the wide adoption of social media. New forms of bullying have since emerged within this new digital environment that are deepening the challenge. In the United Kingdom, it was reported recently that "more than a million young people are subjected to extreme online bullying every day" due to the massive increase in the use of social media, especially Facebook.[19] This translates into seven out of ten young people between the ages of thirteen and twenty-two being bullied online, and almost three out of ten characterizing the bullying as "extreme."[20]

The most common form of cyberbullying is reported to be the unauthorized sharing of a private message or photo with others.[21] Two in five parents report that their child has had a role in online bullying such as this. Teachers know about cyberbullying and consider it important enough to rank it as their issue of "highest concern out of six listed options — 89 per cent said bullying and violence are serious problems in our public schools."[22]

REHTAEH PARSONS

The highly publicized case of Rehtaeh Parsons is a tangible example of how the educational system needs to take cyberbullying into account in addressing social violence. The Parsons case was subjected to an external review that evaluated and made public the school system's behaviour in the face of this tragic pattern of facts. The facts that follow are drawn from that external review, as well as a collection of media sources in 2013.[23] Rehtaeh was from Cole Harbour, Nova Scotia. In November 2011, at fifteen years old, she was at a party where drinking was going on. Her mother reported that she was sexually assaulted by four boys at the event. One of the four took photos of the crime. Traumatized and frightened, Rehtaeh only told her parents a few days after the incident. What ended up transforming her trauma into mental illness was the wide circulation of the photos of her on social media. At Rehtaeh's school, she was castigated and victimized, perceived as having brought the incident on herself. She was subjected to taunts and harassment that referred to her as "easy" and a "slut." She started skipping school on a regular basis, but this didn't help, because it was on the Internet that she suffered most.

On Facebook, Rehtaeh started receiving text requests for sex. She changed schools several times, but apparently could not escape the harassment. A lewd photo involving Rehtaeh continued to circulate, and the number of people who saw it and messaged about it also continued to grow. School officials did not transfer information to each other regarding her situation. Rehtaeh was admitted to the mental-health unit of the local hospital, then released, but her situation only seemed to deteriorate as, according to her father, she started cutting herself. The cyber harassment continued as well. Almost a year and a half of this abuse was enough for her. She attempted suicide in April 2013 and died a few days later.

What could the educational system have done? Can the overwhelmed and chronically underfunded schools prevent or reduce violence, conflict, and harm, including online harm, among their students?

Two experts reviewed the school's actions relating to the bullying Parsons experienced. They ascertained that although school staff did phone the Parsons home during Rehtaeh's numerous absences and one vice-principal did make some effort to assist, the teen did not receive much support from the school.[24] Interestingly, the same report points out that once the police got involved, the high school took "no further action" to either support Rehtaeh or her family or investigate the student suspects who had allegedly gang raped her in November 2011.

The lead expert said this about the whole situation:

> School systems need to address the whole child, not just academic standing. Young people who have serious mental-health problems need support. They cannot navigate systems themselves. Skipping school should be a signal to the school system, it should be a signal to parents, it should be a signal to friends.[25]

Though the teaching staff at Rehtaeh's school did see and hear many signals, they appear to have let the situation deteriorate, trusting others like Rehtaeh herself to take responsibility for resolving the conflict. The school had no organized manner to investigate and intervene effectively when the initial signs of trouble arose. Just as the schools Reena Virk attended had many chances to intervene, one must ask why Rehtaeh's schools failed to take advantage of the plentiful opportunities they had. We know the answer. It is not that the schools didn't care or that teachers were uninterested. The inquiry concluded that they squandered myriad moments to prevent the tragedy from escalating into a suicide attempt because the educational system simply isn't yet designed or resourced to either reduce the likelihood that bullying and violence will arise in the first place or to forcibly and effectively intervene to prevent further harm when it does. In a sentence: The Canadian educational system is not yet equipped to intervene early.

SOCIAL AND EMOTIONAL LEARNING

One emerging method for early intervention is to include structured and regular social and emotional learning opportunities for students in the school's programming. In a report prepared in August 2013 for the Alberta-based Carthy and Max Bell Foundation, Guyn Cooper Research

Associates said, "Social and emotional learning (SEL) is a framework for developing social and emotional competencies that is gaining interest in Canada and the United States."[26] SEL can be used to address bullying and school violence among other issues.

SEL was featured in the prominent professional magazine *Child Development* in an article in 2011 as a recommended approach to improve school performance in the area of student violence. The article, based on American statistics, made a very clear and sound argument for introducing evidence-based social and emotional learning initiatives into the school environment. The argument is relevant to the Canadian education system, given its similarities to American teaching traditions, performance priorities, and student realities.

Instead of moving toward codes of conduct or stiffer penalties for students and parents involved in or tolerating bullying, the article focused on the social and emotional learning of students.[27] It began with the premise that poor student outcomes and behaviour are related to underdeveloped social and emotional skills. The authors cited a few compelling statistics to this effect:

> *Unfortunately, many students lack social-emotional competencies and become less connected to school as they progress from elementary to middle to high school, and this lack of connection negatively affects their academic performance, behavior, and health. In a national sample of 148,189 sixth to twelfth graders, only 29%–45% of surveyed students reported that they had social competencies such as empathy, decision making, and conflict resolution skills.*[28]

They also posited that schools do not seem to be a place where these skills can be easily acquired. On this topic, the authors referred to a 2004 study that confirmed that:

Only 29% [of students] indicated that their school
provided a caring, encouraging environment. By high
school as many as 40%–60% of students become
chronically disengaged from school.[29]

So most students appear to have a limited emotional range, and most schools are failing to offer an ecosystem to expand that range. The result is not only a greater likelihood of poor behaviour, including violence and bullying, but also poor academic performance. It makes sense. How do we learn about the world if not with others and through others? Being able to manage one's emotions and pick up social cues gives a young person a greater chance to successfully navigate relationships with peers and teachers, and maximize their learning experience. A student unburdened with frustration, fear, anxiety, and jealousy has a huge learning advantage over one struggling to come to terms with these emotions. It is for these reasons that the authors of the report set out to determine "the effects of school-based social and emotional programming on children's behaviours and academic performance."[30]

The study examined programs that promote competencies such as the ability to "recognize and manage emotions, set and achieve positive goals, appreciate the perspectives of others, establish and maintain positive relationships, make responsible decisions, and handle interpersonal situations constructively." The authors analyzed reports involving more than 200 American high-school programs involving almost 300,000 students. The results indicated in general terms that, compared to those who did not participate in the programs, the students showed demonstrably better interpersonal and emotional skills, attitudes, and pro-social behaviours following intervention. These same students were also subjected to fewer disciplinary incidents and experienced less personal anxiety. These abilities translated into significant improvements on scholastic scores.[31]

A few important implications flow from this seminal report. First, it is clear that social and emotional skills can be taught and learned successfully. Parents and teachers who throw their hands in the air about the bad apples in the class being rotten to the core should read this report. Second, a student who is able to calm himself or herself, give space to others, negotiate, and compromise is significantly less likely to be personally involved in bullying among other objectionable behaviours. Last, this emotionally mature and empowered student will perform better scholastically than the student two chairs down who is struggling to understand his or her anger.

MARY GORDON

One social and emotional learning program that has demonstrated a mammoth impact on students, teachers, schools, and communities was created in Canada in 1996. It was founded by a Newfoundland-born teacher named Mary Gordon. Gordon grew up in a loving and progressive household that believed profoundly in giving back to the community. Three generations lived under one roof.[32] One rule in the house was that, during dinner, the conversation had to be centred on ideas and ideas only. It was a constant civics course. "There was definitely a sense that you were a citizen . . . and you were lucky for that," she once said.[33] Her father, a deputy minister in the Liberal government of Joey Smallwood, kept a tin can on the supper table into which he dropped his spare change. Mary's father explained to her one evening at age six that unfortunately neither she nor her sister, eight-year-old Susan, could have the "Mary-Jane party shoes [they] wanted because the money [in the tin can] would go to buy shoes for the little girls in India who didn't have any money."[34]

Another story goes that Mary's mother welcomed newly released prisoners back into society by offering a home-cooked meal. Mary and her siblings were required to sit at the table and interact with each parolee. She summed up her early lessons this way: "Your happiness should include the happiness of others."[35]

Like so many Atlantic Canadians, Mary Gordon left the East Coast after spending three years at Memorial University in St. John's, Newfoundland.

She arrived in Toronto in the late 1960s where she went to teachers' college, following which she began to teach at the kindergarten level. She wanted to work with and improve the lives of young kids. The call to service she had inherited as a child soon manifested itself further. In 1981, she decided she wanted to help young mothers in low-income areas, but she wasn't sure quite how to start a relationship with them that would quickly help Gordon understand the mothers' needs. What she decided to do looks like nothing less than a stroke of pure inspiration in retrospect. She borrowed a friend's baby with the idea of making herself seem less threatening. And she was. Doors opened, conversations commenced, and trusting relationships emerged. What Gordon gleaned from these early days was that student success was inextricably linked to family settings. A teacher's impact could only go so far. Engaged and active parents could make a huge positive difference in a young person's life.

These observations led Mary to create the first Parenting and Family Literacy Centres in Canada. To engage families in their children's learning, one of Gordon's strategies was to have English books translated into the mother tongue of immigrant families, so that parents could follow along the child's development and assist in understanding the stories. As the children's books were very short, Mary would have them translated in some cases by taxi drivers who spoke the native language in question . . . sometimes at red lights during the cab rides! Twelve children's books were translated in this enterprising manner. The result was very positive. Literacy rates of children whose parents participated in Parenting and Family Literacy Centre programs greatly improved.[36] Mary received international recognition for her work in bringing families and parenting into the middle of the learning experience.

Though these centres still exist today, serving thousands of Toronto families, and are now public policy across Ontario in both official languages, Mary Gordon had a new project in mind. By the mid-1990s, she had become distressed about the prevalence of family and school violence and child abuse and neglect. It had become her deeply felt view that the absence or insufficiency of empathy was at the root of this violent behaviour, and she wanted to do something about it. Her experience and credibility in the educational field and with vulnerable families led her to found Roots of Empathy.

ROOTS OF EMPATHY

Roots of Empathy is a school-based social and emotional learning program designed to increase the empathy of students through the presence of a baby and parent in the classroom. Here's the model. With a school's consent, a trained Roots of Empathy Instructor is assigned to a classroom. The instructor will work with the class over the entire school year. Although Roots of Empathy has different curricula for different grades, the core of its program is the same. A neighbourhood parent and baby visit the classroom nine times over the school year. The instructor guides the students in observing the baby's development and labelling the baby's emotions. In doing so, the instructor is helping the children identify and reflect upon their own emotions as well as those of others. The instructor visits the classroom the week before the baby and parent are due to arrive as well as the week after the baby and parent visit to reinforce the teachings. There are therefore twenty-seven total classroom visits over the year.

In the very first session, the instructor will explain that a parent and baby will be visiting with the children once per month over the school year, and that students will have the chance to see the remarkable changes the baby will experience over that time. During the parent-baby visit, the students will sit in a circle around a blanket to observe the interactions between the parent and the baby — a living model of empathy. For the next thirty to forty five minutes, the baby will greet every student, react to the sound of toys and the parent's cues, attempt to move and make the playful disarming sounds a baby makes. Students have the chance to ask the parent questions about the baby, including what the baby has learned, what sounds the baby can make, and what makes the baby feel happy. The instructor will share with the students how a baby learns and coach them in taking the baby's perspective. They'll talk about the baby's temperament, the relationship between the parent and infant, and how to keep the baby safe and secure.

During the post-family visit, the class debriefs and reflects with the instructor on what they learned from the parent-baby visit, including how it relates to the student's own experiences. For example, on the theme of crying, the instructor will pose questions to the class, such as, "Why does the Roots of Empathy baby cry?", "What does the parent do to soothe the baby?", "When did you feel sad?", "What did you do when you felt that way?", "Who helped you?" and "What can you do to help a friend who is sad?"

Every one of the nine themes covering the nine-month program follows the same pattern: a session to prepare for the parent and baby to arrive, a session with the parent and baby, and a debrief following the visit. The instructor, with the help of the teacher, will use activities, dialogue, children's literature, art, and other interactive techniques to draw out of the students their emotional experiences and opinions over the course of an entire school year.

Here is where the genius of Roots of Empathy lies. A baby and his or her parent together in a classroom create a true and genuine opportunity for school-aged children to discover, name, and articulate their own emotions vis-à-vis another human being. It brings them out of themselves and makes them feel what another person may be feeling. Roots of Empathy plants the seeds of empathy through its structured approach and fertilizes those seeds over the course of an entire school year. Here is the goal of Roots of Empathy in Mary Gordon's own words:

> *Empathy is the key ingredient of competent parenting,*
> *and the exploration of what it takes to be a responsive and*
> *responsible parent opens the door to emotional literacy*
> *for children creating change from the inside out. The skills*

they learn in the program will not only help them with
relationships today but will affect the quality of parenting
we can expect in the next generation.[37]

A more empathic person is more likely to refrain from participating in behaviours that harm others. Increasing empathy reduces bullying and school violence. This is the premise underpinning Roots of Empathy. The premise was specifically tested by Dr. Robert Santos and colleagues in a randomized control trial that began in 2002. Santos randomly assigned a cohort of more than 400 kindergarten, grade four, and grade eight Manitoba students to receive the Roots of Empathy program, while a control group of a nearly equal number did not (the control group was wait-listed and received the program in the next school year). The participating students' behaviour both before the program and for nearly three years afterwards were evaluated on three outcomes: physical aggression, indirect aggression, and pro-social behaviour. In an article published in *Healthcare Quarterly* in 2011, Santos reported that the Roots of Empathy program had a significant and lasting impact on student comportment and attitudes.[38] According to the authors, "Roots of Empathy had beneficial immediate effects on all outcomes, reducing physical aggression and indirect aggression and increasing prosocial behaviour."[39] Compared to the control group, Roots of Empathy cut school violence in two. The research team concluded by saying the program had an impact into at least the third year following a student's participation.

DARREN

In Mary Gordon's book about Roots of Empathy, published in 2005, she described the experience of one child named Darren who was profoundly affected by the program. He was fifteen years old in grade eight, having been held back two years. He had been through the child-protection system, bouncing from one foster home to another. He shaved his head clean except for a ponytail, and he had a tattoo on the back of his skull. Darren had seen a lot, probably too much for someone so young. And here he was, stuck in a class of thirteen-year-olds, discussing a baby's emotions. In this case, the baby's name was Evan and, surprisingly, Darren was listening intently during the exchanges about Evan's temperament. At one point, Evan's mom explained that the baby would get fussy and upset if he was faced inward when being toted around in Snugli, a sort of harness to carry a baby upright on one's torso. Evan preferred to face outward. When the class ended, the mom asked the students if any of them wanted to try on the Snugli. Darren raised his hand and proceeded to slip on the green and pink brocaded harness. Darren then dared to ask if he could carry baby Evan around in the device. The mom hesitated at first, but decided to let him, in essence, care for and nurture Evan, albeit for a short moment. Instead of putting him in facing outward, Darren put the baby in facing his chest. This is how Mary Gordon described what happened next:

> *That wise little baby snuggled right in, and Darren took him into a quiet corner and rocked back and forth with the baby in his arms for several minutes. Finally, he came back to where the mother and the Roots of Empathy instructor were waiting and he asked, "If nobody has ever loved you, do you think you could still be a good father?"*[40]

Since its inception in 1996, the Roots of Empathy program has been offered to more than half a million children in eleven different countries. It is operating in every Canadian province. The research continues to confirm this particular social and emotional literacy initiative is world-class.[41] Participating students show an average increase of 78 per cent in helping behaviours, a 39 per cent drop in social aggression, and huge increases in sharing and peer acceptance.[42]

American neurobiologist Dr. Sue Carter theorized that the Roots of Empathy program is so effective because of a hormonal response of participating students to the presence of the baby. Carter had performed pathfinding hormone studies and found that one hormone in particular, oxytocin, seems to drive behaviours such as caring and trust. In a recent interview, she said that Roots of Empathy "may be an oxytocin story." She added this: "I believe that being around the baby is somehow putting the children in a biologically different place. We don't know what that place is because we haven't measured it. However, if it works here as it does in other animals, we would guess that exposure to an infant would create a physiological state in which the children would be more social."[43]

Professor Stuart Shanker argues that Roots of Empathy's success is founded on its ability to help children develop self-awareness and self-regulation. He suggests that, in creating an environment of safety and inquiry, children can be calm enough and alert enough to acquire empathy. And because the experience "feels good, you want to repeat the experience."[44]

Roots of Empathy acts as a "behavioural vaccine."[45] In other words, by repeated exposure to an empathic environment, an inoculation of sorts is administered to participating students. We vaccinate against polio, measles, mumps, and the flu. Why not violence?

The program's results recently led the government of Scotland to adopt Roots of Empathy as one of its cornerstone initiatives for increasing school safety for all Scottish children. Roots of Empathy is in every school in Scotland because Scotland has set as an objective for itself to be the best place in the world to grow up. There's also an interesting economic argument for buying Roots of Empathy for all kids.

THE RETURN ON AN EARLY INTERVENTION

In Manitoba, the cost of bringing a Roots of Empathy program into a classroom is approximately $108 per child per year (which includes instructor, materials, and transportation costs).[46] The cost for a classroom of thirty children is about $3,500 per year.[47] To complete the math, the cost for a 1,000-student school would be in the range of $100,000.

Now let's look at the cost of bullying. It has direct and indirect facets. The direct costs are many and include suspensions, expulsions, and alternative school placements that flow from the school's legal obligations to address incidents of violence. As we've seen, truancy and dropping out also rise in direct proportion to increases in violence. Spikes in vandalism also produce additional financial burdens on schools that face increased bullying. The actual value of the direct costs will, of course, vary from one school to the next. In the United States, the National Association of Secondary School Principals (NASSP) published a study that calculated the typical cost of bullying for a 1,000-student public high school using the above cost factors. They generated the staggering figure of $2.3 million, with the largest part due to lost school revenue from student dropouts and expulsions.[48] The NASSP invites all schools to calculate their own costs by downloading their School Climate Loss and Cost Calculator.[49]

The Roots of Empathy program cost of $100,000 for a 1,000-student school would appear to be a sound economic investment when weighed against the costs it serves to diminish. Though Roots of Empathy won't and doesn't claim to eliminate all problems of school violence, it would appear to easily pay for itself in the same year the investment is made from the reduction in direct costs (e.g. suspensions, explusions, and alternative school placements) a participating school would otherwise be obliged to incur.

What about the indirect costs, such as increases in health-care costs and productivity loss? One estimate puts the cost of conduct disorders at about $8,000 per child per year.[50] This figure includes policing, judicial, and correctional services. Millions were spent on prosecuting the offenders in the Reena Virk case (three times in the case of Kelly Ellard). If Roots of Empathy only succeeded in discouraging thirteen students in a 1,000-student school from engaging in violence, the entire cost of introducing the program to the entire school would be paid for.

Roots of Empathy has been offering its program in the province of Manitoba since 2001. Its presence in the province is in part due to economics. In 2013–14, Manitoba Children and Youth Opportunities Minister Kevin Chief announced that more than $350,000 would be spent on Roots of Empathy programs across the province. In an article in the *Winnipeg Free Press* on May 23, 2013, the minister justified the spending in the following way: "The positive behaviour that comes from having compassion is worth the investment . . . Every dollar invested in early childhood programs results in $17 saved."[51]

FINAL REFLECTIONS

There is an interesting denouement to the Reena Virk case. Kelly Ellard fought her repeated convictions three times at trial level: twice at the British Columbia Court of Appeal and once all the way to the Supreme Court of Canada. Warren Glowatski, on the other hand, confessed to his part in the murder and served as a witness in the prosecution of Kelly Ellard. His background was not easy. Raised in a difficult home with a severely low income and moving all the time, he was left to his own devices at age sixteen when his father decided to take a job in California. He doesn't really know why he helped Ellard commit the crime, other than the fact that violence was what he knew and understood. He started to feel great remorse about his role quite soon after the event. While incarcerated, he spent a great deal of time with the prison psychologist reflecting on the kind of person he had become. He decided he wanted to change, and the youth correctional services staff asked if he'd like to start by apologizing to the Virk family. He did, indeed, meet with Reena's parents who, without forgiving him, were impressed by his sincerity. Manjit tried to convey the message that one life was already lost, and that Warren, who served his term, should be allowed to begin again. The point is that there was empathy in Warren Glowatski. It just came out too late to prevent the Reena Virk tragedy.

CHAPTER 6

Healthier Health Care

Canada spends more than $200 billion on health care every year. Health-care services are used about 400 million times a year by our population.[1] That our system has a sustainability challenge, especially in light of changing demographics, is not in question. This challenge was encapsulated in the *Huffington Post* in February 2014:

> *A little over 2 months ago, the Society of Actuaries
> and the Canadian Institute of Actuaries released their
> "Sustainability of the Canadian Health Care System
> and Impact of the 2014 Revision to the Canada Health
> Transfer," report, outlining the viability of our health
> care system over a 25-year horizon. While the report
> seemed to slip under the media radar, the results
> are nonetheless daunting. Actuarial analysis of the
> Canadian health care system concludes that, at current
> growth rates, a staggering 97 per cent of total revenues
> available to provinces and territories will be spent on*

health care expenditures by 2037, compared to 44 per cent in 2012.[2]

Calling none of them "appealing," former Bank of Canada governor David Dodge laid out the following options for addressing the issue in a recent report for the C.D. Howe Institute:

1. *a sharp reduction in public services, other than healthcare, provided by governments, especially provincial governments;*

2. *increased taxes to finance the public share of healthcare spending;*

3. *increased spending by individuals on healthcare services that are currently insured by provinces, through some form of co-payment or through delisting of services that are currently publicly financed;*

4. *a major degradation of publicly insured healthcare standards — longer queues, services of poorer quality — and the development of a privately funded system to provide better-quality care for those willing to pay for it, as in the UK and many European countries.[3]*

This chapter is about a fifth and more appealing option, namely reducing the pressure on and cost of the existing system through the scaling of evidence-based early intervention measures. The existing health system is largely a traditional late-intervention one, as evidenced in part by the fact that its largest area of expenditure is hospital services.[4] As Jeffrey Simpson said in his book *Chronic Condition*, "The Canadian health care system was originally designed around hospitals and, to a fault, it remains so today."[5] Could an early intervention approach across health care improve the system's long-term sustainability and improve health outcomes for its millions of users?[6] I'll make an attempt to answer this question by examining four different health-care settings, namely youth mental health, stroke, dementia, and falls.

YOUTH MENTAL HEALTH
The Bilermans

The experience of the Bilerman family in Fredericton, New Brunswick, will set the scene for a look at the youth mental-health system in Canada. Maureen Bilerman is an articulate parent-activist who has spoken widely on her family's encounters with the existing institutions mandated to deal with mental illness. Her family's story is typical of how the existing mental-health services are organized and provides the necessary narrative to query whether an alternative to the status quo wouldn't be both more effective and less costly over time.

Sarah Bilerman was a typical, shy thirteen-year-old when she started losing interest in school, family, and her normal activities.[7] She became intense and even appeared manic at times. Defying her parents, Maureen and Shawn, on all fronts, she started destroying furniture and screaming dramatically about the smallest things. Her confrontational attitude was stark and out of character. Her parents brought her to see a psychologist, who concluded she was too young and lacked sufficient insight to allow for a clear diagnosis. Late one night, Maureen received a phone call from Sarah. After everyone had gone to bed, Sarah had packed a bag and slipped out of the house. She walked out of her neighbourhood and then made her way to a major highway without having a destination in mind. As she left the outskirts of Fredericton, walking on the shoulder of the highway, she stopped in her tracks with the realization that she didn't know where she was going. She called her mother from her cellphone and asked her for a lift home. Driving in the foggy night, Maureen recalls feeling like events were about to come to a head. And they did.

Here's what happened next in Maureen's own words:

> *It took eight months for the situation to completely*
> *unravel. It took Sarah coming into our bedroom one night*
> *to tell me she had taken an entire bottle of Extra Strength*
> *Tylenol. We took her to Emergency where she was treated*
> *for the overdose. Although she was still suicidal there are*
> *only six beds in all of New Brunswick [in Moncton] where*
> *children and youth in need of a mental health diagnosis*
> *can go. The beds were full and they sent us home.*
> *   I spent the next six weeks on suicide watch with*
> *Sarah, sleeping with her, following her into the washroom,*
> *hiding medications and razors. Almost every week she*
> *would become so distraught I would take her back up to*
> *the hospital where we would spend the night sitting up*
> *in Emergency, waiting for the psychiatrist to arrive in*
> *the morning. Sarah would be assessed and although she*
> *was still feeling suicidal they would send her home again*
> *because there simply was no place for her to go.*[8]

After a long waiting period, Sarah was finally seen by professionals at a specialized facility for children and adults two hours away in Moncton. Maureen describes the physical space as "right out of *One Flew Over the Cuckoo's Nest*," and as a "truly terrifying place" for a thirteen-year-old. Sarah stayed at the facility for a month and was finally diagnosed with bipolar disorder. She was then referred to a psychiatrist in Fredericton. Though kind and caring, the psychiatrist's only mode of treatment was medication. The family was on its own again. Sarah overdosed three more times on painkillers, and she plummeted again and again into the hospital system.

Maureen and Shawn hung on. They continued to do everything in their power to help their daughter. Maureen asks how much worse off

Sarah might have been if she and Shawn weren't a loving couple who were devoted to each other and if they weren't wealthy enough to afford the kind of home and environment they were blessed to have.

Over and above the agony of untreated mental illness Sarah has endured and the distress the Bilerman family has suffered, Sarah has cost the New Brunswick health system, its hospital budget in particular, a load of money.[9] The system wasn't designed to address Sarah's condition from its onset. Specialists thought Sarah might be simply acting out and seeking attention like so many teenagers. They didn't trust her. They let Sarah's condition deteriorate until it was an emergency. The New Brunswick hospital treated her for an overdose several times, but had no resources, methods, or protocols to prevent the self-harm from recurring. They were not organized to intervene the first time Sarah was wheeled in and to avert the repeated episodes that cost the system so much.

Youth Mental Illness in Canada

The Canadian Nursing Association (CNA) summed up the mental illness situation concisely in 2013:

> *The needs of people living with mental illness are not being adequately met by the Canadian health system. Far too many Canadians are turning up at our emergency departments or being hospitalized unnecessarily for health conditions that could and should be managed in the community. This is a function of insufficient system-wide capacity.*[10]

A 2013 report of the British Columbia Representative for Children and Youth chillingly entitled *Still Waiting* confirmed the CNA's observation, stating,

*Families and caregivers strongly indicated that they are
not well-served by the system. Those surveyed consistently
identified wait times as a significant barrier, with about
half of parents and caregivers indicating that their child
had been placed on a wait-list. Said one parent: "We had
to wait until my daughter became violent before even a
semblance of help appeared."[11]*

Based on 2011 data, in excess of six and a half million people were living
with symptoms of mental illness in Canada, representing approximately 20
per cent of the population. Of this total, more than one million were children and adolescents between the ages of nine and nineteen.[12] Although
these young people represent only 15 per cent of Canadians living with
depression, anxiety, psychosis, and other disorders, 70 per cent of such ill-
nesses begin prior to the age of twenty-five.[13] This means that of the five
and a half million adults with mental illness, four million or so faced the
onset of their disease in their youth and have lived with it ever since.

Only about one in four young people with a mental-health condition
gets any treatment at all.[14] And of those who receive treatment, a small
minority receive adequate service.[15] The reason for this situation is quite
simple. Canada is comparatively good at emergency, acute, and intensive care, the kind of care that a hospital can deliver industrially, like
piecework. Provinces have invested heavily in hospital infrastructure,
hospital machines, and hospital professionals. And hospitals can play
an important role in addressing the emergencies associated with youth
mental illness, like sedation, stomach pumping, and surgery. However,
families like the Bilermans are doomed to an overreliance on hospitals
because there are often no other choices. This limited vision drives the
inappropriate repeated use of hospitals for chronic care and the cost
escalation that accompanies it.

Canada spent $3,329 per person on health services in 2010, of which
$244 was spent on mental-health services (primarily hospitals, medication,

general and specialized services, and income support).[16] This direct spending by government is only accessible to one in five young people in Canada and provides a fairly gruesome quality of care. The actual costs of mental illness are higher than health-care spending alone. In a study commissioned by the Mental Health Commission of Canada (MHCC), the total cost from mental-health problems to the Canadian economy is estimated to be "at least $50 billion per year. This represents 2.8% of Canada's 2011 gross domestic product."[17] This total cost translates into a little more than $1,500 for every Canadian and more than $7,500 for every person having symptoms of mental illness (20 per cent of the population).

Early Psychosis Prevention and Intervention Centre

Dr. Patrick McGorry was named Australian of the Year in 2010. Normally, this prestigious and singular national award goes to pop stars, actors, athletes, or musicians. In 2010, it went to a fifty-eight-year-old physician-psychiatrist-researcher who had been working with young people with mental illness his entire career. Back in the early 1970s, when he began his career, colleagues tried to dissuade him from heading into psychiatry because of the profound stigma attached to the field. Dr. McGorry describes the mental-health field at the time as "apartheid-like" because it was viewed and funded as a second-class system in comparison to the way the "physical" health system was treated. Those were the days when patients were sometimes handcuffed in the back of ambulances and brought to the psychiatric hospital, where the care they received resembled "veterinary" medicine. Yet, Dr. McGorry sensed this was the domain in which he could make a real difference. "Mental health was a total greenfield opportunity in the '70s," he said.[18]

Describing himself as a "clinician who does research," Dr. McGorry has concentrated mainly on treating severe mental illness, including schizophrenia and bipolar disease, the two most-common forms of the condition known as "psychosis," which share the symptom of disconnectedness from reality.

Not one to mince his words, Dr. McGorry describes the last century's treatment of psychosis as "a corrosive blend of pessimism, stigma, and neglect [that] has confined therapeutic efforts to delayed and inconsistent palliative care."[19] Building on some earlier research successes in the 1980s, Dr. McGorry and his colleagues posited that by intervening with patients at the onset of the disease (or even earlier), when delusions and hallucinations were first being experienced, they could avert the symptoms from fully developing into a permanent, chronic condition. He had seen too often in his clinical practice the tragic consequences of doing nothing. Because onset occurred mostly in late adolescence or early adulthood, the disease might end up lasting a full lifetime. As Dr. McGorry says:

> *Without appropriate early intervention, significant disruption to the young person's psychosocial development becomes the norm. Maturation is put on hold, social and family relationships are strained or sometimes severed, and educational and vocational prospects are derailed. Secondary problems such as substance use, unemployment and behavioural problems may develop or intensify and the illness itself may become more deeply entrenched. Early intervention aims to either prevent the onset of psychosis, or if this occurs, to facilitate recovery and allow the young person to achieve to their full potential.[20]*

Using a variety of clinical interventions, including psychotropic medication and psychotherapy, Dr. McGorry and his team determined that reducing the duration of untreated psychosis (DUP) could substantially help young people toward a trajectory of recovery.[21] Other studies confirmed the finding.[22] The evidence produced by Dr. McGorry and his team led to the creation of one of the first early psychosis programs: Melbourne, Australia-based Early Psychosis Prevention and Intervention

Centre (EPPIC).[23] EPPIC's success in helping many young Australians facing psychosis get back on the wire of their lives has spawned other such programs around the world, including several in Canada.[24] As well, EPPIC is being rolled out from Melbourne to all parts of the country,[25] not only because it works to impede the progression of disease, but also because it saves money for government.

EPPIC's own calculations show that adolescents receiving faster attention can end up costing the government as little as a third of the price tag of those with longer DUPs, every year over the course of their lifetimes.[26] Other cost-effectiveness studies confirm that early intervention in the field of psychosis is a good investment. One such study examined the returns of a Danish early psychosis program called OPUS, which was inspired by Dr. McGorry's work in Australia. The name OPUS was drawn from the world of music "in order to express the necessity for different instruments to play together according to a carefully prepared plan that is organized and coordinated by a conductor."[27] The program offered a suite of interventions to young people having symptoms of psychosis, including enriched assertive community treatment, psycho-educational family treatment, and social-skills training. Against a randomly controlled group with the same profile, the researchers concluded "that there was a high probability of OPUS being cost-effective compared with standard treatment." As a result of these studies, the government of Denmark has increased the number of OPUS teams serving youth with first-episode psychosis by tenfold from 1998 to 2013; however, more coverage is necessary to serve all Danish youth.[28] Many other studies have confirmed the financial argument in support of early psychosis intervention.[29] Interestingly, the authors of the OPUS study added that a richer suite of early interventions produces a higher likelihood of economic returns.[30]

This goes to an important point we've seen in other areas, like early intervention in autism. It's not just speed that matters. Quality counts, too. The big payoff in early intervention generally requires a firm and tenacious attention to the quality of the programs themselves.

Glimmers

In June 2013, the Canadian Wait Time Alliance reported that although the Canadian Psychiatric Association's (CPA) recommended wait times of no more that two weeds for assessment referral for first-episode psychosis, not a single Canadian province was able to report on its ability to meet this standard.[31] Though young people get a real chance at recovery and the government gets a real chance to save money, early psychosis programs are not available everywhere in Canada. New Brunswick didn't have an effective one to help Sarah Bilerman and her family when they needed it.

Many early psychosis programs have been launched in Canada since then that are meeting CPA standards, including programs in Montreal[32] and London.[33] Fraser Health in British Columbia is also reporting success

> *with 13 per cent more people seen within one week of referral, and 60 per cent of first treatments occurring in the community instead of in the hospital. Health outcomes have been positive as well, with 71 per cent of people experiencing significant improvements in psychiatric symptoms at six months, and 21 per cent having complete remission of symptoms at one year.[34]*

However, there is still a great deal of work to be done to make quality early psychosis programs available to all youth in a timely way. A forthcoming peer-reviewed article made this observation on the topic:

> *In Canada, specialized EI (early psychosis) services emerged in the late 1990s. While EI [Early Intervention] services exist in most provinces, much remains to do on*

the policy front to make them universally available to Canadians. Many Canadians, especially those in rural and remote areas, still cannot access EI services as many are based in urban academic institutions. Canada also lacks national-level policy/funding commitment to EI services. This is in stark contrast to the UK's policy-driven scaling up of EI services to cover the entire population.[35]

So, although there are Canadian centres of excellence in addressing the onset of psychosis in youth, there are simply not enough of them.

STROKE
Brain Attack

Dr. Vladimir Hachinski, a renowned Canadian neurologist specializing in stroke care, has suggested that the very name of this health condition be changed to "brain attack."[36] He says that the term "stroke" makes this very serious condition sound gentle and unobtrusive, like stroking your pet cat or dog. He wants it renamed to reflect the urgent health crisis that it is. Dr. Hachinski has said that "to give the best chance of limiting damage, brain attacks should be heeded even more urgently than heart attacks."[37] Describing the event as an "attack" makes it sounds as if it requires immediate attention. And it does. It is not widely known that early intervention can save stroke victims.[38]

Stroke, which is a leading cause of death in Canada and the United States, has two varieties. The most common is an artery blockage that deprives the brain of the oxygen it needs to survive. This is called an ischemic stroke. The longer the blockage remains, the more brain damage that occurs. This type of stroke represents 85 per cent of all incidents. The other type is the rupturing of the blood vessels into and in the brain. This hemorrhaging diverts blood destined to feed the brain to parts unknown. This type is called a hemorrhagic or bleeding stroke. Victims respond to strokes differently, depending on which part of the brain has been affected. In the case of Dr. Jill Bolte Taylor, it was the left lobe of her brain.

Dr. Jill Bolte Taylor

Dr. Bolte Taylor is a Harvard brain scientist.[39] Her attraction to neuroscience resulted from tending to her schizophrenic brother. She decided to devote her life to mapping the microcircuitry of the human brain. She toiled away in research for many years, while also volunteering for the American National Alliance on Mental Illness. Then, on December 10, 1996, at the age of thirty-seven, Dr. Bolte Taylor woke up in the morning with a bad headache. She didn't think much of it at first and tried to start her day as usual with a cardio workout. She looked at her hands as she gripped her workout machine and they were bent out of shape like animal claws. Everything seemed to be slowing down. She was having trouble figuring out where the boundaries of her body were as they seemed to be blending in with the walls. Her headache intensified, and she finally realized she was having a stroke.

In the space of four hours, Dr. Bolte Taylor lost the ability to walk, talk, read, and remember. She felt like an infant in a woman's body. The stroke had affected the left side of her brain. The left and right lobes play different roles related to lateralized control of the body, perception, and language, among others. Though the left side of her brain had essentially gone silent, the right side, the only functioning side, exploded with colour and importance, offering a truly different experience of the world. Dr. Bolte Taylor explains that she felt expansiveness and beauty all around her, a world without limits. Released from left lobe control, the right side of Dr. Bolte Taylor's brain offered her the gifts of lightness, peacefulness, euphoria, and love all at the same time and with an intensity she had never felt before.

She said to herself, "How many brain scientists get to experience this kind of brain event?" It was, she noted, a stroke of luck to have the chance to tap into the full power of brain's right side.

She tried to phone her office, but she couldn't recognize the numbers on her business card. So for forty-five minutes, she attempted to match the shape of the numbers on the card to the identical shape on the phone. She finally succeeded in dialling her office, but she had lost the capacity to both speak and to understand what her colleague was saying to her. All the sounds came out sounding like "DUOH." Her colleagues did realize she was in trouble and the ambulance finally arrived to take her to Massachusetts General Hospital in Boston. On her way to the hospital, she knew she might not survive, so she "let her spirit soar free to Nirvana."

But she did survive. However, the hospital didn't finally intervene until the next day. It took protracted surgery to remove a golf ball–sized clot from an artery in her head, then a full eight years of occupational therapy to completely recover her functionality. It had taken the Boston health system more than twenty-four hours to fully recognize what Dr. Bolte Taylor was experiencing and take action. This was, admittedly, 1996. We know a lot more now about the value of faster treatment. If she had been treated the same day, the length of her recuperation might have been significantly shorter. The organization Power to End Stroke has adopted the following slogan to encourage early intervention: "Learn to recognize a stroke, because time lost is brain lost."[40]

Why is time so precious? If a clot-busting drug such as Alteplase is administered within approximately three hours of the onset of an ischemic stroke (the most common type of stroke), the likelihood of long-term disability is reduced significantly. This treatment is called thrombolysis.[41] It would appear that Dr. Bolte Taylor would have greatly benefited from this procedure.

Even more effective is recognizing the early symptoms that most often occur prior to the onset of a full stroke. A "mini-stroke" happens in a great deal of cases. It's officially titled a transient ischemic attack (TIA) because the blood flow to the brain is only interrupted for a short time. The symptoms are the same as for a stroke, but they usually last only a few minutes or hours, and disappear altogether within twenty-four hours. Total stroke prevention is achievable if intervention occurs at the TIA stage.

Stroke Care in Canada

A total of 50,000 strokes occur every year in Canada, about one every ten minutes. While 14,000 people die from such brain attacks, 315,000 people are living today with the effects of stroke.[42] The good news in Canada is that the number of hospital visits and the rate of hospitalization has been declining since the mid-1990s, and so has the rate of death due to stroke.[43] The bad news is that two-thirds of patients who have an ischemic stroke do not arrive at a hospital that is in a position to provide optimal care.

Even worse, only 22 per cent of patients who arrive within three and a half hours of the onset of stroke symptoms receive the necessary care to prevent most long-term disabilities associated with stroke.[44] A University of Toronto study released in October 2014 uncovered a related problem. The researchers studied stroke care delivery and outcomes for two cohorts; namely, those who had a stroke while in the community (about 32,000 people), and those who had a stroke while already hospitalized for other reasons, such as a hip replacement (more than one 1,000 cases). They were surprised to find that relative to community patients, people with in-hospital strokes

> *waited significantly longer from the time stroke symptoms were recognized to neuroimaging (i.e., a CT scan), waited longer from the time a stroke was confirmed to getting clot-busting drugs, and were less likely to receive clot-busting drugs than those who were admitted following strokes outside of hospitals, even when they were eligible.*[45]

"There is evidence that people do worse when they have a stroke in the hospital, and not just because they are already sicker,"[46] said the lead author.

A 2011 report prepared for the Canadian Stroke Network looked into the net costs of implementing an optimal-care regime across the country that included early and effective stroke intervention. It concluded that such a regime would not only lead to a 20 per cent reduction in acute-care services, a 15 per cent reduction in deaths, and a 5 per cent reduction in institutional care, but we would also save $302 million in direct service costs and $436 million in lost productivity.[47] In 2013, Australia's National Stoke Foundation asked Deloitte Access Economics to investigate the same issues as the Canadian Stroke Network, and they reported similar findings.[48]

Dr. Bolte Taylor is back at work, mapping the human brain and sharing her amazing personal story about the power of the right hemisphere. It took an enormous amount of time, struggle, pain, and money to get her fully back on her feet. But now, we know how much spending can be avoided by providing early intervention and other services to Canadians experiencing what Bolte Taylor experienced in 1996. We know that early intervention radically reduces the likelihood of subsequent strokes; it also reduces readmission rates to hospitals, number of bed days for readmissions, acute care costs, and disability costs. In the United Kingdom, savings from early intervention are estimated to be in the order of £624 (approximately $1200) per patient per year.[49] The change has begun, but is slow to get fully off the ground. More strategic investment in early intervention will save more lives and save more money.

DEMENTIA

Early intervention for dementia patients can be an equally sound investment. British Columbia's Jim Mann, a dementia patient himself and advocate for other Canadians with the same medical condition, has put his own story into the public domain in a rich and transparent way. It will serve as the backdrop to how orienting our services toward earlier intervention produces many positive returns.

He was not ninety-eight or eighty-eight or even seventy-eight years old when, travelling on business as an executive for Canadian Airlines, he went up and down the escalators twice trying to remember why he was at the airport and where he was supposed to go. Fifty-eight years old and thoroughly embarrassed, Mann had to ask airport staff for help figuring out where he was going and when his flight was.

Mann's mother had had Alzheimer's, and he learned about the condition from her. He also learned about the stigma attached to it, the training health-care workers need to diagnose and treat it, and the fact that it doesn't only hit elderly people.

He made it to retirement, and even though he was starting a consulting business, Mann had to give up the effort. As he became uncharacteristically disorganized, he lost confidence in his abilities to adequately serve his clients. He finally sought help after driving off to do an errand, forgetting why he had ventured out, and in his confusion, almost hitting a pedestrian. He surrendered his driver's licence after he received his diagnosis and doesn't drive to this day. He actually felt somewhat relieved to know about the condition as he could start getting organized to fight it. He started deferring more responsibilities to his wife (as hard as he says that was). He never turns the stove on without her around. He writes everything down, including messages reminding himself to clean his glasses and take a drink of water.

Mann's frustrations are endless. He gnashes his teeth over computer navigation. He has to refill the coffee machine, often many times, because he's forgotten how many scoops he needs to put in it. He's gotten lost in the neighbourhood he's lived in for eighteen years.

He says he lives the "split personality" of Alzheimer's disease; one-half of the personality is the real Jim, and the other, a forgetful and incompetent man he and his family don't recognize. One day he lives independently, and the next, he's childlike. He calls this the "ever-changing landscape of eggshells" as everyone is walking on them, not knowing which person Jim will be today.

There is life after the diagnosis, Mann says, if it's diagnosed early enough.

Rising Tide

Alzheimer's disease is named after Dr. Alois Alzheimer. A German doctor born in the mid-1800s, Dr. Alzheimer was part of the medical staff at a state-run asylum in Frankfurt. Over the years, he became a widely published neurologist with interests in such areas as epilepsy and syphilis. He became particularly adept at tracking clinical developments in his patients and then correlating them with alterations of the brain post-autopsy. In 1901, Dr. Alzheimer met a patient code-named "Auguste D.," a woman in her early fifties. Auguste D. was his patient in Frankfurt for many years. As her condition steadily deteriorated, she displayed "memory loss, difficulty with speech, confusion, suspicion, agitation, wandering, and screaming when bedridden. She became incontinent and unaware of her surroundings."[50] After her death, Dr. Alzheimer conducted an autopsy and found that Auguste D.'s brain had shrunk and brain cells had died. He also discovered neurofibrillary tangles and senile plaques, characteristics that he linked to dementia. These are the telltale signs of the disease that, as of about 1906, bears his name — the disease Jim Mann lives with every day.

According to a study called *Rising Tide*, about a half-million Canadians were living with Alzheimer's disease as of 2010.[51] That number is expected to triple by 2038. This seminal study estimates that, if we continue to manage the disease in a reactive last-resort way (namely through hospitalizations and nursing home care), the economic burden to Canada will increase from $15 billion in 2008 to $153 billion in 2038 (adjusted for inflation). The authors of *Rising Tide* made the following three recommendations to lower the tide:

- Increase physical activity.
- Provide caregiver training and support.
- Improve system navigation.[52]

The authors suggested that implementing these four measures aggressively across the population and across the country offered the "potential for dramatic reductions in economic impact over the next 30 years."[53]

A study commissioned by the Ontario Brain Institute recently found that physical activity alone is able to prevent one person in seven from ever getting the disease at all.[54] Moreover, the study found that, "in older adults without Alzheimer's disease, those who were very physically active were almost 40% less likely to develop Alzheimer's disease as those who were inactive." Exercise seems to have a protective impact on the brain. It can even slow the progression of Alzheimer's symptoms after onset.[55] And the cost savings? Up to $52 billion dollars over the next thirty years in health-care costs.[56]

Declaring War

Jim Mann is a prolific speaker. Six years after his diagnosis, he travels the province of British Columbia to get his message out that the stigma that is still attached to Alzheimer's needs to be lifted. We can no longer afford to live in an environment in which we hide the early symptoms in a closet. The clinical and financial benefits we gain by immediately telling our families and doctors about memory loss, disorganization, and lack of focus are too great to allow the stigma attached to dementia to persist.

The accepted best practice to determine if Alzheimer's-type brain deterioration is present is to interview family and friends of the patient and conduct an office-based clinical assessment.[57] By using standard cognitive tests and listening to family and friends, the primary-care physician can make a reliable clinical diagnosis more than 90 per cent of the time.[58] There is a consensus in the field that the diagnosis of Alzheimer's disease is one of "inclusion rather than exclusion." What this means is that physicians should, if there is any doubt at all, make a diagnosis of Alzheimer's disease and prescribe a care regimen accordingly. This is contrary to past practice.

Mann talks about his war on the stigma of Alzheimer's disease, which is discouraging thousands of people from seeking a diagnosis and obtaining a care regimen that might stanch the progression of the disease. This is Mann's purpose in life, and it amounts to the core part of his own treatment. It is why he is as functional as he is today.

FALLS

It may sound trivial at first, but when a person of a certain age falls, moderate or serious injury will occur in 20 to 30 per cent of the cases.[59] An ambulance will be called, assessment, treatment, and rehabilitation will follow, and gradually the person will return to his or her dwelling and regain most if not all functionality. The person in question is in pain, possibly in traction, and in a state of dependence until the requisite time has passed. The cost to the health system is massive, considering one senior in three takes a fall every year. These falls occur in spite of protocols that have been developed to assess a person's risk of falling, as well as the numerous prevention aids that have been developed, including railings, bathroom grips, fall alarms and sensors, anti-slip socks, vision exams, and even fall cushions.

Falls are the leading cause of hospitalizations of seniors due to injury in Canada, representing 85 per cent of such hospitalizations. More than 53,000 seniors were hospitalized due to falls in 2008–09 in Canada.[60] Falls like these cost Ontario taxpayers alone $1.5 billion in health-care costs in 2011.[61] Forty per cent of admissions to nursing homes were due to falls.[62]

The American Association of Retired Persons (AARP) published a list of six key steps that, if implemented widely in an aging population, might have a serious positive impact on the numbers of falls that occur:

1.   Offer free bone-density tests.

2.   Promote muscle fitness.

3.   Promote protein diets.

4.   Offer fall-risk assessments.

5.   Offer home-safety appraisals.

6.   Promote carefulness.[63]

Ann Taggert

Ann Taggert is a retired person with two hip fractures behind her. The first was about nine years ago when she fell down her front stairs. The second was three year ago when she fell in her driveway. Ann uses a walker, but continues to live in her own home. She's determined not to fall again. With the support and counsel of her family and general practitioner, she's reducing her risk of a repeat incident. She's taking pills for osteoporosis and calcium supplements. She's made her home a low-risk fall environment by removing all obstacles in the main walking areas and putting frequently-used items like cereal on the counter instead of in high cupboards. She says she's also actively trying to be more cautious, in particular, by walking more slowly. "I'm trying to reduce sudden movements, which led to my falls in the past," she says.[64]

A comprehensive program to enable all seniors to reduce their risks of falling or falling again, like Ann Taggert's efforts, in combination with access to affordable anti-fall devices, could result in a big payoff for provinces. One estimate yields $6.25 in savings for every $1 invested in prevention.[65] Another suggests that a "20% reduction in falls would translate to an estimated 7,500 fewer hospitalizations and 1,800 fewer permanently disabled elderly over the age of 65. The overall national savings could amount to $138 million annually."[66]

It's interesting and important to note that these savings will be generated for fall prevention as a whole, not just for people who've never fallen before. Even though Ann Taggert has experienced two falls and fractures, her efforts to prevent a third fall, together with those of her family and the health system, are right and good both for Ann and the government's pocketbook. It's never too late to intervene early.

IMPATIENCE

Add up the savings that early intervention approaches in all sectors of the health-care system could generate and examine the budget difficulties that governments in Canada (especially provincial governments) complain about, and things start to look a lot more manageable in the long term. We need to look beyond annual provincial budgets or four-year election cycles. The quality of our health is a lifetime concern, and a new decision-making framework that calculates the benefits of a given intervention over the course of the citizen's life is therefore the only one that makes sense.

Another key challenge to overcome is the science. The medical system is aware that certain drugs, treatments, or procedures will work in, say, 30 per cent or even 50 per cent of cases, but it doesn't yet know in general which 30 per cent or 50 per cent of the affected population will benefit. This means that patients are sometimes subjected to a lot of trial and error, side effects without benefits, and uncertainty and worry. This will continue to be the case until personalized medicine, which can customize care to an individual's genetic, physiologic, and social makeup, is further developed and widely available. Until then, the system will have some reluctance to introduce new approaches if their benefits are not clear and apparent. It is unfortunate that this justifiable reluctance or scientific conservatism regularly bleeds into even manifestly proven interventions like the ones discussed in this chapter. Put another way, a therapy, program, or intervention that doesn't work in all cases, or even for only a minority of patients, can still be very worthwhile medically and more than pay for itself, despite it not having overwhelming efficacy. The research, including the health economic aspects of it, should guide the policy development in this regard.

Will we need emergency, intensive, and acute specialized services in a system that gives priority to early intervention? Of course we will. But the promise of high-quality early intervention is that expensive late-stage intervention will serve an ever-smaller population at a shrinking cost because demand will decrease. If the population is healthier for longer time periods due early intervention, the supply of late-intervention services can be reduced. Early intervention requires early investments. Setting up the systems to address health issues as they arise requires extensive planning, new staffing, new training, methods of outreach, and delivery. It also requires new mechanisms to track performance and progress. As well, the payoff sometimes takes time. The transition period from last resort to early intervention can be expensive as both systems are being financed intensively at the same time. However, in time, the investments on the early interventions produce a healthier population and positive financial returns to the state.

CHRONIC CONDITION

In his 2013 book on the deep challenges the health-care system in Canada is facing, entitled *Chronic Condition*, Jeffrey Simpson gives short shrift to the idea that a health promotion and prevention agenda could make any real dent in reducing the cost of running the country's health-care system.[67] Health promotion and prevention would be considered among the earliest forms of early intervention. Simpson is not wrong to be skeptical about emphasizing this strategy to the exception of others, given many failed political initiatives to improve wellness in the past. He said, "If governments and their citizens were truly serious about health promotion, they would confront the social determinants of health, which would include employment and working conditions, housing, standards of living, early child development."[68]

Simpson is absolutely right. Making a health system early intervention–oriented is not enough. There are so many factors outside the control of the existing health system itself that contribute to illness, including the ones Simpson mentions above, but also many more, such as poverty, homelessness, family health, and safety, that a truly whole-system approach needs to be taken to make health care itself sustainable. For example, reducing poverty can, indeed, assist in reducing health-care costs over time. The opposite is also true. Effectively improving health and wellness can reduce poverty by, in particular, allowing adults to get back into the workforce. Indeed, the entire social safety net has to be considered when thinking about health-care reform (and other reforms across the welfare state). An evidence-based early intervention approach to the entire net may be a way to get at Simpson's concern.

Simpson concludes this topic by stating that a wellness agenda "is alluring and important but not likely to produce anytime soon the results sought by its most ardent proponents." Right again, unless the Canadian federal government and our provincial governments imagine their priorities differently across the whole of the social safety net, including the health system.

IMAGINE

We've looked at youth mental illness, stroke, Alzheimer's disease, and falls in this chapter. In each area, the research shows that early intervention can reduce the need for more expensive ongoing services and their attendant costs. It turns out these are only a few examples of the potential power of a new mantra for the health system. Research is emerging in virtually every area of medicine, from arthritis to zinc deficiency, showing that waiting to make a difference is costly to us all. Deaths from heart disease are starting to be averted because we are diagnosing and treating coronary artery disease before the heart attack strikes. The symptoms in Parkinson's appear only after 80 per cent of dopamine cells have been lost. In contrast, intervening before 40 per cent of these cells have died can actually prevent the onset of any symptoms. The research supports the conclusion that, across the health system, an early intervention approach makes a lot of sense.

CHAPTER 7

Proactive Poverty Reduction

In the aftermath of the back-breaking poverty of the 1930s, Canadians drove their political leaders to create a social safety net for the poor. Poverty was so widespread and so daunting that it became both politically possible and politically necessary to intervene. It was poverty that brought the state dramatically into the health and social service realm, and over time, its role came to greatly exceed that of charities and the church. Federal and provincial governments of different political stripes and persuasions have come and gone over the years, but virtually none has put into question the fundamental mandate of the state to alleviate poverty. It is one of the bedrocks of Canadian political reality. While balancing political dynamics in different ways, the federal and provincial governments, whether led by Liberals, Conservatives, New Democrats, Social Credit, or Parti Quebecois, have respected a deep moral and historical obligation to ensure that poverty is not a death sentence.

MEASURING POVERTY

We tend to define poverty in terms of the amount of money an individual or a family possesses. Accumulated wealth may be a useful measure when comparing large fortunes, but for most Canadians, income gives the best picture of what resources are available, which is why income is the focus of Statistics Canada's attention. The agency has produced reports for decades on the low income cut-off (LICO), which has been used for decades as an unofficial poverty line in Canada. (The United States has an official poverty line set by the American government.) LICO is a relative measure of poverty in the sense that it is based on a comparison of household expenditure at different income levels. Statscan states that LICOs "are intended to convey the income level at which a family may be in straitened circumstances because it has to spend a greater portion of its income on the basics (food, clothing and shelter) than does the average family of similar size."[1] A family just below LICO will tend to spend about two-thirds of its income on just the three necessities of food, clothing, and shelter. LICO is adjusted according to the size of the community. This makes sense, as poverty in high-cost Vancouver looks a lot different from poverty in Sherbrooke, Quebec. The LICO will also change depending upon how many people are in the family. This also makes sense, as a single person will have different challenges from a single parent or a two-parent, two-child household.

Other measures of poverty used by the Canadian government include the Market Basket Measure (MBM), which tracks a comprehensive basket of goods necessary for a modest lifestyle in a given part of the country, and the low income measure (LIM), which indicates the proportion of Canadian families making less than 50 per cent of the median income.[2] LICO has several advantages over other poverty measures. Preferably, a poverty measure should have a relative aspect so that policies can target the segment of the population that needs more help than the average household. It is also useful to have a poverty measure that shows when families are struggling to get the basic necessities. LICO accomplishes both of these goals by indicating the point at which families are having a much harder time feeding themselves, clothing themselves, and keeping a roof over their heads than the average family of a similar size in a similar place.

LICO is not without its critics. The Fraser Institute's Christopher Sarlo has made a career of arguing against measures of poverty that are in any way relative.[3] The measure he prefers is similar in approach to the MBM described above, but with less-generous estimates of what it costs to get by. For example, in his 2013 analysis, Sarlo budgeted $820 for a year's worth of public transportation for a family of four in Halifax (a sum less than the annual cost of a transit pass for one person in Halifax) and made no provision for people in areas without public transit.[4] The Stats-can MBM considers the cost of two passes for urban families or the cost of a modest used vehicle for rural ones. Of course, any estimate of this type is fraught with value judgments as to what people need in order to live decently. We might be forgiven for expecting that the official MBM more closely reflects Canadian values and more accurately measure costs than Professor Sarlo's approach, which, in constraining the definition of who is poor to only those in a state of abject deprivation, promotes the Fraser Institute's world view that government intervention in poverty alleviation can and should be held to a strict minimum.

Given that after-tax LICO approximates the official MBM and, unlike the MBM, has the benefit of statistics available back to 1959, it will be used throughout this chapter.

There were just under three million poor people in Canada in 2011, representing 8.8 per cent of the population.[5] In rough terms, this breaks down to half a million children, a quarter of a million seniors, and more than two million adults between the ages of eighteen and sixty-four. These were actually the lowest poverty figures in twenty years. The highest level during this period was 15.2 per cent in 1996. In historical terms, even these latter figures look pretty good. During the Depression, before poverty statistics were actually gathered, Canada's gross national expenditure fell by 42 per cent between 1929 and 1933 and unemployment stood at about a third of all working-age people.[6] They were all living on the precipice. Into the 1960s, poverty rates hovered in the 20 per cent range.[7] By 1982, poverty had fallen to about 12 per cent of the population and would rise and fall slightly within that range, depending largely on economic swings.[8]

This appears to be an interesting truth about poverty: it follows the economy to a significant extent. Former American president Ronald Reagan's claim that "the best social program is a job"[9] is largely accurate. The recent recession of 2008 pushed the poverty numbers up by more than half a per cent, representing more than 100,000 Canadians. On the other hand, poverty fell to its 2011 level as the economy recovered. In other words, well-paying, full-time jobs or multiple part-time jobs can be salves to poverty.

WELFARE

The programs Canada has developed to alleviate poverty are multi-faceted, but it is probably fair to say that, just as we have defined poverty in income terms, governments have implemented the mandate to alleviate it largely through income-assistance measures. These measures include the federally run Employment Insurance program for working-age Canadians and the Old Age Security, Guaranteed Income Supplement, and Canada Pension Plan for seniors. At the provincial level, it includes disability support programs, workers' compensation, student aid, and housing allowances. All of these programs are targeted to specific demographic groups that have demonstrated histories of income vulnerability. The program that sits under these and all others is what is called "social assistance" or simply "welfare." If a household has no other source of income, it can apply to the provincial government for a monthly welfare cheque. Unlike many income-assistance programs that are time-limited (like Employment Insurance), welfare can continue indefinitely. A person or family can receive state welfare support continuously if they continue to meet the eligibility requirements.

Those requirements, in short, are that the household has depleted all its financial assets (with some exemptions such as furniture or a car) and has no other source of income (like wages or income assistance from another program) whatsoever. In other words, welfare is there as a program of last resort if the individual or family is utterly broke. It is the quintessential late-intervention program that is only available to Canadian residents when they are truly in dire straits.

The amount of social assistance an eligible household is entitled to receive will depend on the circumstances. In general, an adult with children will receive additional sums for each child in his or her care. These sums will change with the children's age to take into account the family's evolving financial needs. Moreover, a person with a diagnosed disability will receive additional amounts on his or her welfare cheque to compensate for the supplementary costs associated with having a disability.

However, regardless of the category, almost everyone dependent on welfare is poor. Though welfare payments differ from province to province, not one of them, with one remote exception, is generous enough to lift the household out of poverty.[10] For example, in Ontario in 2012, a single, unattached individual received $8,067 in annual welfare payments (a little under $700 a month) from the province, while the LICO for such a single person without dependents was $19,597. This means the Ontario welfare recipient was approximately 60 per cent, the equivalent $11,500, under the poverty line.[11] A single parent with one child on welfare in Alberta did similarly in 2012. She or he received total social assistance payments for the year in the amount of $16,333 (about $1,360 a month), while the LICO was $23,850. This put the recipient more than 30 per cent below the poverty line, or $7,000 short of being able to avoid constantly "straitened circumstances."[12]

The state's mandate to alleviate poverty falls short when it comes to households with no other place to turn but the state-run local welfare office.

In 2009, over 1.7 million people relied on welfare payments in Canada.[13] There were over 3.1 million people in poverty that year, so more than half the poor population at the time was state-funded through welfare. Of the rest, 227,000 were seniors and the remaining 1.2 million or so were mostly working individuals and families (and their children). These latter, the working poor, are certainly too great in number, but represent only a small fraction of all workers (roughly 5 per cent).[14] The point is that for those who are able and have the opportunity, employment has proven from the Depression to today to be one of the best cures for poverty. Welfare has proven to be the opposite, a toxin with paralytic qualities capable of locking people in a state of poverty.

JUANITA BLACK

Juanita Black's story is representative of this struggle within a system that is designed, in Juanita's words, to "imprison" those in its clutches. Juanita landed on welfare as a young woman and didn't emerge from it for a long time. She is an expert in how the welfare system works from the point of view of the beneficiary. She shared her expertise with me in a series of interviews and email exchanges over the course of 2014. The narrative that follows is an insider's look at the workings of the provincial welfare system. Thousands and thousands of people in Canada today face the same challenges Juanita faced, all of whom might benefit from a radically different government approach to addressing poverty.

Born in St. Joseph's Hospital in Saint John, New Brunswick, in 1954, Juanita grew up as the eldest of five children. The younger four were the children of Juanita's mother and her stepfather. Because her mother worked the evening or night shift at the Red Rose Tea Company, Juanita actually grew up mostly in the care of her grandparents, where she would go every Sunday night, returning to her mother after school on Fridays. By the age of fifteen, Juanita was acting largely as the head of her grandparents' household by cooking meals and paying bills.

It was a busy and a happy childhood. Nothing changed as she approached adulthood. In 1971, while going to high school full time, Juanita also started to work at Red Rose. She worked beside her mom on the 4:30 p.m. to 11:30 p.m. shift, processing tea and coffee. She paid her mother a stipend for room and board, and actually managed to save enough to buy a car. She loved driving her friends to Simonds High School in East Saint John and waving to her other friends who had to take the bus. Juanita was progressively busier at Simonds, starting as a member of the student police team and the school's junior field hockey team and moving up to vice-president of the student council in her junior year and finally president of the student council in her senior year. She was so busy with her school activities that she had to quit working at Red Rose in her final year.

Her busy and popular life changed drastically near the end of the graduating year when she got pregnant. She continued to live at home for a while after graduation and then moved into an apartment with a friend when the baby, Joseph Adam Black, was born. She moved into her own apartment in early 1975 and applied for welfare. She qualified as she had no other revenue source and received her first monthly cheque, in the amount of about $270, soon after. Juanita would be on welfare almost continuously for the next 33 years.

A LIFE ON SOCIAL ASSISTANCE
Even in the mid-1970s, $270 was not very much money for a single mom to raise a family. Juanita decided she needed some more income, so she took on some part-time work as a dispatcher at a taxi company on Sunday mornings and, for a short a time, a few midnight shifts a week at Red Rose. Under the welfare rules, she was allowed to earn up to $200 of work-related revenue per month. Any sum over that amount was clawed back dollar for dollar from her welfare cheque. The idea behind this rule, called the wage exemption, was to encourage attachment to the workforce and not shut welfare recipients completely off from the mainstream economy.

To make ends meet, especially at the end of the month, Juanita had to juggle her credit cards, which were almost always "maxed out." As well, while she declared the entire income she earned from Red Rose to the welfare office, she only declared half of what she earned from the taxi company. The other half she took in cash. The welfare rates set by the provincial government department responsible for income assistance were so low that they created a huge incentive on the part of recipients to try to earn additional revenue under the table. To counter this practice, governments have put into place highly sophisticated financial teams to systematically audit recipients. The result has been that welfare departments have been able to terminate payments to beneficiaries caught taking in revenue from other sources without declaring it in violation of the rules. This, in turn, has generated significant savings to provincial governments. Audit teams end up paying for themselves.

Here's the quirky outcome of this policy: the social assistance client who was kicked off the welfare roll is allowed to almost immediately reapply for benefits. The law requires that he or she be granted welfare benefits if the eligibility criteria are met anew. This cloak-and-dagger battle between the welfare office and many welfare recipients takes place in every province in Canada every working day of the year.[15]

Juanita did want to spend time with her child and continue to be extensively involved as a volunteer in her beloved Crescent Valley community, but she also found it was terribly difficult to consider the option of full-time work. Despite the constant oversight of the welfare office and its demands for pay stubs, purchase invoices, and receipts (to monitor her lifestyle in an effort to ensure she wasn't cheating the system), the money was regular and reliable, and the additional financial and non-finanical benefits also came to be very important to her. In addition to her cheque, she received extended health benefits, which covered all her medical needs, including prescription drugs. She also received a small transportation benefit, so she could buy a bus pass and move around the city (she had given up her car before graduation). In 1979, because of her very low-income and the fact she was a single parent, she qualified for public housing, which meant her rent was the equivalent of

30 per cent of her income ($270) or $81 a month. When she added it up, it wasn't a lot, but it was enough. Juanita added, "It had to be enough."

Juanita received no support for child care. When she worked dispatch or Red Rose shifts, she paid babysitters to watch Adam. There could be no returning to full-time work without a way to ensure her child was cared for.

As Adam grew up, Juanita would show him her monthly welfare cheque and tell him, "This is what we've got for rent, telephone, hydro, food, clothes, soap, TV, haircuts, and school materials." Adam once complained that he didn't like his shoes and that his mom should buy him something other than "welfare sneakers." When Adam was older, he'd pick blueberries in August, so he could buy himself a pair of fancy sneakers and go to the exhibition for rides and treats.

There were no extras, no trips, very few meals out, and certainly no luxuries around the Black house. Juanita's uncle once paid for her and Adam to travel to Ottawa. Adam loved Parliament and the Science Centre and wanted to stay longer. Juanita told him they could "if we win the Lotto." Adam graduated from high school in 1993 and took a stab at university, but it wasn't for him. He travelled west to Alberta and worked in the oil patch, making good money. He eventually took up ceramic tile work for kitchens and bathrooms, and settled down in the Ottawa he remembered so fondly.

THE WELFARE WALL

Even after Adam left the house, Juanita stayed on social assistance. Although she says she received no encouragement from the welfare office to seek full-time work, she also admits she was "in a rut." Her self-esteem was low and she had become used to the pattern she was in, including the credit-card shuffling, the scrimping, and the dance with the welfare office. The challenge Juanita was facing has generally become known as the "welfare wall." The Library of Parliament defines the concept in this way:

> *The "welfare wall" refers to the disincentives to work*
> *created by interaction between the system of social*
> *assistance and personal income taxation in Canada.*
> *Canadians who receive social assistance and subsequently*
> *accept low-paying employment face a series of*
> *consequences that could potentially make them worse off,*
> *including: higher income and payroll taxes; new work-*
> *related expenses such as transportation, clothing and*
> *child care; reduced income support in the form of social*
> *assistance and income-tested refundable tax credits; and*
> *loss of in-kind benefits such as subsidized housing and*
> *prescription drugs.*[16]

In other words, Juanita feared, quite rightly, that jumping into the world of work, income taxes, and potential loss of benefits was not worth it. So she stayed put and continued to do limited part-time work, volunteer activities in Crescent Valley, and juggle her credit cards. Then two things happened. Her credit ran out completely, and she met Brenda Murphy.

It was 2008, and her debt load had become so heavy and stressful, she declared personal bankruptcy. Juanita was frustrated, ashamed, and angry at this defeat when she met Brenda Murphy, a local anti-poverty advocate for women, through her volunteer work. She explained her situation to Brenda, who suggested Juanita join Power Up, a ten-week program for women designed to encourage self-discovery, skill building, and preparing for next steps. Juanita jumped in, and over the next few months, she made new friends, found a new system of personal support, learned about credit and budgeting, and found a new lifelong focus: fighting for those in need. With a new-found self-confidence, a plan to dig herself out of debt, and a clear passion to serve, Juanita applied for the job of editor of a new free local publication that would eventually be named *Around the Block*. She got the job and soon nearly doubled *Around the Block*'s bi-monthly circulation from 6,000 to 10,000 copies, with a commensurate revenue increase. She went from twelve hours of work per week to twenty hours per week and got off welfare permanently. She remembers January 2009 as being the first month in decades that the direct deposit into her account from the welfare office was $0. She has since added four additional hours of work to her week, at the local Vibrant Communities office and a few more working on tenant relations for the local housing authority. There is still enough time left in the week for Juanita to volunteer at the Legion and at the Crescent Valley community garden.

Juanita remembers her worries about moving into work. She was a little panicky because she had little experience with taxes, the challenges of transportation, rent increases (though she continued to qualify for public housing), and the loss of her Health Benefits card. On the latter, she was assisted by New Brunswick's freshly minted 2009 poverty reduction plan, which extended health-care benefits for those wishing to climb the welfare wall into work.[17] She continues to enjoy these benefits to this day. Juanita would not be called rich by any measure. In 2013, she earned about $19,000 a year, well above what a welfare recipient would have received (about $6,800) and above the Saint John, New Brunswick, LICO (approximately $16,500). However, she's well under the average income for all single adults in New Brunswick, which sits at about $28,000.[18] She's proud of how far she's come. In 2012, she bought her first car since high school (a used one) and paid cash. She went to see her son in Ottawa and paid her own way. She's become a role model for many in the valley north of Saint John and now tells people who are in their own rut, "If I can do it, you can do it."

Juanita says that welfare imprisons people. To this day, she said, "it's passive and focused on the rules. It doesn't encourage people." She remembers in the early days getting down on herself and losing the will to initiate new projects or change certain of her ways. She asks herself if she was ready to work in the 1970s and 1980s or, rather, if she needed a hand like the one Brenda Murphy gave her thirty years later.

JAMES HECKMAN

James Heckman is a world-renowned economist who won the Nobel Prize in his field in 2000. His personal and professional interests include poverty and what can be done about it. His research has demonstrated that intervening early with quality child care not only helps children emerge in time from the poor homes into which they were born, but also assists the children's parents to join and stay joined to the workforce.

James Heckman was born in Chicago, Illinois, in 1944. At about the age of twelve, his family moved to Lexington, Kentucky. It was here that he first witnessed racial discrimination. He first experienced it when he sat in the back of a municipal bus and was told to move to the front because "that's for these people (African Americans)."[19] Heckman walked through parks with benches marked "whites only" and down streets with water fountains marked "colored only." These disturbing impressions were further reinforced when the family moved again to Oklahoma City, which was also segregated. He attended a whites-only school where the only black faces were the janitorial staff. Although he never saw Klansmen or lynchings, he was simply amazed by the explicit and open racism that was practised with no opportunities at all for interaction. He learned what he called the "racial code in action."

At age nineteen, Heckman began his post-secondary education in the state of Colorado. In late 1963, he took a swing through the south with his Nigerian roommate. They drove to Lexington, Birmingham, then into the Mississippi Delta, eventually arriving in New Orleans. This was about the time of the Birmingham church bombing and a few months before the murder of civil rights workers in Mississippi. Tensions were high as the Civil Rights Movement was picking up speed. In Birmingham, Heckman and his roommate bunked at the black YMCA, breaking local Jim Crow laws and scaring YMCA staff, who feared police repercussions. Heckman remembers being stopped by police in Hattiesburg, Mississippi, and being asked, "Are you guys trying to integrate us? Are you trying to make trouble?" The police then arranged for the two to stay in separate hotels, one for whites and the other for blacks. Heckman was somewhat unnerved by how intensely they were being watched by the authorities.

When the two teenagers finally arrived in New Orleans and walked down Bourbon Street, the shopkeepers closed and locked their doors when they saw them coming. The fear of retribution by the police was universal.

In 1970, as a post-doctoral student at the University of Chicago, Heckman had reason to return to New Orleans. He was participating in his first academic conference, the American Economic Association annual meeting. Heckman had time to tour the same places he had visited seven years previously and he was simply amazed by the total transformation that had occurred. New Orleans was totally integrated.

Heckman became very interested as an academic in the economic impacts of racism. He wondered whether the historic disparity between the achievement of racial groups narrowed post-integration, and he found, in fact, that it did. The historic migration of blacks to the North from the 1880s on reversed in the late-1960s. Migration, Heckman says, is "a movement to opportunity." He studied the textile industry and found that, in places like South Carolina, integration in the workplace and in the community had led to a massive movement of black workers into the sector. Heckman concluded, somewhat controversially to his free market colleagues, that civil rights legislation in the 1960s, not the market, had begun to close the achievement disparity between blacks and whites. He said this on the topic:

> *The blatant discrimination that existed in the South before Title VII was in large part eradicated by civil rights legislation. It's far less of an issue today. There's still disparity, of course, but it's not now primarily due to discrimination. I now think it's much more due to the differentials in family environments and the fact that*

the initial life circumstances of racial and ethnic groups
are very unequal. And understanding that, I think, is the
source of solving the black-white problem, not new civil
rights laws, and certainly not affirmative action laws.[20]

Though he found that civil rights improved outcomes for many in the black community, it has not been nearly enough to even outcomes to the norm. Heckman wanted to know what would have the biggest impact on long-term social and economic performance of disadvantaged children, so he turned to early childhood education.

Heckman's work in the field of early learning has been nothing less than groundbreaking. He and his colleagues at the University of Chicago (and elsewhere) have made some startling findings. The first is on the effects of high-quality early-learning environments. Heckman has said this about early learning:

Enriched early intervention programs targeted to
disadvantaged children have had their biggest effect on
non-cognitive skills: motivation, self-control and time
preference. We know that there's a scientific basis for this
finding . . . Non-cognitive skills are powerfully predictive
of a number of socioeconomic measures (crime, teenage
pregnancy, education and the like).[21]

The other main finding complemented the initial discovery regarding early learning; namely, that no amount of programming for older children from disadvantaged backgrounds in skill or educational training can possibly open the door to higher levels of social and economic success:

If we don't provide disadvantaged young children
with the proper environments to foster cognitive and

noncognitive skills, we'll create a class of people without such skills, without motivation, without the ability to contribute to the larger society nearly as much as they could if they'd been properly nurtured from an early age. Neglecting the early years creates an underclass that is arguably growing in the United States. The family is the major source of human inequality in American society.[22]

One of the two primary longitudinal studies Heckman relied upon was the North Carolina Abecedarian early learning study that calculated not only the gains children from poorer families experienced, but also the effect on their mothers. The results in terms of female labour rates of participating mothers, including a sub-sample of single teen moms, were remarkable: 92 per cent of teen mothers whose children were registered in high-quality early-learning programs were employed when the children turned fifteen (against an employment rate of 66 per cent for the control group). Overall, all participating mothers were ten percentage points higher in terms of employment when their kids were fifteen compared to the control group (85 per cent in jobs versus 74 per cent).[23]

Heckman concluded that, from an economist's perspective, the most effective way to attack poverty is "to invest in children when they are young." His studies on the economic returns from government-funded GED (General Education Development) programs, convict remediation programs, public job training programs, and other late-in-life skills-development initiatives "cannot make up for 17 years of neglect."[24] Heckman's work led him to produce what is now known as the Heckman Equation. The equation reads like this:

Invest (Invest in educational and development resources for disadvantaged families to provide equal access to successful early human development).

+

Develop (Nurture early development of cognitive and social skills in children from birth to age five).

+

Sustain (Sustain early development with effective education through to adulthood).

=

Gain (Gain a more capable, productive, and valuable workforce that pays dividends to America for generations to come).[25]

In economic terms, he's proven that every dollar of investment in quality early-learning programs yields approximately $7 in long-term gains or an annualized return of about 12 per cent.[26] Spending a dollar today on high-quality early-learning environments means not spending dollars tomorrow (or often ever) on welfare, correctional services, GED, and even health services. He cautioned that the investments had to be in quality early-learning environments; poorer quality environments where staff were poorly trained, managed, and remunerated, among other standards, would not produce the expected returns.[27]

Bloomberg business magazine said this recently about Heckman's findings, following an extensive interview with him:

> *Focused, personal attention paid to the young children of poor families isn't some warm, fuzzy notion, [Heckman] argues. It's a hard-nosed investment that pays off in lower social welfare costs, decreased crime rates, and increased tax revenue. And he has the numbers to prove it. He calls this the Heckman Equation, and shares it relentlessly in public lectures around the country and the world. "The argument is not just an appeal to the poor," he says. "We're saving money for everyone, including the taxpaying middle class and upper class. Right now they're supporting prisons, health, special education in schools.*

The benefit is broadly shared . . . It's something that
would actually accrue to the whole country."[28]

Heckman's work is a call to intervene early.

THE QUEBEC MODEL OF CHILD CARE

No jurisdiction in North America has taken Professor Heckman's advice more to heart than the province of Quebec.

Following the Quebec sovereignty referendum in 1995, Quebec Premier Jacques Parizeau resigned and Lucien Bouchard took his place. About a year into his mandate, Bouchard announced perhaps the most radical and progressive social program the province had seen since the 1970s: the Quebec $5-a-day child-care program. The initiative was launched by the Parti Quebecois government in September 1996 and was couched in a new provincial family policy that Bouchard said would support a number of the government's primary goals:

> *the fight against poverty, equal opportunity, the*
> *development of the social market economy, transition*
> *from welfare to the workforce and increased supports to*
> *working parents. In addition to being at the centre of the*
> *Government's strategy, these new measures reinforce the*
> *most important values of our society: sense of family and*
> *love of children.*[29]

The new family policy had three main components; namely, a child benefit for low-income families, an improved parental insurance plan, and the signature universal early childhood education and child-care program. The Minister of Education at the time was Pauline Marois. The Ministry of Education was given the initial responsibility for the implementation of this new three-pronged policy about which Minister Marois had this to say:

In Québec, as elsewhere in the world, society revolves around the family. It is where our children learn the values that help them grow and open to the world. Despite the fact that a majority of families consist of two parents and their children, the picture is progressively changing. We find more and more lone parent families and blended families, and more women are active in the labour force. The Government needed to adapt its policies to the changing needs of families. This is why our new family policy measures aim at insuring all children in Québec benefit from conditions that promote, through early childhood intervention and care, their development and success in school.[30]

Since the introduction of the program in 1997, thousands and thousands of Quebec families have been able to access to low-cost child care. The program was introduced gradually, with the initial focus on opening spots for four-year-olds and extending kindergarten to all five-year-olds.[31] Pre-school and after-school services for five- to twelve-year-old children were introduced in 1998. Finally, in 2000, early childhood education spaces for children up to age four were opened on a mass scale. The cost to parents was established at $5 a day per child to be paid directly to the child-care centre or home-based agency. The balance of the cost of services, including administration, rent, staffing, meals, books, and other materials, was paid to the service provider by the Quebec government based on regulated norms. A new department of government was created to oversee the new programming: the Department of Children and Families.

Interestingly, the government made the program universally accessible at the $5-per-day rate. James Heckman argued that early learning targeted at the disadvantaged should be the priority given its higher rates of economic return. However, Quebec accepted the argument that it was in children's best interest to draw together families from all income spectrums into the fulcrum of the child-care experience. This intermixing of parents and children from different socio-economic backgrounds was intended to create new bridges of awareness and new points of reference.

The program proved fabulously popular. Though the new Liberal government increased the fee to $7 in 2003, demand did not stop growing.[32] In 1998, only 16 per cent of Quebec families with preschool-aged children (up to age five) had access to daycare; by 2008, a total of 43 per cent had access. As of 2014, it had reached more than 50 per cent of families, with more on waiting lists. This compares to a Canadian average of 18 per cent in 1998, increasing to only 26 per cent in 2008. In harder numbers, from 1998 to 2005, Quebec added an average of 16,000 new spaces every year, slowing somewhat thereafter and landing at approximately 215,000 total spaces in 2011, representing enough spots for the children of about half of Quebec families.[33] No other Canadian province has yet been able to reach this level, though some have targeted it.[34]

The participation of poorer families was of specific concern to the government. Low-income families were, therefore, given the additional benefit of a waiver of daily fees for up to twenty-three hours per week per child (hours are used instead of days as parents often modulate the amount of time per day their child or children spend at a child-care centre). For middle- and higher-income families who were required to pay the full daily charge, the savings per child since the introduction of the program have been substantial. In some cases, families now pay four or even five times less than the cost of child care prior to the introduction of the program.

The impact of widening access to state-funded child-care services has not been consistent in Quebec. There are early learning centres in the province delivering demonstrable success, while others struggle to deliver results. In a 2010 presentation on the quality of early learning centres in Quebec, Professor Christa Japel underscored that only 26 per cent of 1,574 early learning centres subjected to a quality evaluation between 2000 and 2003 were judged to be of "good" quality, while 61 per cent were judged to have only met a "minimum standard," and 13 per cent were scored as "inadequate."[35] This is the challenge Heckman issued in terms of implementing early learning programs to a high-quality standard. The full returns on investment Heckman calculated in his equation only apply when the service provided exceeds a certain level of quality. Quebec appears to have some ways to go to achieve this objective across its network.

LABOUR FORCE PARTICIPATION AND POVERTY REDUCTION

Having said this, Quebec's affordable daycare programming has increased women's participation in the labour and reduced their poverty quite significantly. In fact, "superlatively" may be a better description.

From 1996 to 2011, the percentage of women joining the workforce increased across North America. However, in Quebec, the rate at which women were finding and keeping employment was higher than elsewhere. The Quebec child-care program was one of the main reasons for this success. Quebec mothers with children under six went from 63 per cent labour participation to 74 per cent from 1996 to 2008 (an eleven percentage point increase), while Ontario mothers only rose 4 per cent, from 67 per cent to 71 per cent. Single Quebec mothers blasted up from 46 per cent participation in 1996 to 67 per cent in 2008.[36] Pierre Fortin and colleagues calculate that roughly 60,000 Quebec women joined and stayed in the workforce during this period who would not otherwise have been able to if the Quebec child-care program did not exist. This represents more than half of the total increase in the labour participation of Quebec mothers from program inception to 2008. Fortin and his team further estimated that the program had the overall effect of increasing the female labour rate in Quebec by almost 4 per cent and overall employment by almost 2 per cent from 1996 to 2008.[37]

The entry of so many women into the workforce had a major effect on the welfare rolls and on poverty, one of the objectives of the program articulated by its authors. Once again using the period 1996 to 2008, the number of single mothers on welfare nosedived from 99,0000 to 45,000.

It is also estimated that "the relative poverty rate of single mother families went down from 36% to 22% and their median after tax income shot up by 81%."[38]

These numbers suggest that, though the Quebec child-care program was open to all regardless of income, it did have a significant positive impact on poorer mothers. Single mothers, in particular, were finding affordable child-care spaces for their children and, in turn, were finding work in large numbers. Significant employment opportunities were generated by the opening of hundreds of new child-care agencies. In sum, there was a general net positive effect on the incomes of mothers in lower socio-economic brackets.[39]

Would Juanita Black have fared differently if she'd had her child in Quebec in the early part of the twenty-first century? If she could have almost doubled her disposable income, even taking daycare costs into account, would she have had to wait thirty years to poke her head over the poverty line? These questions can't be answered. However, we do know that affordable child care is a route out of poverty for many women. It is not the only route out of poverty and not even the pathway many women would choose to take. However, it is unquestionably one that has demonstrated its effectiveness in achieving a sizeable reduction in Quebec poverty rates.

Some might say, that given its high cost to taxpayers, "it better work." The Quebec low-fee child-care program is, indeed, very costly. The provincial government spent approximately $300 million on subsidized daycare spaces in 1998. By 2008, the cost had grown to about $1.65 billion. As of 2014, the price tag had reached more than $2.2 billion. However, the influx of a large number of women into the workforce resulted in an approximate increase in the gross domestic product of the province by $5.1 billion (or 1.7 per cent) in 2008, in addition to new income tax and sales tax revenues for the province. Economists estimate that tax revenue increases at the same rate as GDP, meaning tax revenues also went up by approximately 1.7 per cent. These new tax revenues, combined with decreases in applicable tax credits, welfare payments, and other social benefits available to non-working people with low incomes, led to a positive global provincial budgetary impact of $1.7 billion in 2008.[40] In other words, the program ended up netting the province about $50 million ($1.7 billion in revenue, minus $1.65 billion in costs) in fiscal 2008.[41]

This progressive early intervention measure developed in 1997 to improve early childhood outcomes ended up putting considerable downward pressure on rates of poverty for Quebec women, especially single mothers, and more than paid for itself in the process. As the quality of services in each centre increases, families across the province, not only in the best centres, will also start to see improvements in educational and cognitive development scores.[42] In time, Quebec society, not just poor families, will be a huge beneficiary of these investments. As Heckman has written:

> *Early interventions that partially remedy the effects*
> *of adverse early environments can reverse some of the*
> *damage done by disadvantaged families and have a*
> *high economic return relative to other policies. They will*
> *benefit not only the children themselves, but also their*
> *own children as well as society at large.*[43]

Investing in high-quality early intervention programming at the youngest ages is a recipe for continuous returns and savings. It can solve poverty for many families in the short term due primarily to the opportunities for women to participate in the workforce, and in the medium and long term due to the increased preparedness and ability of those children who accessed quality early learning experiences.

RETURNS

Wide access to early learning experiences can both prevent poverty and reduce poverty for those (mostly women) already experiencing it. There are many other ways of achieving this objective. One of them is actually reforming the welfare system.

In 2012, Canadian provinces spent more than $12 billion on supporting clients on welfare. The cost is actually higher in years when there is an economic downturn, as it was in 2009 and 2010. Canada undoubtedly needs to retain income-assistance programs for those who fall through the cracks of our economy or whose personal and social challenges make it too difficult to find and keep employment or other forms of work (e.g. self-employment or contractual work). However, as we have seen in Juanita Black's story, the design of the system creates the bizarre incentives that make it irrational for recipients to seek full-time or regular part-time work if they are able, while "imprisoning" them in a state of poverty. Many provinces have started to recognize the perversities inherent in the current system that, in effect, yields only costs and no returns. Welfare payments continue to be treated by governments as expenditures and not investments. It is for this reason that the audit teams in each provincial welfare office are seen as money-makers as they have the effect of catching the welfare rules violators, removing them from the rolls, and thereby temporarily reducing social assistance expenses. What if welfare were, instead, framed and analyzed as an investment? What could provinces do with an investment fund with an initial capitalization of $12 billion and an objective to create deep attachments to the economy and reduce poverty? The answer is, "a lot."

Juanita's native home, New Brunswick, initiated a bipartisan poverty reduction process in 2008 that led to a provincial plan entitled Overcoming Poverty Together. The plan included a strong welfare reform component that called for measures to "move from passive assistance to employment orientation," "move from focus on income poverty to social and economic inclusion," "provide more opportunities to keep earned income as individuals transition to work," "reform wage exemptions to include a working income supplement," and "link benefits such as child care, home heating and health to household income to the extent possible."[44] The last provision is the most exciting of the proposed policy changes as it would mean that entitlements to many non-financial benefits would be made available to all people with low incomes, whether they're on social assistance or not. This measure would go a long way to tearing down the welfare wall. The province has begun to implement these reforms, but the bulk of the work is still ahead. Nonetheless, New Brunswick's integrated poverty plan has succeeded in driving down child poverty rates by 12 per cent since 2008, one of the best results in the country.[45] The problem is no province, or any other jurisdiction in North America, has attempted a full-scale welfare reform that seeks to intervene early with new recipients to help them get attached or stay attached to the economy without getting stuck in a welfare lifestyle. The evidence of how to successfully reduce poverty in North America through welfare reform is simply not available yet.

THE POVERTY GAME

A final word about Juanita Black. One of her ongoing volunteer activities is to teach the Poverty Game, a project of Brenda Murphy's Urban Core Support Network, to students and other interested audiences. Juanita begins the activity by describing her own life in poverty and her long journey out of its talons. She then hands out a sheet of paper that asks participants what spending choices they would make if they were welfare recipients receiving a cheque in the amount of about $650 per month. Participants then break into groups to discuss the different alternatives to make it through the month. They have to decide how much to spend on rent, food, transport, and going out to the movies. Juanita forces them into the life a welfare recipient, albeit for only a few hours. In mid-discussion, Juanita stops them and introduces a problem that's just arisen. "Your fridge is broken. What do you do, and how does your budget change?" For the students, this is just a game. For Juanita, it's more than thirty years of memories.

CHAPTER 8

Homes for Homeless People

Canada has witnessed a massive rise in homelessness over the last twenty years. Organizations like the Old Brewery Mission, which I mentioned in Chapter 1, have been serving homeless people for almost 125 years, but have had to significantly increase the number of beds and buildings under management in the last two decades to meet demand. The Old Brewery, where homeless men were served hot soup by Mrs. Mina Douglas and her team of Methodist volunteers around the turn of nineteenth century, went from 150 or so beds in the mid-1990s to more than 450 today. The irony is that these organizations were meant to be temporary. They were supposed to shrink and cease to exist as homelessness and poverty gave way to homes and jobs. Instead, the shelters have become some of the biggest non-profit organizations in any city. Some are bigger than the city psychiatric hospitals. The Calgary Drop-In Centre, for example, manages more than 1,000 beds in its network; Seaton House in Toronto, more than 700.

This surge in homelessness beginning in the mid-1990s was propelled by at least four interrelated causes. The first was the elimination of the

Canadian Affordable Housing Program by the Liberal government soon after it returned to power in 1993. The second was a series of cuts to numerous federal transfer programs to the provinces, including health and welfare grants. The third was the ongoing deinstitutionalization of mental-health patients and the fourth the intensive cuts made by the provinces to housing, income support programs, and community supports following federal spending cuts.[1] Until the mid-1990s, provincial governments and the homeless shelters in Canada's larger cities seemed able to keep the clientele safe, warm, fed, and out of the headlines. Homelessness was discrete and somewhat hidden before the surge. Then the number of homeless people spiked. In Toronto, between September 1992 and September 1998, the average daily hostel occupancy for single adults increased by 63 per cent. In the same six-year period, the increase in shelter use in Toronto was 80 per cent for youth, 78 per cent for single women, 55 per cent for single men, and a shocking 123 per cent for families.[2] In Calgary, the homeless population rose by 122 per cent between 1994 and 1998.[3] Homelessness started to hit the front pages as the media began to cover the issue more actively, which, in turn, drew public attention to the growing social problem.

Homelessness is dangerous to your health. A 2009 study by Dr. Stephen Hwang, an epidemiologist based in Toronto, estimated that homeless men in Canada have about the same remote chance of reaching the age of seventy-five as an average man in 1921, before the advent of antibiotics.[4] Another Hwang study, from 2000, showed that, on average, homeless men in Toronto die at the age of forty-six and homeless women at thirty-nine, more than thirty years sooner than the Canadian average.[5]

Provincial government reaction to this burgeoning public health challenge was predictable. They started doing more of what they were already doing. They grew emergency shelter funding and transitional housing programs. The clearest illustration of this was the increase in homeless shelters. For the one-year period 2006-07, the number of known shelters in Canada grew from 859 to 1,020, and the number of beds increased from 21,988 to 26,872.[6]

This reaction to the growing population of homeless people was consistent with the workings of the late-intervention model, namely expand emergency-type services to meet the basic needs of those in trouble. No attention was given to stemming the demand for such services during the period from the beginning of surge in the mid-1990s to about 2008.

The increase in shelter services papered over a thinning of the traditional social service net that occurred in the deficit-busting 1990s. Provincial governments chose to manage the surge in homelessness by boosting funding to the community sector and hoped it was enough to help the homeless population survive the winter and get a hot meal and a shower. This minimalist approach didn't take into account that the homeless population had drastically changed. It was becoming younger, more diverse, and more complex. A cot, a meal, repeated visits to the ER, and encouragement from local shelter staff and community services were no longer going to suffice.

PETE MONTOUR

Pete Montour's story is just one example of how this policy backfired.[7] This story came to me from the team at the Homeless Hub, a part of the non-profit Canadian Homelessness Observatory based at York University in Toronto.[8] It is one of many personal stories the Homeless Hub has collected and published to put a human face on a population that has often been labelled rather homogeneously "the homeless." I've chosen it from among several options offered to me by the Hub because of the variety of institutions Pete came into contact with throughout his travels into and within the world of homelessness.

Pete Montour and his two brothers were taken into the care of the Catholic Children's Aid Society in the outskirts of Toronto in 1979 when Pete was three years old. His parents were addicts, his mother to alcohol, his father to intravenous drugs. They were young, poor, and poorly educated. His father was abusive to both his wife and his children when money was tight or when he was "having a bad trip." Pete's mother had fled the family prior to the intervention of children's aid. He remembers there being painfully little love in the household. In fact, in trying to piece together his very early life, Pete characterized the one clearly loving event being the same one that led to the final break with his father.

His father was suffering from "dope sickness," or withdrawal, and desperately needed money. He elected to rob a corner store with a knife. He told his son that "he would be back in five minutes and not to worry." He apparently succeeded in robbing the corner store, but either it wasn't enough of a haul or he felt luck was on his side, so he decided to rob a second one. The unknowing cab driver who was waiting for him after both robberies finally realized he was abetting a series of crimes and called the police.

When the older Montour was taken into custody, he didn't tell the police that there was a threesome of young boys back at his house. (Pete's brothers were five and six at the time.) Pete felt his father refrained from sharing this fact because he was afraid of losing the kids. He said this about his father:

> It took me many years to understand why he didn't
> tell anyone we were there, but I eventually came to the
> conclusion that my father did it because he loved us. I
> figure he thought if he didn't tell anyone about us being at
> the apartment, he hoped he could post bail, get out of jail,
> and take us away without Children's Aid being involved
> — thereby preserving the nucleus of our dysfunctional
> family. Unfortunately for him and us, things did not turn
> out as he had planned, and regardless of his intentions,
> his misunderstanding of the severity of his crime left my
> brothers and I grossly neglected. His desire to rescue us did
> exhibit a twisted form of protection guided by fatherly love;
> as fantastically desperate and unrealistic as his rescue plan
> was, it is the only love I have ever known from the man.[9]

The three little boys were left to themselves. There was no food in the house, and they became very hungry. They went to the hockey arena around the corner and begged for change to buy a hot dog or two to share. Then they'd return to the empty house. This pattern lasted three weeks until by chance a social worker who brought her own child to the arena noticed the Montour boys begging on a number of occasions for money. It was not long afterward that child welfare swooped in and took over.

Pete's brutal childhood, his abandonment, his hereditary risk of substance abuse, and his formative years without strong affective relationships were certainly among the causes of his own eventual homelessness. As Pete said in his own words, "When I look back at my horrible childhood, it's little wonder I ended up addicted, homeless, and fighting for my life."

Pete never finished high school, never retained solid employment, or enjoyed a meaningful personal relationship. By the age of thirty, he had already had a long experience with addiction and homelessness. The foster-care system was not able to prevent these co-occurrences. Nor was the health system.

In 2006, Pete was in the hospital for a post-surgery checkup. He had badly injured his lower right leg and foot during a drunken stupor, and St. Michael's Hospital had casted the injury three weeks previously. Pete moved his appointment up because the pain had become intense, and his toes had become discoloured. The triage nurse at the hospital gasped when she removed the cast. The sight and smell were awful.

The surgeon had originally advised Pete that it would be important for him to keep the area around the injury clean and to avoid smoking, drinking, and drugs. The problem was that following these instructions was impossible for Pete. He was homeless (surfing between friends' houses and the shelter system) and addicted to alcohol. He lived in what he calls a "veritable cesspool of microbes and bacteria" and had no hygiene options at his disposal. As for the addiction, he says, "I just couldn't quit." Most addicts can't "just quit" without a lot of time, patience, and counselling. Pete's environment and habits colluded to bring about the infection that worsened his injury.

The attending physician took the staples out and examined Pete's swollen and multicoloured shin and foot. He said the leg was not just infected, but that gangrene was setting in. The surgeon cleaned the affected area, cut off the rotting skin, and trimmed the bone. The procedure was so painful, Pete vomited and passed out. He awoke with a new cast and in a fresh set of clothes. The surgeon gave Pete a prescription for antibiotics, a suction pump to improve circulation, and a schedule for a nurse to come to his dwelling to change the dressings twice daily. He also told Pete that he was at serious risk of losing his leg "if you don't take care of yourself." The doctor was ashen when Pete told him he was staying at a large shelter run by the city of Toronto. They both knew following the directives would be difficult.

Pete was knowingly discharged from the hospital to the homeless shelter. Although he filled the prescription, the antibiotics were stolen in the shelter. So was the circulation pump. To make matters worse, the nurse never showed up to change the bandages. A week after discharge, the infection had returned. Pete remembers just giving up. He got high on crack and a bottle of mouthwash. He was trying to forget "my rotting leg and pitiful homelessness."

Staff at the shelter did their best. They gave Pete fresh socks, free bus passes, and cigarettes. His friends at the shelter also gave him what they could, namely free tokes of crack. Finally, when he could no longer feel his toes and they had started turning black, Pete returned to the hospital.

At St. Michael's Hospital, the same physician who treated him on his previous two visits was on call again. Pete recalls the doctor being furious and saying, "Do you know how sick you've made yourself?" Pete was very sick, and the doctor was very worried the severity of the infection was such that it could spread to the heart and brain. After examining the injury, the surgeon told Pete he wanted to amputate the leg.

Despite his extremely frail health, Pete stood up, retrieved his crutches, and staggered out of the hospital. There was no way he was going to lose his leg. He returned to the shelter, packed his donated clothes in a garbage bag, took a hit of pain-relieving crack, and fumbled his way to the subway. He decided to head to his native Brampton "to get as far away from St. Michael's and the thought of amputating my leg as I could."

He arrived at Bramalea City Centre with an idea. He describes it this way:

> *If neither the hospital system nor the shelter system would help me I was going to force the jail system to do it. I had to use the system to my advantage. I knew the state couldn't let me lose my leg, not while I was incarcerated. It would make them look bad. And everyone knows that the government will spend billions not to look like fucking assholes. Besides, and sadly I thought, no one gives a shit about a homeless guy with a rotten leg, but they do care about a guy willing to do anything to survive. And everybody loves a guy who is willing to sacrifice themselves by throwing a Hail Mary pass in the dying seconds of the game. I had my plan.*

Pete had never robbed anyone before. He had never wanted to rob anyone. Now, he felt he had no other choice. Like his father several decades previously, he entered a Brampton corner store on July 9, 2006, and stole all the money in the cash register after threatening to kill the staff if they failed to comply. He was apprehended, charged, and convicted of theft and uttering death threats. He spent the next three and a half months at Maplehurst Correctional Complex.

This chapter will end with the denouement of Pete's story. It will give nothing away to say it is one of flagrantly missed opportunities. So is Murray Barr's story.

MURRAY BARR

A now-famous American story about the absurdity of homelessness was written by well-known Canadian author and essayist Malcolm Gladwell in *The New Yorker* magazine in 2006.[10] He wrote about a Nevadan named Murray Barr in his now-seminal article on how the cost of managing a social issue like homelessness often exceeds the costs of solving it. Gladwell described Barr as a loveable mountain of a man, an ex-soldier, and an uncontrollable alcoholic who had been diagnosed with a mental illness. If Barr had cash in his pocket, he would spend it on his drink of choice, vodka (beer he apparently looked down upon as "horse piss"). If broke, he'd wander through the casinos of Reno and lap up the drinks left over by blackjack and Keno clients.

The police were never far from Barr. They'd often have to pick him up two or three times a day when he was on a big binge. Gladwell interviewed the officers who had the most contact with Barr, and in his *New Yorker* article, he reported the police's frustration at having only two available responses, the detox or jail. They'd admit him to one or the other, and then, inevitably, he'd be released, sometimes just a few short hours later. Then Murray would start up again. One of the officers, a fifteen-year Reno beat cop, told Gladwell he'd been picking up Murray Barr from the city's streets his entire career.

Often, the police would have to bring Barr to the emergency room at the local hospital as he'd been in a violent altercation, a traffic event, or some other dangerous incident. The hospital would stitch him up, sober him up, and plead with him to stop drinking, but he never did. Except once.

Under house arrest, Barr was ordered to participate in a local treatment program. The program included employment and case management. He apparently thrived in the structured environment where he had specific tasks, someone to report to, and daily expectations. Barr not only showed up for work, he showed up on time. He performed his functions effectively and was a solid and dependable team member. He accumulated savings, around $6,000, stayed sober, and was in what we would call "recovery." The program came to end, and Barr was sent out into the world to fend for himself. Gladwell reports that the program managers said, "Congratulations," and put him back on the street. Not surprisingly, it took Barr a week or so to spend his entire accumulated savings.

Gladwell said this of the financial illogic of the situation:

> When someone passed out on the street, there was a "One down" call to the paramedics. There were four people in an ambulance, and the patient sometimes stayed at the hospital for days, because living on the streets in a state of almost constant intoxication was a reliable way of getting sick. None of that, surely, could be cheap.[11]

The Reno police calculated the cost of managing Murray Barr, of essentially riding side saddle with a person living in absolute chronic homelessness. Policing, transporting by ambulance, hospitalizing, jailing, and judging Murray cost Nevada taxpayers about $100,000 per year, a million over ten years. Gladwell's article was entitled "Million-Dollar Murray" for this reason. He asked rhetorically in the article whether the state of Nevada might not have better spent its resources on initiatives like the structured therapeutic program that had appeared to work so successfully in Barr's case. Gladwell speculates that paying for an apartment and a full-time nurse for Murray (and solving the problem) would have cost less than doing nothing (and solving nothing).

This is a key point about the existing social safety net. By waiting until specialized security, health, and social-service officials need to be called in to sort out the intense and dramatic emergencies that are really just the apex of a long and sad climb into chaos, the government is making a choice in how it spends its resources. If governments think they are saving money by waiting and doing nothing as the catastrophe nears, they are in profound error. There are options even for the most difficult of cases, like "Million-Dollar Murray," and those options often cost less than the tired model currently in effect.

PATHWAYS TO HOUSING

This is exactly the frustration that animated the work of a Canadian clinical psychologist based in New York named Dr. Sam Tsemberis. Dr. Tsemberis, the founder of a leading housing organization for homeless people in New York City called Pathways to Housing, is one of the foremost innovators in the world on the subject of housing and services for homeless men and women with mental illness. I interviewed him for this chapter in late 2013.

Dr. Tsemberis was born in the village of Skoura in the Greek Peloponnese, about ten kilometres from the ancient warrior city of Sparta. For the first seven years of his life, he lived in the embrace of "an extended sense of community." In Skoura, the villagers of his parents' generation were addressed as "aunts and uncles," and were respected as such. Everybody took care of everyone else. Dr. Tsemberis described it as, "whether they were rich or poor, sick or well, saints or sinners, they saw themselves as one community."[12] The cultural milieu of Skoura was all about inclusiveness. There was no judgment or pre-qualification for community membership. Everyone socialized at the same village café in the centre of town. Births, weddings, and funerals were common knowledge. You looked out for your neighbours, and they looked out for you. You were cared for if you needed caring. This early upbringing was determinative of Dr. Tsemberis's approach to solving homelessness.

In the spring of 1956, he and his family landed at Pier 21 in Halifax, where they embarked on a train for Montreal. Living on Esplanade Street, young Sam attended English elementary school in the Plateau Mont-Royal. After graduating from West Hill High School in Montreal's west end, it was on to Sir George Williams University (now Concordia University) from 1966 to 1970, where he majored in English literature and psychology. After graduation, he was hired by Pierrefonds Comprehensive High School in Montreal's West Island, where he taught courses in special education and drama. A couple of years later, he decided that he wanted to be a better teacher, so he enrolled in a master's program in psychology at the New School for Social Research in New York City, and after completing it, he pursued a doctorate in clinical psychology at New York University.

As part of his training as a clinical psychologist, he completed an internship at Bellevue Psychiatric Hospital in New York City, where he came into regular contact with people diagnosed with severe mental illness. He was soon hooked on figuring out better methods of care for this hard-to-serve clientele. Dr. Tsemberis decided to detour his initial goal of teaching into practising clinical psychology. In 1983, he received his doctorate in clinical psychology as well as an offer to work at Bellevue Psychiatric Hospital, which he readily accepted. To Dr. Tsemberis's profound dismay, newly elected president Ronald Reagan was conducting as assault on social programs in the country, including severe cuts to social housing programs.

Dr. Tsemberis was the attending psychologist for hundreds of patients flowing in and out of Bellevue's in-patient wards. Many of the patients he treated on the ward he would later see sleeping on the streets of New York. He was dismayed by the number of men and women he would have to treat over and over again in the wards, because after each hospitalization, they were discharged back into homelessness. Their mental and physical health quickly deteriorated on the street, and they would be rehospitalized, starting the cycle over again.

In the mid-1980s, greater and greater numbers of mentally ill New Yorkers were living on the streets, with their access to housing, benefits, and community supports reduced by government cutbacks, out of reach, or altogether eliminated. Dr. Sam Tsemberis, the man from Skoura, the clinical psychologist who never judged his patients but rather tried to accompany them on their journey back to psychological wellness, was ashamed by the way his patients were being treated by the mental-health system. It was difficult to walk past people he recognized from the wards, familiar faces now homeless, in need, and in pain. To this day, he can't walk by a homeless person on the street, begging or sleeping, as if he or she were not there. They are his brothers and his sisters, his neighbours, and they need his help.

In 1988, New York Mayor Ed Koch, under political pressure to stem the negative publicity around the rising tide of homelessness in general and a raft of street deaths in particular, launched Project HELP[13] (Homeless Emergency Liaison Program), and Dr. Tsemberis was hired to direct it. It was essentially a mobile psychiatric emergency service whose mission was to prevent homeless men and women from dying on the streets.

Now in the media spotlight as the mayor's lead in the fight against homelessness, Dr. Tsemberis spent the next five years running a team of outreach workers, including psychiatrists, nurses, and social workers mandated to determine if a homeless person who had a mental illness was a danger to himself or herself (as defined in the New York Mental Hygiene Law) and whether or not involuntary hospitalization should be ordered. As the lead clinician on the team, Dr. Tsemberis had to approve every admission. He had to determine whether the client in question was sufficiently unaware of how critical his or her condition was to justify a decision to admit. Some of his stories about this work are disturbing: a man who was delusional and believed he was in fine form as puss leaked from his feet out through his sneakers; a man standing in the middle of the intersection preaching to no one in particular as the cars raced by; a woman sitting on the sidewalk next to the steam vent trying to stay warm in the cold of winter, the front of her clothing wet and soaked and her back covered in ice. Project HELP was essentially a hospital emergency room on wheels and conducted thirty assessments per day, admitting, on average, one to two of these assessed clients to Bellevue.

Dr. Tsemberis was in the perfect spot to observe how the system processed these admissions. He observed that about 30 to 40 per cent of these patients soon returned to the streets upon discharge. This reality he describes as a "system failure." It was also a wake-up call for him and his colleagues. A thirty-day admission, at a system cost of about $1,500 per day, or $45,000 total, was the equivalent of three years' rent or the down payment on an apartment house. Worse, the Project HELP team would often have to readmit clients very shortly after discharge and the meter would then start again. Dr. Tsemberis says, "It was a revolving door of hospitalization, stabilization, and a return homelessness. And it was wrong."[14]

In 1992, he decided to do something about it. Instead of trying to address homelessness as a mental-health issue, he wanted to address it first as a housing issue. Project HELP and Bellevue, as governmental bodies, were highly risk averse in terms of assuming any responsibility and would therefore not consider trying to rent an apartment for their patients. The hospital wouldn't fund or support a patient's lease unless he or she was psychiatrically stable, clean, sober, and had all their benefits; this is, someone who would pay the rent on time, not create a disturbance and not damage the apartment. This profile excluded a large majority of the patients Dr. Tsemberis wanted to help.

So he started a not-for-profit organization called Pathways to Housing and wrote a grant application to the New York Office of Mental Health requesting state funding to test a new approach to housing homeless people who were mentally ill, some of whom were not on medication, some with addiction problems, and all with a long history of homelessness. His mission was to help homeless people with the most difficult and highest-risk conditions find and maintain housing in New York City. The state approved the application for Pathways, and Dr. Tsemberis launched his inaugural Housing First anti-homeless program in America. Dr. Tsemberis left the relative comfort and security of state employment and became the leader and sole clinician on the Pathways team. He put his reputation on the line by advancing the risky and counterintuitive methodology Pathways proposed.

Over the course of the next year, with five staff, the Pathways team housed one homeless person per week. After one year, they had housed fifty people, some of the most downtrodden, mentally ill, so-called hard-to-handle patients in the entire medical system. At the end of the year, Dr. Tsemberis reported to his board of directors that 80 per cent of the (formerly) homeless participants in the program were still housed. Asked why he thought it was working, he replied that the key was not simply providing the apartment itself, although that was essential, it was also the process the Pathways team developed of working with the whole person in a respectful manner.

Dr. Tsemberis's Housing First program was based on the a philosophy of client choice he had learned from his friend and colleague Bill Anthony. Pathways offered clients choices they had never had before: choice to participate in the program or not; choice in selecting where to live and what type of housing to live in from a one-person apartment to congregate accommodation; choice in the type and sequence of services after the person is housed. The program supported the person's choice of how to decorate and organize the apartment. In this way, the participant developed decision-making skills and self-confidence, contrasting with most social programs that develop the singular skill of respecting the institution's rules. The Pathways team soon understood that exercising choice does not build compliance and dependency, but rather, the skills for autonomy and independence that are the cornerstones of recovery.

Implicit in the program was the need to practice harm reduction for users of drugs and alcohol (e.g. needle exchange and alcohol management programs), and it was equally important to permit failure. These are two core practices that many programs won't tolerate. The Pathways team gambled by that treating participants with the same dignity and regard anyone would want, they would see a payoff in less, not more, damage and loss to the rental properties they controlled than typically occurred in the more common coercive structured initiatives. The gamble paid off as Pathways results started beating all other programs providing housing and services for this clientele. Over the next five years, Pathways grew its program in terms of services offered (including Active Community Treatment) and number of clients served. They worked out the kinks and learned to operate an efficient and effective Housing First model.

In 1997, Dr. Tsemberis felt the model was sufficiently robust to pitch an idea to the American federal Substance Abuse and Mental Health Services Administration (SAMHSA) to conduct a randomized control trial testing its performance against treatment-as-usual programs. Pathways Housing First and six other programs were awarded research grants from SAMHSA. They conducted a multi-year randomized control trial comparing Housing First to traditional treatment first, then to housing programs in New York City. The New York Pathways cohort numbers were very impressive in terms of improved housing stability and reduced use of emergency services, and once those numbers were published, the Housing First model was on everyone's lips.[15] Cities across the United States started asking, "How do we start a Housing First program?"

The studies continued and the results continued to be impressive. In a 2007–08, thirty-six chronically homeless men and women in Washington, DC, participated in a Pathways program and were followed for two years.[16] All thirty-six individuals suffered from a major mental illness (either schizophrenia or bipolar disorder) and were alcohol dependent. All were offered a variety of apartments to rent in their own name and were given a rent supplement by the federal government to be able to afford a dwelling in the neighbourhood of their choice (about a $1,000 per month, the balance being paid out of their own disability benefits). After the first year, with Pathways providing ongoing support to all clients, 97 per cent of the participants were stably housed in the apartment they had selected. After two years, 84 per cent of the participants remained housed. While the Pathways program doesn't insist on abstinence from alcohol, the study showed clear reductions in the negative impact of participants' alcohol addiction. Psychological distress was also greatly reduced as a result of housing stability and the predominance of choice in the clients' lives. One participant said, "It took me a year to believe that the apartment was mine. It took a long time to accept it."[17]

In 2002–03, the United States Interagency Council on Homelessness adopted the Pathways approach as its primary model for reducing chronic homelessness in America. Its head, Philip Mangano, was a

Republican appointee with a zeal for social change, whom Dr. Tsemberis describes as an "abolitionist" inasmuch as Mangano compared the fight to eliminate homelessness to the struggle to abolish slavery in the United States. In 2003, Mangano announced that his agency would be investing $35 million in Pathways-type housing programs across the country. The large-scale replication of Housing First had begun.

Today, there are more than seventy American cities that have adopted Housing First programs. Some cities and states, like Salt Lake City, Utah, have made it the centrepiece of a full municipal or state plan to end chronic homelessness. Other countries, including Australia and eleven Western European nations, are now using the approach. The US Veteran's Administration is using Housing First as the core strategy to end veterans' homelessness and has shown a 33 per cent reduction since adopting the model in 2011. Dr. Tsemberis's own organization, Pathways to Housing, has expanded its operations to Washington, DC; Burlington, Vermont; and Philadelphia, Pennsylvania, in order to make sure it can help budding Housing First programs get off the ground correctly, train new staff, and advocate for sufficient state and federal funding to make the incipient initiatives effective from the beginning.

Another country that is in the process of adopting Housing First as a national policy for ending chronic homelessness is Canada.

MENTAL HEALTH COMMISSION OF CANADA

In 2007, Health Canada committed $110 million to study the Housing First concept in a Canadian context. It tasked the Mental Health Commission of Canada (MHCC) to examine whether Dr. Sam Tsemberis's model of addressing homelessness might help reverse the burgeoning of the homeless population, which has been increasing relentlessly over the recent decades. Over the next five years, under the research leadership of Dr. Paula Goering of the Centre for Addiction and Mental Health in Toronto, Ontario, the MHCC initiated At Home/Chez Soi, the largest Housing First randomized control trial in the world. With five sites (in

Vancouver, Winnipeg, Toronto, Montreal, and Moncton), the MHCC deployed assertive community treatment teams for those participants with high clinical needs, and Intensive Case Management (ICM) for those with moderate needs. MHCC secured rent supplements to ensure access to market housing options, identified clients, and went on to house more than 1,000 chronically homeless, mentally ill Canadians between 2009 and 2012. The study recruited an extremely vulnerable clientele. In the Montreal sample, alcohol addiction was present in almost 80 per cent of all cases. Ninety per cent also had at least one chronic physical health condition, and seven of ten had childhoods like Pete Montour, which were defined by abuse, violence, and alcoholism.[18]

Unlike many other Housing First research projects, the MHCC-led study benefited from a large sample with a comparative group. Outcomes for those who received Housing First services were compared to those of a randomly selected treatment-as-usual cohort to not only determine how well the test group did, but also to see the difference between their improvements, if any, and those of the group that received no more than would be typically offered in their community. This feature makes the Canadian study, in addition to being the largest anywhere, perhaps the most meaningful of any such research project to date.

The final results of the initiative were reported in 2014. The conclusion included this observation: "In terms of housing stability, Housing First was found to be unequivocally more effective than existing programs accessed by Treatment As Usual participants for finding housing and staying housed." In the last six months of the study, 62 per cent of the Housing First group were housed all of the time, 22 per cent were housed some of the time, and just 16 per cent were completely homeless. By contrast, only 31 per cent of the treatment-as-usual cohort were housed all of the time and 46 per cent of them had no housing at any point in the previous six months. Over the full course of the study, the treatment-as-usual group spent more than two-thirds of their time in shelters, on the street, or in some sort of transitional dwelling (compared to slightly just over a quarter for the Housing First group).[19] This positive result was not terribly surprising, given Pathways results a decade earlier.

The cost implications of the study were particularly interesting. The research team priced the services participants typically consumed such as health care, justice, and social services and compared the sum to the cost of the Housing First services that were offered (e.g., housing and assertive community treatment teams). In essence, the economics team was trying to determine if Housing First costs more or less than providing a typical basket of emergency services to this clientele.

For the high-needs system users, the research team calculated that the average cost of government services consumed before they entered the Housing First program was approximately $80,000 per person per year at baseline. This would include emergency room visits, trauma care, ambulance transport, police intervention, incarceration, court costs, and welfare and disability payments. And the average annual cost for Housing First services? While the new housing and housing support interventions cost about $22,000 per person per year, the cost of other services typically used by homeless people was halved. The net result was that for each $10 invested in Housing First, $9.60 was saved in reduced spending on other services.[20] In other words, to successfully house a usually desperately sick and lost homeless person costs about the same as doing nothing more than the system did for Pete Montour and "Million-Dollar Murray." For these high-end users, government can choose whether to intervene immediately with housing and support, and actually solve the problem, or to let this clientele linger *ad nauseum* on the street or in the shelter without any resolution and without it making a difference to the public purse. Stable housing, compassionate professional support, and respect for the participant's choices, the primary services contained in the housing first basket, appear to radically reduce the need for expensive government services.

For other homeless people, those who are not high-intensity users of services, the financial portrait is different. The government only recoups $3.42 in reduced service use for every $10 spent on Housing First, although savings related to the justice system might increase over a longer time frame when old arrest warrants become less of a factor. However, this masks an important shift in the services used by homeless people when they are given stable housing. For example, users of the Housing First approach were far more likely to start using food banks and showing up to regular medical appointments.[21] The formerly homeless clients stopped being prolific users of emergency stop-gaps and started accessing services that let them improve their nutrition, health, and self-sufficiency. It could, therefore, be said that it costs government in the first two years of implementing Housing First a net amount of $20,000 to successfully house and sustain an average homeless person and ensure he or she has a chance to get his or her life back on track instead of becoming a chronic consumer of emergency government services.

EDMONTON

If the early 1990s were the beginning of the first modern wave of homelessness in Canada, the city of Edmonton, Alberta, experienced a second wave in the first decade of the twenty-first century, culminating with Tent City in 2007.[22] Erected by 200 people who, having no other place to go, set up their tents in a vacant lot in the downtown core, Tent City was the symbol of the dangers of rising rents and the mass conversion of apartments to condos to feed an oil-driven economic boom. Without housing alternatives, these homeless people decided to squat in public and declare it their right to do so. Within a space of three months, there were forced off the vacant lot. But a clear message had been sent to local and provincial officials to the effect that doing nothing was no longer an option.

Casting around for options, Edmonton leaned on its sister city, Calgary, for inspiration. Midway into the first decade of the twenty-first century, Calgary had begun the process of developing a ten-year plan to end homelessness with Housing First as its centrepiece. Edmonton officials attended a Housing First conference in Red Deer, Alberta, in 2007, at which both Dr. Sam Tsemberis and Philip Mangano were speakers. It wasn't long afterward that Edmonton began developing its own strategy to reduce homelessness at the behest of then-Mayor Stephen Mandel. A wide-ranging and inclusive process led to the adoption in 2009 of Edmonton's own ten-year plan to end homelessness through a Housing First focus. Edmonton committed itself to preventing people from becoming homeless in the first place, but also, if someone found themselves on the street or in one of the city's myriad shelters, it would quickly offer them permanent housing options, according to the Tsemberis method.

A strong, stable, and professionally managed non-for-profit organization called Homeward Trust was asked to lead the implementation of the plan. According to the results of Edmonton's 2012 count of homeless people, just under 2,200 distinct individuals were found to be sleeping in a shelter, on the street (or in such places as doorways, abandoned buildings, or parks), or otherwise had no housing of their own. This is a remarkable 30 per cent reduction from the results of the 2008 count ,when more than 2,750 people were found to be homeless. By following the Housing First mantra of intervening early to accompany homeless people on the journey toward sustainable permanent housing, Edmonton, like Calgary, Lethbridge, and a growing number of other Canadian cities, is finally reversing the upward trend in homelessness it had been experiencing over the previous twenty years. As we have seen, it has been saving the city and the province of Alberta a lot of money in the process.

CHARLES

One person who directly benefited from the Edmonton campaign to reduce homelessness was Charles, a forty-two-year-old man who described himself as the "baddest guy around."[23] He was also one of the most ill people in and around the Edmonton area. Homeless for more than twenty years and long-addicted to cocaine, Charles had contracted both Hepatitis C and HIV over his years on the street and in crack houses. He knew a common cold could kill him, so fragile was his immune system.

Then he met the staff of one of the Edmonton agencies offering Housing First to chronically homeless people like him. Charles was invited to join the program. Having chosen an apartment, he needed to sign a lease. The landlord required Charles's credit history, tenant history, and references, as would any landlord. Charles had no history and no references. He thought, "I might as well hand the form back blank." He needn't have worried. The agency stepped in, as it did for all participants in the program, and said to the landlord, "We're the credit check, we're the reference." In addition, the organization agreed to work with Charles if there were ever a problem, fix the apartment if it were ever damaged, and be available on call to the landlord if there were any problems at all concerning the apartment. And, finally, the agency would be present to support Charles and the landlord for as long as Charles would reside there, even if it was for the rest of Charles's life. Their commitment was as permanent as the housing.

The non-for-profit agency states: "It's not our job to stop someone from doing drugs." The client has to be ready and willing to get treatment, but the organization is present to support that choice when it's made. This is the magic of Housing First. It treats clients as adults and respects their choices, even if they lead to failure. It doesn't give up. It anticipates the problems and provides the supports necessary to succeed. It also supports the landlord to make the relationship with sometimes-difficult tenants work. This is what homeless people need, especially gravely sick addicts like Charles: a genuine and relentless sponsor.

Charles says with assurance that the agency saved his life. He is now forty pounds heavier, his HIV barely registers, and his Hepatitis C is also under control. He's learned to shop and cook for himself. He possesses all necessary ID to live independently. Charles is even cautiously optimistic he'll be able to attend his child's graduation ceremony. He's resurrected this dream because he finally has what he's always wanted: a home of his own.

FINAL WORDS

As Dr. Sam Tsemberis says, "Housing First ends homelessness. It's that simple."[24] But Housing First can't end homelessness alone. The state continues to regularly fail to assist clients, patients, and wards under its care and protection to find and keep permanent housing on discharge. Housing First doesn't "do prevention," but prevention most certainly needs to be vastly improved.

As well, Housing First doesn't work for all clients. Charles is the rule inasmuch as 80 per cent of homeless people can be stably located in long-term permanent housing, but 20 per cent of clients need alternative approaches to escaping homelessness.

However, the Pathways Housing First model provides the strongest evidence-base in the world and is the rightful basis for developing any anti-homelessness strategy. For this reason, it was vaulted into the centre of the Canadian federal government's Homelessness Partnering Strategy, which, although underfunded in terms of both programming and housing development, now has a firm and sensible direction for years to come.[25] It is now up to the Canadian provinces to adopt, implement, and bring to scale Housing First programs as part of comprehensive and integrated strategies to end homelessness. Only four of the five host provinces to the MHCC trial have actually gotten organized to pursue the program (British Columbia, Manitoba, Ontario, and New Brunswick), while Quebec has, so far, been reluctant to include Housing First in its array of anti-homelessness measures. The most impressive province to date on deploying Housing First is surely Alberta, which was not even part of the trial. Edmonton is evidence of the true promise of this approach.

A full and committed rollout of Housing First across Canada will not end the need for shelters, halfway houses, facilities for women fleeing violence, and other emergency-type services. However, a rollout would, in time, drastically reduce the burden on these agencies and in the process, through system savings, potentially fund complementary initiatives in prevention and alternative housing programs for clients not receptive to Housing First methods.

The system would finally be equipped to help people like Pete Montour the first time he slipped into homelessness. Medical staff at Maplehurst Correctional Complex saved Pete's leg. Counselling staff helped Pete get into a rehab, where he finally got the assistance he needed to sober up (after fifteen years of addiction).

Pete went on to complete his high-school diploma and is currently an undergraduate student at York University. He's also run numerous marathons on the leg he almost lost.

The state spent a lot of time and money on him. The child-care system, the health-care system, the homeless shelter system, and the correctional system all came into contact with Pete. Could those systems have done a lot better spending the kind of resources Maplehurst Correctional Complex ended up investing in Pete to fix the problem much earlier? Almost certainly. We have few details about child protection's efforts, but we do know St. Michael's Hospital fixed up Pete's leg with a temporary mindset, without treating the known causes of the injury and reinjury: homelessness and addiction. The hospital seemed powerless to work beyond Pete's immediate physical needs and practically invited him to return for subsequent rounds of painful and expensive surgery and treatment. Instead, the hospital system could have adopted a Housing First model and reorganized to properly staff and implement such a program (or properly partner with a Housing First organization to accompany patients like Pete immediately into housing).

The shelter system didn't work for Pete, either. Cigarettes and socks seem to be a poor substitute for a professional Housing First program. As for the correctional services, they seemed to have accorded Pete the kind of attention that ensured he wouldn't be their client again. They appear to have dealt with the whole Pete Montour the first time, and the payoff was the elimination of repeat offences and incarcerations.

Pete said this about his jailers:

> *The state does care more about criminals than they do*
> *about the homeless. To prove it, I have my leg, and my*
> *life. Inside, I received stellar treatment. I got all the rest I*
> *wanted, all the food and medication I needed, and my leg*
> *healed up about half way through my sentence . . . It should*
> *be known that I do not condone criminal behaviour, and*
> *this story shouldn't be read as a validation to go and rob*
> *stores to make your life better, but before you judge my*
> *actions ask yourself: "What would I have done?"*

The savings to the system would have been significant if child welfare had adequately supported Pete and his brothers through their formative years. If the health system was organized to treat not just Pete's leg, but also his whole self through a Housing First program, savings would still have flowed. The same logic holds true for the homeless shelter. It, too, could have intervened to help Pete more adequately if it had been organized and funded to do so. The fourth system Pete had contact with, corrections, ended up saving Pete and putting him on the road to personal success, and that is really three systems too many to deal with the same individual. Even so, it is still worth it to the state both morally and financially to organize itself to intervene early at whatever stage a citizen like Pete is at. It would have yielded the greatest return, of course, at the stage of child welfare if those investments had prevented further ones being necessary. It would have still produced benefits at the second and third stages. Pete's story is demonstrative of the idea that it's never too late to intervene early.

CHAPTER 9

A Better Social Safety Net for Canada

Early intervention in the health and social services is starting to produce social benefits for citizens and families in trouble and financial benefits for the state in many parts of the world. The Herculean efforts of people like Mike Doolan, Dr. Ivar Lovaas, Mary Gordon, Dr. Patrick McGorry, James Heckman, and Dr. Sam Tsemberis are beginning to bear fruit. However, across Canada and, to a large extent, across the world, early intervention is the exception in terms of addressing complex health and social issues, and late intervention remains the rule.

The twin purposes of this final chapter are to sum up the early intervention approach, including how its different parts might fit together, and to offer some ideas on how such an approach might become more broadly accepted and implemented in Canada.

THE EARLY INTERVENTION APPROACH

There's a great television ad from the 1980s, about Fram oil filters, that is still available on YouTube.[1] A mechanic is telling his customer that his colleague, Joe, has been fixing a lot of engines recently. To avoid this cost, the mechanic affirms in a friendly and confident way that it is important to change the oil regularly and "put in a new Fram filter when you're supposed to." The ad concludes with these words:

> Mechanic: "You can pay me now [for the filter]."

> Joe: "Or you can pay me later [to fix your engine at a much higher cost].

The mechanic represents the early intervention approach, and his colleague, Joe, the late-intervention path that Canada currently follows in terms of managing most of its health and social services. This book has attempted to contrast the two approaches and answer the question, "When should the state intervene to make services available?" In health and social services terms, I have been arguing that intervention should take place as early as possible. Systems should be organized to intervene early because it is both morally right and financially smart.

The moral case is fairly straightforward. When there is a chance of completely avoiding risk through a universal program, such as Roots of Empathy in schools, it should be taken, provided the evidence has shown it works. When there is a chance of reducing risk of greater harm through a targeted program (i.e., a program directed at a specifically defined group that has demonstrated characteristics of risk), such as the professional administration of clot-busting drugs in the event of stroke, it should be taken (again, if the evidence has proved its effectiveness). As a general rule, effectiveness is amplified because, at its early stages, the problem is easier to resolve and the menu of alternatives available to address the health condition or the social problem are much more numerous. Effectiveness decreases as the condition or problem deteriorates because that condition or problem becomes increasingly complex and the availability of options to address it are fewer. In other words, early intervention is better because the problem is addressed when it is manageable. These are, perhaps, self-evident propositions, but it is their contrary proposition that makes the case. It is profoundly difficult to argue that we should not intervene when we have the knowledge and the experience to do so effectively. To refrain from making evidence-based early intervention services available when we know they work is to deny many fellow citizens and families the chance at better, longer, and happier lives.

The financial case for early intervention rests on comparing the costs of the two approaches. The status quo is not free. We've seen in every chapter of this book that doing nothing or waiting until there's an emergency does not come cheap. The early intervention approach isn't free, either. However, using child protection as an example from Chapter 3, the evidence shows that paying for early intervention social workers to help a family at the first signs of trouble costs less than waiting for the trouble to deepen and, in time, require more resources, including foster care and litigation, to deal with it. It ends up costing less to set up a system to act quickly, as soon as a child's welfare is put at risk, than waiting for the situation to spiral out of control, requiring the child to be fostered and the case to be litigated.

The math has to be done on a program-by-program basis. Governments need to know the financial implications of the decisions they're making. When both positive clinical or social outcomes and financial returns from an early intervention program are indicated, there is little basis, save for ideology, in not making it available to the entire population who may benefit from it. However, what about a scenario where an effective early intervention costs more than the status quo? This is a more difficult issue. A decision needs to be made on a case-by-case basis about the degree and duration of the benefit against the cost, including the opportunity cost of investing the same amount in another health or social service area where there may be a positive financial return.

For example, from the At Home/Chez Soi study of homelessness we looked at in Chapter 7, we saw that it cost no more for the government to provide housing and supports to high-needs, chronically homeless clients than the cost of the late-intervention services, including shelter costs, ER, and ambulance costs. In contrast, clients who were not high needs ended up costing more to the government to house than to sustain in a homeless lifestyle. This is a moral dilemma. Does the government direct early intervention programs only to those who save them money?

The At Home/Chez Soi team argued that the marginal increase in relative cost to house a non-chronically homeless person was justified as the government at least generated a positive outcome for the client. The existing way it was spending its budgets on this group generated no positive outcome, other than making ER and shelter services available to prevent a tragic end.

Should the government direct its early intervention efforts only at those clients who produce economic benefits? My answer to this question is yes, but only for the initial period of implementing early intervention approaches across the entire system. There are so many financially advantageous and evidence-based early intervention opportunities available for scaling, including those highlighted in this book, that prudent governments, with adequate research resources, will prioritize them. Some early wins will generate more wins. The time will come, earlier rather than later, one would hope, that political and financial resources can be directed to other initiatives that, while not so clear and convincing economically, can make a big difference in the lives of struggling Canadians and their families.

DESIGN FEATURES

Taking the example of autism services from Chapter 4, while it is true that some families have the time and wherewithal to help an autistic child through his or her early years and even successfully into school, most families need assistance. A design feature of the late-intervention system is to wait and see which families can cope alone and which need assistance. This is one purpose of a waiting list. The problem is that once the determination is made, it's often too late to make a big difference in the functional capacity of the child. The design feature in the early intervention system is the exact opposite. It doesn't set up its eligibility criteria to deny services; rather, it is inclusive in its methodology. Ideally, it proactively seeks out clients to whom services should be offered. It does this not only because the autistic child and family will be better off, but also because, in providing funding for more children to receive early behavioural training not less, the government actually saves money over the child's lifetime. An early intervention approach appreciates that there is a payment to be made or cost to be assumed one way or another, and paying or assuming it earlier rather than later makes for a more-effective and less-expensive system over the long term.

An early intervention approach, in its efforts to catch everyone who may be at risk, may end up serving many people who either didn't need the service or could have overcome the obstacles in their way without assistance. This is another design feature. Take the example of bullying from Chapter 5. Roots of Empathy is a program that is universal in nature. While not every child in every classroom in a school will need expo-sure to the Roots of Empathy program to develop his or her empathic skills, every child nonetheless receives it. A late-intervention approach waits until the telltale signs of aggression, anger, and poor grades would emerge in a student, then puts the child into intense remedial training, often in a separate facility with the minority of other children with the same profile. Somewhat counterintuitively, it turns out that the univer-sal Roots of Empathy program, though serving all children, even those kids who don't need it, costs less in reducing a school's record of student violence than programs that zero in on only the students manifestly needing remediation support.

Successful early intervention approaches share this feature. Services don't have to be required or even successful with every person receiving them to be cost-effective. Take the example from Chapter 7 on poverty. We saw that providing child-care spaces in Quebec at an affordable daily rate helped a large number of mothers with low incomes join the workforce and escape poverty. However, not every woman with a low income and with children could access an early learning placement for the children or even wanted to participate in the program. Nonetheless, we saw a noticeable drop in the poverty rate among this demographic group and increased attachment to the workforce. The resulting tax contributions went a long way toward covering the cost of the early learning program itself.

Service quality is another key feature. Indeed, the benefits of early intervention in many areas are very dependent upon the quality of the intervention. The training of the early intervention workforce is particularly pivotal in this regard. For example, the positive results from early intervention in child protection are predicated on the work of highly trained family-enhancement social workers. The same is true in autism. Without skilled early behavioural intervention workers, neither the functional nor the financial returns can be expected. As James Heckman pointed out in the chapter on poverty, only high-quality early learning environments will springboard children forward in life and generate the system savings he calculated. More evidence of the importance of quality can be found in the health chapter in terms of dealing with early psychosis, strokes, Alzheimer's, and falls (particularly with regards to professional assessment).

To summarize, a health and social service system built on early intervention will be characterized by proactivity, inclusivity, and service quality.

A SYSTEM PERSPECTIVE

In this book, different aspects of the social safety net have been analyzed, but the question remains how the different parts fit together. The answer to this question begins with the reality that there is no single or simple response to every health or social challenge faced by Canadians. No one program, even the most effective early intervention program, will be effective for the totality of a population every time it is administered. Indeed, as we saw above, none of the early intervention measures on display in this book had total success with the population group it targeted. People slipped through the cracks of even the best programs. While it takes sometimes only a minority of successful clients to make an early intervention program cost-effective, what happens to those who don't benefit? What service is left to assist those who are left behind? If we were managing the entire system on an early intervention basis, the answer to the question is obvious. It has two steps. First, the successful program would be expanded so all people who fit the program's target population could access and benefit from it. Second, another high-quality early intervention program would be implemented for those who did access the original program, but didn't benefit from the initial intervention. And so on. Under no circumstances would the system let clients free fall until hitting rock bottom.

For example, we saw from the Ontario study of autism services in Chapter 4 that the provincial government would benefit financially if the services were extended from approximately 37 per cent of the population to the entire population of kids aged two to five with autism. Step 1 would, therefore, be extending the existing successful early intervention to all those who would benefit from it. Waiting lists for the program would be eliminated. Step 2, for children who did not achieve full functionality by age five, would be to implement another program in kindergarten that also has the design features of a successful early intervention. In other words, we'd look to designing, implementing, then scaling up a proactive, inclusive, and high-quality intervention for autistic children who are of school age. It might be a mentoring or shadowing program with behavioural treatment components; but, like the Lovaas-type training that preceded it, it should be adjusted and adapted until it is effective both in individual and financial ways.

This latter program, be it mentoring, shadowing, or otherwise, will also not be successful for all autistic children of school age, so research and educational leaders, in a system built on early intervention, will be looking to making another service available for these particular children. Layering of evidence-based interventions turns a mishmash of disconnected programs into a truly systemic approach to care.

Another example of an early intervention system in action is in the poverty and homelessness field. The successful poverty-reducing program in Quebec explored in Chapter 7 was particularly beneficial to mothers with low incomes. But not all mothers with low incomes. Step 1 would be to expand it so all parents (including all single mothers) wanting access to affordable high-quality daycare for their children could get it. If, despite having such access, a parent's poverty (as well as, in all likelihood, other factors like mental illness) led to homelessness, how then would a system based on early intervention react? Hypothetically, Rosemarie, the mother I introduced in Chapter 1 who spent much time at the Old Brewery Mission's Patricia Mackenzie Pavilion, might have been one such person. At Step 2, the system would intervene early and offer Rosemarie a Housing First program of the kind described in Chapter 8. She would be rehoused and, in due course, because of having a stable housing arrangement, be newly eligible to get her kids back into her care and, if she wanted, have spots for them in quality daycare spaces, so that she could attempt to join the workforce.

A system driven by early intervention might, therefore, be operated based on the mantra that "it's never too late to intervene early." To continually expand existing effective early interventions to all who would benefit from them and tenaciously go about exploring and implementing services for those whom the system did not adequately help in the first place is to develop a system that is no longer disjointed and often ineffectual, but rather, one that is logical, sensible, and effective.

A system of early intervention would, thus, tether together evidence-based proactive programs across the lifespan. If each pays for itself, as we've seen from the examples in chapters 3 to 8, the overall cost of the maintaining the system drops over time because each successful early intervention program contributes to reducing demand for a more expensive late-intervention program. The cumulative effect of systemically introducing and scaling up early intervention programs that produce the clinical and economic results we've witnessed in this book means we can reduce the supply of late-intervention services over time that currently overwhelm governmental budgets.

LATE-INTERVENTION SERVICES IN AN EARLY INTERVENTION WORLD

As the quantity and quality of early intervention services increase, the need for existing levels of emergency and other last-resort services diminishes. Lower demand for emergency room staff, code red child-protection social workers, homeless shelters, and special education and remedial programs means governments can reduce the supply of these services and either pocket the savings or redirect them into other early intervention initiatives. An early intervention approach is admittedly a threat to major interest groups because it proposes a gradual shift of resources away from these existing late-intervention services. This is the theory of change, but it's easier said than done. As I have said elsewhere, it is not easy politically to reduce the size of late-intervention infrastructure for fear of not being able to address unexpected spikes in demand for emergency response with all the political exposure and fallout that may ensue.[2] It was this logic that entrenched the late-intervention ethos in the first place.

One of the hardest things for politicians to do is downsize emergency-service capacity. However, it is plain that such reductions become easier if a system-wide early intervention approach is adopted because, instead of citizens losing out, there is simply less demand for late-intervention services.

The other important point to make here is that though reduced and, in some cases, greatly reduced (e.g., late-intervention child-protection costs, including foster care and litigation costs in New Zealand, were reduced by 90 per cent within a few years of the introduction of early intervention measures), late-intervention services cannot and should not be eliminated. They remain necessary for two primary reasons. First, emergencies happen, and we need to have effective emergency responses. Second, despite best efforts, some individuals and families will not benefit from any early intervention program, and the system needs to have a response that can save life and limb, and address all forms of violence and immediate danger when it is present. In this sense, late-intervention services actually become a coherent part of a much more effective overall system of care. These services are not left alone to try to assist all complex and vulnerable people and families, avoid or manage a difficult situation, or a condition they were never designed to address.

BROADENING ACCEPTANCE

How can the tables be turned to make early intervention the rule and late intervention the exception to the rule (though an important and necessary exception)?

It would be easy to say that all that is necessary is to convince political leaders in Ottawa and our provincial and territorial capitals to snap their fingers and order their civil servants to implement early intervention approaches in all health and social services for all population groups across the lifespan. Unfortunately, if it were so easy, it would have already been ordered, implemented, and accomplished. As we've seen, politicians since the inception of the welfare state in the 1930s and 1940s have addressed these issues cautiously and carefully. This reality is no different in 2014 when annual governmental budgets, scrutinized surgically by the Opposition, the press, and lobby groups, are evaluated on the immediate results they produce. Nor are four- or five-year political mandates helpful as they create incentives to short-term successes, not long-term returns. They create an ecosystem of impatience, not the patience required for system change.

However, as this book also demonstrates, some early interventions have been successfully birthed and grown right here in Canada. Child protection in New Brunswick, Manitoba, and elsewhere is increasingly early intervention–based. Autism services are also early intervention–based in Alberta. Manitoba has made significant strides in making Roots of Empathy available in its schools. There are pockets of successful early intervention in the field of early psychosis in Quebec, Ontario, British Columbia, and several other provinces. The same is true in the case of stroke where some parts of Canada are massively reducing both mortality and morbidity rates. Quebec is leading the way on poverty reduction for single mothers through its child-care investments. The federal government's core homelessness reduction strategy is based on Housing First, an archetypal early intervention program that is bringing down the homeless numbers in several cities in Canada, including Edmonton. For those wanting to develop, pilot, or scale up these early intervention approaches or others, are there lessons to be learned from these early successes?

There is an emerging area of research inquiry on this very topic, called implementation research. It is a field that is interested, in particular, in how to bring proven or promising practices to scale. The Fogarty International Center, an arm of the National Institutes of Health in the United States, uses the term "implementation science" and defines it in this way: "Implementation science is the study of methods to promote the integration of research findings and evidence into healthcare policy and practice. It seeks to understand the behavior of healthcare professionals and other stakeholders as a key variable in the sustainable uptake, adoption, and implementation of evidence-based interventions."[3] There is now a considerable body of research from a variety of sectors on the multiplicity of means and methods to deploy knowledge effectively in policy and practice. However, it seems there is no single mousetrap that will work in all cases. Successful implementation seems to depend greatly on the setting and the sponsor. The case studies in this book suggest a number of factors that contribute to successful implementation of early intervention initiatives.

There seems to be four important determinants that contribute to bringing about an early intervention policy. The first is that engaging an experienced thinker and practitioner steeped in the issues can be extremely helpful in developing the case for an early intervention approach. For example, Mike Doolan managed the frontlines of New Zealand's child-welfare services, and saw and experienced personally and professionally the ravages of a late-intervention or child-rescue approach on Maori families, in particular. He then spent the next few decades of his life championing the benefits of an early intervention alternative, both inside the country and outside. His efforts, including his writing, consulting, and speaking, were picked up in many places across the world, including New Brunswick. Doolan was hired by the province to accompany it on the journey to develop an early intervention system for families in trouble, including visiting Fredericton on several occasions to meet with political and departmental leaders and provide key training to all of the province's child-protection staff. Without Doolan's credibility and support, it's unlikely the province would have had the confidence and resolve to push the reforms forward as quickly and as completely as it did.

Such engagement was also present in Manitoba (and Scotland, among other places) where Mary Gordon and her Roots of Empathy team helped the jurisdictions develop and implement their anti-bullying approaches. She has committed her life to such work, which is bearing fruit for the well-being of children across the world. Dr. Patrick McGorry's work in early psychosis and Dr. Sam Tsemberis's efforts in homelessness have been capitalized on in many places around the world, including Canada. Credible and committed leaders who have tested and piloted early intervention initiatives and written, travelled, and consulted widely on their efforts and results have the capacity to provide singular assistance to local reform-minded associations, governmental departments, or institutions to test and pilot early intervention-based programs.

Another ingredient in some of the successful early intervention stories we've heard appears to be, unfortunately, crisis. Mike Doolan was able to crowbar the New Zealand government into action in the child-protection field, in part, because of the crisis level of Maori children who were being taken away from their families and put into the state's care using the traditional approach. The Phoenix Sinclair case in Manitoba contributed to a movement that is bringing a system of early intervention in child protection to the province (i.e. differential response). The CEO of the agency responsible for child welfare in the Winnipeg area at the time of Phoenix's birth, Lance Barber, testified during the public inquiry into the case about the greater context in which the agency was then operating. CBC filed this report, respecting his testimony:

> Barber stated that a very high percentage of the agency's clients were aboriginal single-parent families, headed by women living in poverty. Most lived in 55 small inner-city neighbourhoods. Within those neighbourhoods 40 to 50 per cent of open CFS [child and family services] cases were concentrated in public housing. "There was," Barber said, "a large level of the population in crisis . . . needing our service." And that need, Barber noted, was growing. The agency's budget, however, was not.[4]

Mediatizing this crisis was, no doubt, a contributing factor to the reform movement.

The world of public health offers graphic examples of crisis driving the take-up of effective early intervention. Polio is one such example. Approximately 6 per cent of all deaths among those aged five to nine in the early 1950s were due to poliomyelitis.[5] Even if it didn't kill, its effects could be deadly, including crippling or serious breathing difficulties. In 1953, of the 9,000 Canadian children who had contracted polio, 500 lost their lives to the disease. Polio was considered a crisis of epidemic proportions at the time.[6]

Then, in 1954, the March of Dimes funded the largest health experiment the world had ever seen, involving more than a million children in both the United States and Canada, to test what would come to be known as the Salk vaccine. The success of the drug trials led the Canadian government, under the leadership of Health Minister Paul Martin Sr., who had polio in his youth, to provide financial assistance to the provinces to assist them to widely implement an immunization program by the mid-1950s. Though there were bumps on the road, the vaccine eradicated polio in North America by the early 1960s, within half a decade of its introduction.[7]

By the way, polio immunization has paid off handsomely. An American study estimates that the 1.7 billion vaccinations given to American children prevented approximately 1.1 million cases of paralytic polio and more than 160,000 deaths from 1955 to the present. The authors found that,

> Due to treatment cost savings, the investment implies
> net benefits of approximately US dollars 180 billion
> (1955 net present value), even without incorporating the
> intangible costs of suffering and death and of averted fear.
> Retrospectively, the U.S. investment in polio vaccination
> represents a highly valuable, cost-saving public health
> program.[8]

The highlighting of this dire epidemic clearly contributed to eventual elimination.[9]

Examples from this book show that a third potential ingredient to the wider adoption of early intervention measures is the presence of an engaged governmental insider. Mike Doolan was the chief social worker for New Zealand. Then-Mayor of Edmonton Stephen Mandel, now Alberta's Minister of Health, played a pivotal role in bringing the Housing First approach to fighting homelessness in Edmonton. The

Edmonton Homeless Commission described the latter's role in the following way:

> *Edmonton's mayor Stephen Mandel understood that*
> *something had to be done. He struck up the Edmonton*
> *Committee to End Homelessness. Mayor Mandel*
> *wanted innovative thinking applied to the problem*
> *of homelessness, so he appointed a wide spectrum of*
> *community leaders to the Committee: business people,*
> *labour leaders, managers of philanthropic organizations,*
> *social agency directors, politicians and faith leaders. The*
> *Plan that this Committee came up with set an ambitious*
> *goal — ending chronic homelessness in 10 years. It's based*
> *on the Housing First principle.*"[10]

In the polio vaccination case mentioned above, it was Health Minister Paul Martin Sr. who undertook to universalize the program across Canada through negotiations with the provinces. The record shows that finding that key insider, whether a politician or a passionate bureaucrat, can be extremely helpful in advancing the cause of early intervention.

A fourth element is strong data, both social and economic. Each case study in this book is based on data relating to the individual impact of the intervention as well as its cost relative to the existing approach. Along with the personal stories that humanize a social challenge, it is these numbers that end up being the most powerful weapons local leaders can wield in making the argument for reform. The people who produce the data, whether they are statisticians, epidemiologists, health economists, or otherwise, become indispensable contributors to making the case for wide implementation of the proposed early intervention.

SCALING UP EARLY INTERVENTION

There is a big difference between testing potential life- and money-saving early intervention and scaling them up so they are available to an entire population who may benefit from the intervention. Having a credible and committed leader like Mike Doolan or Mary Gordon in your camp, a crisis to make the case for reform, a passionate insider, and strong social and economic research results may go a long way to convincing a funder, usually a government funder, to test the initiative, but it usually takes more to scale up the initiative and make it available to everyone who needs it. Monique Begin, former federal Health Minister, once famously said that Canada is a "country of perpetual pilot projects," which are never translated into wider usage.[11] Canada is demonstrably poor at ramping up innovations for the benefit of the population. A recent Conference Board of Canada report underlines this point as a key message:

> Despite a decade or so of innovation agendas and
> prosperity reports, Canada remains near the bottom of
> its peer group on innovation, ranking 13th among the 16
> peer countries. Countries that are more innovative are
> passing Canada on measures such as income per capita,
> productivity, and the quality of social programs.[12]

When it comes to scaling up early intervention pilot initiatives that have been proven to work in both moral and financial terms, it is up to the federal or provincial government to make it happen. Governments in Canada are the keepers and managers of the social safety net as a whole and they have the responsibility of making early interventions available to the whole population who would benefit. It admittedly takes political courage to invest in scaling the evidence-based practices across the entire system because, as we have seen, the investments are being focused on people who are not at the stage of desperation, when life or limb may be at stake. Disproportionate early intervention investments, made to avoid greater costs later on in the course of the condition, disease, or disability's pathology, are simply a harder political case to make than spending on emergency room capacity, homeless shelters, and social assistance rate increases.

Thus, in addition to the four key success factors described above, I posit that two others should be considered. They are bipartisanship and citizen advocacy. I believe both these ideas can be very helpful in scaling up early intervention such that they do, in time, displace late intervention as the rule in health and social service management.

BIPARTISANSHIP

If the returns promised by early intervention are only determined to show up in governmental budgets in the years beyond the current government's lifespan, when the Opposition party may (or may not) form the government, it becomes logical to consider an approach that involves both the government and the Opposition in the transformation of massive systems of health and social services we currently have in place. Is it possible for two or more political parties to be convinced to lock arms in a combined effort to reinvent the social safety net? Taking such a bipartisan or multi-partisan approach to public policy development, though exceptional, is not unheard of.

In New Brunswick, the Liberal government and Progressive Conservative Opposition co-developed and oversaw the implementation of the province's poverty reduction plan in 2008–09. Despite changes in government, the plan continues to be implemented and was, in fact, renewed in 2014 through political cooperation and consensus. As I've said elsewhere, "Treating poverty reduction in a bipartisan way was arguably the key to allowing the plan to be developed without overt political interference and boosting its chances of being implemented for the long term."[13]

There are many examples in Canadian history where a bipartisan approach was used to produce important outcomes for the country, including Confederation itself and winning the First World War.[14] Advocates looking to catalyze long-term fundamental change in the way health and social services are managed might consider asking leaders in both or all political parties whether a conversation could be commenced to co-design a reform process that not only tests, but also scales up early intervention approaches.

CITIZEN ADVOCACY

It is rare in Canada that those directly affected by social reform have a large say in the reform process or proposed policy changes. However, when such a demographic group does manage to get organized and properly resourced, the speed and quality of reform can be vastly increased. The best recent example of this phenomenon is in the field of HIV-AIDS. While stigmatized badly in the 1980s when the disease was identified, it wasn't until HIV patients themselves started to structure an advocacy agenda, including research and service reform, that real change finally materialized. In a *Wall Street Journal* health blog, journalist Amy Dockser Marcus sums up the role of patients in driving change in HIV research and care in the United States in the following way:

> *There are some specific steps taken by yesterday's HIV/*
> *AIDS advocates that could help today's advocates be more*
> *effective. Among them: focusing on specific problems that*
> *hold back research or drug development and proposing*
> *solutions; creating a sense of community among advocates*
> *so that different groups are driving towards a common*
> *goal; training patient advocates to understand the*
> *scientific and policy issues in their disease and figuring*
> *out the key issue limiting research progress and then*
> *developing an approach to fix it.*[15]

New York–based HIV advocacy group ACT UP took a more confrontational and dramatic approach. Here's how *FOX News* described the group's efforts:

In order to get their message heard, ACT UP went to extremes. In one famous incident, members of the organization stormed New York City's St. Patrick's Cathedral during mass to protest the Catholic Church's stance against safe sex education. On another occasion, they even went so far as to sprinkle the ashes of people who had died of AIDS on the lawn of the White House. While many considered the actions of ACT UP to be radical, the activist group accomplished a number of significant changes throughout its history. Through the efforts of its members, ACT UP was ultimately responsible for lowering the price of HIV drugs, transforming the U.S. Food and Drug Administration's drug approval process and pushing for the inclusion of people with AIDS in drug trials.[16]

Groups of patients, citizens, or families can build the advocacy structures necessary to drive the political and media messaging needed to increase the pressure for change. It is harder for certain communities, like people with low incomes and those who are homeless, to create and resource advocacy organizations, but not impossible, particularly when they have the help of the philanthropic community.

Bipartisanship and citizen advocacy might possibly be the extra ingredients necessary to help push successfully tested early intervention trials into full-scale usage.

ROAD SAFETY: A PRECEDENT FOR EARLY INTERVENTION

Canada has seen the scaling up of early interventions in many fields outside of health and social services, including road safety.

Firstly, seat belts and child restraints are having a marked impact on both highway fatalities and serious injury. Here's what Transport Canada says on the topic:

> *In 2009, there were 2,209 fatalities and 11,451*
> *serious injuries (requiring hospitalization overnight),*
> *representing a decline of 25% in both measures compared*
> *to the period from 1996 to 2001 (in Canada) . . . The*
> *annual social costs of the motor vehicle collisions in terms*
> *of loss of life, medical treatment, rehabilitation, lost*
> *productivity, and property damage are measured in tens*
> *of billions of dollars.*[17]

Wearing a seat belt reduces the chance of death or serious injury from a car crash by around 50 per cent, and a huge majority of Canadians (around 95 per cent) are wearing them.[18] Public awareness, advertising, and fines have had a large impact on these figures.

Another powerful early intervention in the road-safety area is compulsory bike helmet usage. The past twenty years have seen a dramatic increase in helmet wearing and the gains have been great. The Canadian Paediatric Society tracks this issue closely and summarizes two global research reviews on the subject. Here's what it says:

> *In one Cochrane review, helmets were estimated to*
> *reduce the risk of head and brain injuries by 69%,*
> *severe brain injuries by 74% and facial injuries by 65%,*
> *with similar effects for cyclists in collisions with motor*
> *vehicles and across all age groups. Another study found*
> *that helmets reduced head injury risk by 60%, brain*
> *injury risk by 58%, facial injuries by 47% and fatal*
> *injury by 73%.*[19]

Seeing the potential health and social cost savings from such reductions, many Canadian provinces acted expeditiously to legislate on the issue and compel the usage of helmets. Here's the result:

A Canadian study compared time trends in head injury rates among children and adolescents five to 19 years of age between provinces that had introduced legislation with those that had not. While their head injury rates were similar before legislation (approximately 18 per 100,000 population), these rates fell by 45% in provinces that introduced helmet legislation compared with only 27% in provinces that did not.[20]

Drunk driving and speeding laws have also positively influenced the downward trend in motor vehicle accidents. A recent British Columbia study determined that "in the 2 years after implementation of the new laws, significant decreases occurred in fatal crashes and ambulance calls for road trauma. We found a very large reduction in alcohol-related fatal crashes and the benefits of the new laws are likely primarily the result of a reduction in drinking and driving."[21]

Many provinces have also implemented asset management programs for their road networks.[22] "Asset Management is the art and science of making the right decisions and optimising the delivery of value. A common objective is to minimise the whole life cost of assets but there may be other critical factors such as risk or business continuity to be considered objectively in this decision making."[23] In short, asset management improves the quality of roads and, in turn, road safety, while concurrently reducing the lifetime cost of maintaining the road.

Fencing to prevent large animals from crossing main arteries,[24] clear and visible road-safety signage, and safer cars themselves, particularly through the installation of airbags, are further measures that are employed to improve road safety.

The combination of seat-belt and child-restraint requirements, bike-helmeting laws, drunk driving and speeding measures, regular asset management respecting roads, moose fencing, effective signage, and safer cars makes for the seeds of a systemic approach to preventing injuries and saving lives, while at the same time reducing costs to government. Accidents, however, continue to happen, so ambulances and surgical suites continue to be crucial parts of the system. We just need a lot less of them now for road safety than we used to. This is how early and late-intervention services should fit together.

Though implemented in a mishmash way over time, through the layering of multiple early interventions, Canada has succeeded in dramatically improving road safety and saved a lot of lives and money in the process. In December 2014, a federal government spokesperson said this on the topic:

> *Regulatory improvements made under the authority of the* Motor Vehicle Safety Act *are a key reason that progressively fewer people are killed or injured on the roads each year, despite the ever-increasing number of motor vehicles being used. We are encouraged by the information we derive from our national crash data, which shows steady and impressive progress toward a vision of Canada having the safest roads in the world.*[25]

This example shows that changing policies to generate better outcomes through early intervention can be done successfully, and has been done in Canada (though, of course, more can and should be done in the road-safety file).[26] It is a valuable precedent for what might be done to Canada's social safety net.

HABITS

My last word is about habits. The weight of decades of political caution sits on the shoulders of those bearing the day-to-day responsibility for designing and managing Canada's social safety net. Civil servants, hospital administrators, front-line nurses, doctors, teachers, and social workers, as well as the vast swaths of non-governmental agencies funded by government, have collectively come to accept life in a last-resort system. They quickly put aside ambitious notions of systemic reform because they know what the response of the political apparatus will be. Up the chain of command in health and social services, there exists a reflexive negative reaction to bold and provocative recommendations that would shake the status quo. Thus, no recommendations of this kind are made. Suggestions to tweak and improve the status quo are greatly preferred. Decades of political caution have dulled the zeal for profound change and the better world it envisages for all first articulated by Leonard Marsh in the 1940s and last acted upon with vigour in the 1960s under the federal Liberal administration of Lester B. Pearson. In a word, to a large extent, it has become the habit of the system to think small and do little other than tinker with the late-intervention service array we've inherited.

Habits can change. Governmental and corporate cultures can change. Not easily and not quickly. Political leadership, urged on and supported by concerned and organized citizens supported by strong research and data, tenacious world-class reformers and thinkers, and guided by pas-sionate insiders, can create expectations within their structures that demand new approaches that over a longer period produce better results for vulnerable Canadians and reduce the cost of governmental services. If the habit is formed, and the entire system starts to think reflexively about intervening ever earlier, the great gains for Canadians and govern-ment pocketbooks will then commence. On this topic and in this book, Gandhi will have the last word: "Your beliefs become your thoughts. Your thoughts become your words. Your words become your actions. Your actions become your habits. Your habits become your values. Your values become your destiny."

ACKNOWLEDGEMENTS

I'm deeply indebted to a number of people for assisting me with *Early Intervention*. John Aylen has been with me on the project from seedling to harvest with advice, encouragement, networks and review. My readers, Jane Wheeler and Ian Boeckh, were intuitive, dedicated and timely in their feedback. Chapter-specific support came mainly from the people whose stories I recount and the subject matter experts who are highlighted. I want to acknowledge the precious time and honest exchange we shared. They include Mike Doolan, Lisa Bayrami, Maureen Bilerman, Patrick McGorry, Juanita Black and Sam Tsemberis. I also want to offer my thanks to Dr. Guy Rouleau , Dr. Ashok Malla and Dr. Mark Smilovitch for their feedback and counsel. Daniel Urbas has been a constant source of support in getting this project off the ground and helping it land. The Graham Boeckh Foundation, particularly Tony, Ray and Ian Boeckh, gave me the latitude and encouragement to write this book. I am forever grateful to them for this generosity. The brilliant Kierstin Lundell-Smith, wise and capable beyond her years, saw to the research sources, footnotes and selected bibliography in a meticulous and creative way. I can't thank Jim Lorimer enough for his steadying presence and finely tuned ear. I'm grateful to his team as well. A new author could not ask for a better publisher. Finally, a work of this kind requires the patience and forgiveness of family. To them, Jane, Nicholas, Jenna and Frances, thank you for both.

ENDNOTES

CHAPTER 1: CANADA'S SOCIAL SAFETY NET: A SNAPSHOT

1   Teghan Beaudette, "Treatment wait times for kids with autism 'excruciating,'" *CBC News Nova Scotia*, May 22, 2014. www.cbc.ca/news/canada/nova-scotia/treatment-wait-times-for-kids-with-autism-excruciating-1.2649993.

2   *CBC News Toronto*, "Ontario affordable housing wait list hits record high," September 9, 2014. www.cbc.ca/news/canada/toronto/ontario-affordable-housing-wait-list-hits-record-high-1.2761042.

3   Wait Time Alliance, *Time for Transformation: Canadians still waiting too long for health care. Report Card on Wait Times in Canada*, June 2013. www.gov.nl.ca/HaveYouHeard/wta.pdf.

4   Andre Picard, "Health system 'makes a mockery' of medicare values," *The Globe and Mail*, March 9, 2011. www.theglobeandmail.com/life/health-and-fitness/health-system-makes-a-mockery-of-medicare-values/article623023.

5   Dr. Paul Taylor, "Overcrowding in Canadian emergency departments," *Personal Health Navigator*, April 1, 2014. healthydebate.ca/personal-health-navigator/canadian-emergency-departments-overcrowded.

6   Ibid.

7   *Torstar News Service*, "Toronto to Open More Homeless Shelter Beds," *Metro*, March 18, 2013. metronews.ca/news/toronto/599805/toronto-to-open-more-homeless-shelter-beds.

8   Mark Kennedy, "Canadian prison overcrowding going to get worse in long-term, auditor general reports," *National Post*, May 6, 2014. news.nationalpost.com/2014/05/06/canadian-prison-overcrowding-going-to-get-worse-in-long-term-auditor-general-reports.

9   *CBC News Manitoba*, "Mental Illness Patients Strain Canada's Police Forces," August 21, 2013. www.cbc.ca/news/canada/manitoba/mental-illness-patients-strain-canada-s-police-forces-1.1396267.

10 Terence Brouse, "Half of all Canadians are Bullied as Child or Teen," Big Brothers Big Sisters Canada, February 15, 2012. www.bigbrothersbigsisters.ca/en/home/newsevents/halfofallcanadiansarebulliedaschildorteen.aspx.

11 UNICEF Canada, *Canadian Companion, Stuck in the Middle: Child Well-Being in Rich Countries: A comparative overview* (2013), 7. www.unicef.ca/sites/default/files/imce_uploads/DISCOVER/OUR%20WORK/ADVOCACY/DOMESTIC/POLICY%20ADVOCACY/DOCS/unicef_rc_11_canadian_companion.pdf.

12 Canadian Mental Health Association, "Fast Facts about Mental Illness." *CMHA* website (2014). www.cmha.ca/media/fast-facts-about-mental-illness/#.VJ20ql4AKA.

13 Ibid.

14 Katie Hyslop, "BC single Moms the Poorest of Them All," *The Tyee*, November 26, 2013. thetyee.ca/Blogs/TheHook/2013/11/26/BC-single-moms-the-poorest-of-them-all-First-Call/#sthash.dLU0qXIX.dpuf.

15 Juha Mikkonen and Dennis Raphael, *Social Determinants of Health: The Canadian Facts*, Toronto: York University School of Health Policy and Management (2010), 35. www.thecanadianfacts.org/The_Canadian_Facts.pdf.

16 William Temple was the Archbishop of Canterbury from 1942 to 1944 as well as a social activist and writer in Great Britain throughout the first half of the 20th Century. See William Temple Foundation website: williamtemplefoundation.org.uk/about-the-

foundation/archbishop-william-temple.

17   Melissa Bellerose, "Renverser le cours de l'itinérance ensemble," *Annual Report 2012–2013*, Montreal: Old Brewery Mission (2013), 13.

CHAPTER 2: THE DEVELOPMENT OF CANADA'S SOCIAL SAFETY NET

1   Statistics Canada, "Population, urban and rural, by province and territory (Canada)," *2011 Census of Population*, Ottawa (February 4, 2011). www.statcan.gc.ca/tables-tableaux/sum-som/l01/cst01/demo62a-eng.htm.

2   Dennis Raphael, *Poverty and Policy in Canada: Implications for Health and Quality of Life*, Toronto: Canadian Scholars (2007), 29.

3   Allan Moscovitch, *The Welfare State in Canada*, Waterloo: Wilfred Laurier University Press (1983), 20.

4   Dennis Guest, *The Emergence of Social Security in Canada*, UBC Press, 3rd edition (2003), 4.

5   Guest, *The Emergence of Social Security in Canada*, 77.

6   Allan Moscovitch, *The Welfare State in Canada*, Waterloo: Wilfred Laurier University Press (1983), 21–22.

7   Dennis Raphael, *Poverty and Policy in Canada: Implications for Health and Quality of Life*, Toronto: Canadian Scholars (2007), 29.

8   Pierre Berton, *The Great Depression: 1929–1939*, Toronto: Anchor Canada (1990), 2.

9   For a summary of the theories relating to the emergence of the welfare state across the developing world, including the role of economic development and the labour movement, see Jill Quadagno, *The Transformation of Old Age Security: Class Politics in the American Welfare State*, University of Chicago Press (1988).

10   See: Jay Makarenko, "Employment Insurance in Canada: History, Structure and Issues," *Maple Leaf Web* (September 22, 2009). mapleleafweb.com/features/employment-insurance-canada-history-structure-and-issues#history.

11   Antonia Maioni, "New century, new risks: the Marsh Report and the post-war welfare state in Canada," *Policy Options* (August 2004). policyoptions.irpp.org/issues/social-policy-in-the-21st-century/new-century-new-risks-the-marsh-report-and-the-post-war-welfare-state-in-canada.

12   Ibid.

13   See Health Canada, "Royal Commission on Health Services, 1961 to 64 (the 'Hall Commission')," *Health Canada* website (October 1, 2004). www.hc-sc.gc.ca/hcs-sss/com/fed/hall-eng.php.

14   Allan Moscovitch and Glenn Drover, "Social Expenditures and the Welfare State: The Canadian Experience in Historical Perspective" in *The Benevolent State: The Growth of Welfare in Canada*, edited by Moscovitch and Albert, Toronto: Garamond (1987), 31.

15   Jim Coutts, "Windows of opportunity: social reform under Lester B. Pearson," *Policy Options* (November 2003). policyoptions.irpp.org/issues/corporate-governance/windows-of-opportunity-social-reform-under-lester-b-pearson.

16   James Hughes, "Homelessness: Closing the Gap between Capacity and Performance," *Policy Options* (December 2012). mowatcentre.ca/wp-content/uploads/publications/56_homelessness.pdf.

17   See: Canada, Office of the Parliamentary Budget Officer, *Renewing the Canada Health Transfer: Implications for Federal and Provincial Territorial Sustainability*, Ottawa (January 12, 2012).

18   The "Fiscal Imbalance" negotiations resulted in a not insignificant bump in federal transfers and tax points to the provinces in the early 2000s. See: Canada, Department

of Finance, "Restoring Fiscal Balance in Canada: Focusing on Priorities. Canada's New Government Turning a New Leaf," *Budget 2006,* Ottawa: Public Works and Government Services Canada (2006), 108. www.fin.gc.ca/budget06/pdf/fp2006e.pdf.

19   Canada, Department of Finance, "Putting Transfers on a Long-Term, Sustainable Growth Track," *Canada's Economic Action Plan.* actionplan.gc.ca/en/initiative/putting-transfers-long-term-sustainable-growth.

20   *Loi sur l'aide aux personnes et aux familles,* LRQ 2005 c. A-13.1.1, ss. 74–78.

21   Allan Moscovitch, *The Welfare State in Canada,* Waterloo: Wilfred Laurier University Press (1983), v.

22   In *Regulating the Poor,* Frances Piven and colleagues demonstrate convincingly that expansion of state benefits occurs to stem civil disorder, while contraction takes place during economic growth periods when work norms need reinforcement. See: Frances Fox Piven and Richard A. Cloward, *Regulating the Poor: the Functions of Public Welfare,* New York: Pantheon (1971).

CHAPTER 3: SAFER CHILD PROTECTION

1   Public Health Agency of Canada, *Canadian Incidence Study of Reported Child Abuse and Neglect — 2008: Major Findings,* Ottawa (2008), 23. cwrp.ca/sites/default/files/publications/en/CIS-2008-rprt-eng.pdf.

2   Public Health Agency of Canada, *Canadian Incidence Study of Reported Child Abuse and Neglect — 2008: Major Findings,* Ottawa (2008), 2. cwrp.ca/sites/default/files/publications/en/CIS-2008-rprt-eng.pdf.

3   Public Health Agency of Canada, *Canadian Incidence Study of Reported Child Abuse and Neglect — 2008: Major Findings,* Ottawa (2008), 2. cwrp.ca/sites/default/files/publications/en/CIS-2008-rprt-eng.pdf.

4   Ontario. Commission to Promote Sustainable Child Welfare, *Realizing a Sustainable Child Welfare System in Ontario — Final Report,* Toronto (September 2012), 17. www.children.gov.on.ca/htdocs/English/documents/topics/childrensaid/commission/2012sept-Final_report.pdf.

5   Ibid.

6   U.S. Department of Health & Human Services, Administration for Children and Families, Administration on Children, Youth and Families, Children's Bureau, *Child Maltreatment 2012,* Washington (2013), xiii. www.acf.hhs.gov/programs/cb/research-data-technology/statistics-research/child-maltreatment.

7   Wulczyn, Hislop and Goerge, *Foster Care Dynamics 1983–1998,* Chicago: Chapin Hall Centre for Children (2000), 23. www.chapinhall.org/sites/default/files/old_reports/75.pdf.

8   King et al. *Child Protection Legislation in Ontario: Past, Present and Future?,* London: Western (2003), 4. www.edu.uwo.ca/cas/pdf/child%20welfare%20legislation%20aug%20technical%20report.pdf.

9   See, for example: Lynne Marie Kohm, "Tracing the Foundations of the Best Interests of the Child Standard in American Jurisprudence," *Journal of Law and Family Studies,* vol. 10 (2008): 1–40.

10   King et al. *Child Protection Legislation in Ontario: Past, Present and Future?,* London: Western (2003), 14.

11   Linda Graff, *Better Safe . . . Risk management in Volunteer Programs and Community Service,* Hamilton: Linda Graff and Associates (2003).

12   Ted Hughes, *The Legacy of Phoenix Sinclair: Achieving the Best for All Our Children,*

vol. II, Winnipeg: Commission of Inquiry into the Circumstances Surrounding the Death of Phoenix Sinclair (December 2013), 115.

13   At just two months old, Echo died of pneumonia.

14   *CBC News Manitoba*, "Phoenix Sinclair's Death 'Unimaginable,' Says RCMP Officer," April 18, 2013. www.cbc.ca/news/canada/manitoba/story/2013/04/18/mb-phoenix-sinclair-inquiry-rcmp-investigator.html.

15   Christie Blatchford, "Allegation of 'altered' report in Phoenix Sinclair fiasco only a tiny part of CFS bureaucracy's sheer ineptitude," *National Post*, December 10, 2012. fullcomment.nationalpost.com/2012/12/10/christie-blatchford-allegation-of-altered-report-in-phoenix-sinclair-fiasco-only-a-tiny-part-of-cfs-bureaucracys-sheer-ineptitude.

16   James Turner, "CFS response in Phoenix Sinclair case 'deeply disturbing': Inquiry told," *Toronto Sun*, January 16, 2013. www.torontosun.com/2013/01/16/cfs-response-in-phoenix-sinclair-case-deeply-disturbing-inquiry-told.

17   New Brunswick. Ombudsman and Child & Youth Advocate, *Broken Promises: Juli-Anna's Story*, Fredericton (January 2008). www.gnb.ca/0073/PDF/JASPFinalReport-e.pdf.

18   Mike Doolan and Marie Connolly, "Care and protection: Capturing the essence of our practice," *New Zealand Child, Youth and Family.* www.practicecentre.cyf.govt.nz/practice-vision/care-and-protection/capturing-the-essence-of-our-practice/care-and-protection-capturing-the-essence-of-our-practice.html.

19   Mike Doolan, "The Family Group Conference: Changing the Face of Child Welfare" in *Diversity and Community Development: An intercultural approach,* ed. Clarijs, Guidikova and Malmberg, Amsterdam: SWP, 2011, 60. www.coe.int/t/dg4/cultureheritage/culture/Cities/Publication/BookCoE08-MikeDoolan.pdf.

20   Mike Doolan indicated to me in an email exchange that credit for the New Zealand reforms needs to be shared with many including his colleague, Jackie Renouf, who led the child welfare policy team which prepared the detailed planning leading to the adoption of the family group conference model. Email from Mike Doolan, February 11, 2015.

21   Ibid, 57–68. www.coe.int/t/dg4/cultureheritage/culture/Cities/Publication/BookCoE08-MikeDoolan.pdf.

22   Ibid, 61. www.coe.int/t/dg4/cultureheritage/culture/Cities/Publication/BookCoE08-MikeDoolan.pdf.

23   Leone Huntsman, *Family group conferencing in a child welfare context — A review of the literature,* Ashfield, NSW, Australia: Centre for Parenting & Research (July 2006), 13. www.community.nsw.gov.au/docswr/_assets/main/documents/research_family_conferencing.pdf.

24   Ibid, 2.

25   Barnardo's , "Family Placement," *Barnado's* website (2014): www.barnardos.org.uk/commission_us/our_services/family_placement.htm

26   Clewett, Slowley and Glover, *Making plans: Using Family Group Conferencing to reduce the impact of caring on young people,* Barkingside, Essex, UK: Barnardos (2010), 14. www.barnardos.org.uk/making_plans_12634.pdf (the last names of the family members were withheld).

27   McRae, Allan and Zehr, *The Little Book of Family Group Conferences New Zealand style,* Intercourse, PA: Good Books (2004), 67.

28   McRae, Allan and Zehr, *The Little Book of Family Group Conferences New Zealand style,* Intercourse, PA: Good Books (2004). Data from 1987 and 2001 show the change

between the time just before family group conferences were implemented and after they had been given a decade to take full effect across the justice system. Now Family Group Conferences have moved well beyond the pilot project stage to become the well-established way that New Zealand handles child protection and youth offences. The government of New Zealand is, of course, always interested in improving its practices. See New Zealand, "Children's Action Plan" government of New Zealand website. www.childrensactionplan.govt.nz/action-plan/. Academic studies of Family Group Conferences are ongoing. See Carswell et al., "Evaluation of the Family Group Conference" University of Canterbury website. www.canterbury.ac.nz/spark/Project. aspx?projectid=288.

29   United Kingdom. House of Commons Justice Committee, "Mediation and other mean of preventing cases reaching court," *Sixth Report Operation of the Family Courts* (June 28, 2011), paragraph 84. www.frg.org.uk/fgcs-quotes-from-official-documents.

30   Ibid, paragraph 86. www.frg.org.uk/fgcs-quotes-from-official-documents.

31   Mandell, Sullivan and Meredith, *Family Group Conferencing Final Evaluation Report*, Toronto: Etobicoke Family Group Conferencing Project (2001), 17.

32   Bernard Richard and Shirley Smallwood, *Staying Connected: A Report of the Task Force on a Centre of Excellence for Children and Youth with Complex Needs*, Fredericton: Office of the Ombudsman and Child and Youth Advocate (March 2011), 19. www. gnb.ca/0073/Child-YouthAdvocate/centre_excellence/PDF/staying_connected-e.pdf.

33   Joseph J. Doyle, "Child Protection and Child Outcomes: Measuring the Effects of Foster Care," *The American Economic Review*, vol. 97, no. 5 (December 2007): 1583– 1610. www.mit.edu/~jjdoyle/fostercare_aer.pdf.

34   Joseph J. Doyle, "Child Protection and Adult Crime: Using Investigator Assignment to Estimate Causal Effects of Foster Care," *Journal of Political Economy*, vol. 116, no. 4 (January 2008): 746–770. www.mit.edu/~jjdoyle/doyle_jpe_aug08.pdf.

35   Nelson et al., "Cognitive Recovery in Socially Deprived Young Children: The Bucharest Early Intervention Project," *Science*, vol. 318, no. 5858 (December 21, 2007): 1937–1940. www.sciencemag.org/content/318/5858/1937.short.

36   Wolfe et al., "Early intervention for parents at risk of child abuse and neglect: A preliminary investigation," *Journal of Consulting and Clinical Psychology*, vol. 56, no. 1 (February 1988): 40–47. psycnet.apa.org/journals/ccp/56/1/40.

37   Kaiser Permanente, "Career areas," *Kaiser Permanente* website (2015): www. kaiserpermanentejobs.org/career-areas.aspx.

38   Robert F. Anda and Vincent J. Felitti, "Origins and Essence of the Study," *ACE Reporter*, vol. 1, no. 1 (April, 2003): 2. acestudy.org/yahoo_site_admin/assets/docs/ ARV1N1.127150541.pdf.

39   Centers for Disease Control, "Injury Prevention & Control: Adverse Childhood Experiences (ACE) Study Major Findings," CDC website (May 13, 2014). www.cdc. gov/ace/findings.htm.

40   Ted Hughes, "Transcript of Proceedings," *Public Inquiry Hearing*, Winnipeg: Commission of Inquiry into the Circumstances Surrounding the Death of Phoenix Sinclair, May 14, 2013: 21. www.phoenixsinclairinquiry.ca/transcripts/public_inquiry_ hearing_may14_2013.pdf.

41   OACAS, *Child Welfare Report 2012*, Toronto: Ontario Association of Children's Aid Societies (2012). www.oacas.org/newsroom/releases/12childwelfarereport.pdf.

42   Australian Institute of Health and Welfare, "Child protection Australia 2011-2012," *Child Welfare Series*, no. 55, cat. no. CWS 43, Canberra: AIHW (2013): 3. www.aihw. gov.au/WorkArea/DownloadAsset.aspx?id=60129542752.

CHAPTER 4: ADDRESSING AUTISM

1   Linda Lee, *Autism Physician Handbook,* Canadian Edition, Bothwell, Ontario: Autism Canada Foundation (2011). www.autismcanada.org.

2   That said, persons with autism often have co-occurring physical and mental-health challenges. See, for example: Matson, Matson and Beighley, "Comorbidity of Physical and Motor Problems in Children with Autism," *Research in Developmental Disabilities,* vol. 32, no. 6 (November–December 2011): 2304–2308.

3   Ontario, Ministry of Child and Youth Services, *The Autism Parent Resource Kit,* Toronto (2014), 9. www.children.gov.on.ca/htdocs/English/documents/topics/ specialneeds/autism/aprk/Autism_Parent_Resource_Kit.pdf. Many studies exist delving into each of these possibilities. For a literature review on genetic factors, see: Judith H. Miles, "Autism Spectrum Disorders —A Genetics Review," *Genetics in Medicine,* vol. 13, no.4 (April 2011): 278–294. For environmental factors, including pollutants and viruses, see: Martha R. Herbert, "Contributions of the Environment and Environmentally Vulnerable Physiology to Autism Spectrum Disorders," *Current Opinion in Neurology,* 23:000-000 (2010): 1–4. And Matsuzaki et al, "Triggers for Autism: Genetic and Environmental Factors," *Journal of Central Nervous System Disease,* 4 (2012): 27–36. For chromosomal abnormalities, see: Faraz Farzin and Kami Koldewyn, "Fragile X Syndrome and Autism" in *Comprehensive Guide to Autism,* ed. V.B. Patel et al. New York: Springer (2014), 2743–2754.

4   Leo Kanner, "Problems of Nosology and Psychodynamics of Early Infantile Autism," *American Journal of Orthopsychiatry* 19 (1949): 416–426.

5   Ontario, Ministry of Child and Youth Services, *The Autism Parent Resource Kit,* Toronto (2014), 9. www.children.gov.on.ca/htdocs/English/documents/topics/ specialneeds/autism/aprk/Autism_Parent_Resource_Kit.pdf.

6   American Psychiatric Association, "Autism Spectrum Disorder Factsheet," *Diagnostic and Statistics Manual 5,* Arlington, Virginia: American Psychiatric Publishing (2013). www.dsm5.org/Documents/Autism%20Spectrum%20Disorder%20Fact%20Sheet. pdf.

7   Allan Grant, "Screams, Slaps and Love: A surprising, shocking treatment helps far-gone mental cripples," *Life Magazine,* vol. 58, no. 18 (May 7, 1965): 90A.

8   Peter Gay, "Per Ardua," review of *The Empty Fortress,* by Bruno Bettelheim, *New Yorker,* May 18, 1968, 160–172. Cited in Mary Beth Walsh, "Top 10 Reasons Children with Autism Deserve ABA," *Behavior Analysis in Practice,* 4(1) (Summer 2011), 72–79.

9   Jim Sinclair, "Don't Mourn for Us," *Our Voice,* vol. 1, no.3 (1993). This piece has become a cornerstone of the online autistic neurodiversity movement and is available at www.autreat.com/dont_mourn.html.

10 Temple Grandin, *Thinking in Pictures,* New York: Vintage (1995). Grandin was blessed with the support of a remarkable mother, mother's helpers, tutors, and teachers at a time, the 1950s, when few with such a diagnosis would have received any support at all. Grandin eventually conquered the main symptoms of autism, which would have otherwise prevented her from writing a doctoral thesis on agricultural science and, in time, designing cutting-edge agricultural equipment, including cattle chutes and dip vats.

11 Scott Sea, "Planet Autism," *Salon,* September 27, 2003. www.salon. com/2003/09/27/autism_8.

12 Susan F. Rzucidlo, *Welcome to Beirut,* BBB Autism Support Network website. www. bbbautism.com/beginners_beirut.htm

13 Centers for Disease Control and Prevention, "Autism Spectrum Disorder (ASD): Data & Statistics," *CDC* website (March 24, 2014). www.cdc.gov/ncbddd/autism/data.html.

14   Solomon, *Far From the Tree*, 222.

15   Ibid.

16   Canadian Institutes for Health Research, "Harper Government Announces New Research Chair Dedicated to Autism Treatment and Care," *Government of Canada Press Release*, Toronto (November 5, 2012). www.cihr-irsc.gc.ca/e/46009.html.

17   Margalit Fox, "O. Ivar Lovaas, Pioneer in Developing Therapies for Autism, Dies at 83," *New York Times*, August 22, 2010. www.nytimes.com/2010/08/23/health/23lovaas.html

18   Tristram Smith and Svein Eikeseth, "O. Ivar Lovaas: Pioneer of Applied Behavior Analysis and Intervention for Children with Autism," *Journal of Autism and Developmental Disorders*, 41 (2011), 375. www.ncbi.nlm.nih.gov/pubmed/21153872.

19   O. Ivar Lovaas, "Behavioral Treatment and Normal Educational and Intellectual Functioning in Young Autistic Children," *Journal of Consulting and Clinical Psychology*, vol. 55, no. 1 (1987): 3–9.

20   Ibid, 3.

21   Ibid, 5.

22   O. Ivar Lovaas, "Behavioral Treatment and Normal Educational and Intellectual Functioning in Young Autistic Children," *Journal of Consulting and Clinical Psychology*, vol. 55, no. 1 (1987): 7.

23   Ibid, 9.

24   Temple Grandin, *The Autistic Brain*, New York: Mariner Books (2013), 4.

25   O. Ivar Lovaas, "Behavioral Treatment and Normal Educational and Intellectual Functioning in Young Autistic Children," *Journal of Consulting and Clinical Psychology*, vol. 55, no. 1 (1987): 6.

26   Dawson et al, "Randomized, Controlled Trial of an Intervention for Toddlers with Autism: The Early Start Denver Model," *Pediatrics*, 125 (2010), e17–e23. www.ncbi.nlm.nih.gov/pubmed/19948568.

27   Ibid, e23. www.ncbi.nlm.nih.gov/pubmed/19948568.

28   Warren et al, "A systematic Review of Early Intensive Intervention for Autism Spectrum Disorders," *Pediatrics*, 127 (2011): e1303–1311. www.ncbi.nlm.nih.gov/pubmed/21464190.

29   Sarah DeWeerdt, "Researchers seek 'active ingredients' of early intervention," Simons Foundation Autism Research Initiative, March 26, 2012. sfari.org/news-and-opinion/news/2012/researchers-seek-active-ingredients-of-early-intervention.

30   Catherine Maurice, *Let Me Hear Your Voice: A Family's Triumph Over Autism*, New York: Fawcett (1993).

31   Steve Buckmann, "Lovaas Revisited: Should We Have Ever Left?," *BBB Autism Support Network* website (May 9, 2002). www.bbbautism.com/pdf/article_40_Lovaas_revisited.pdf

32   O. Ivar Lovaas, Behavioral Treatment and Normal Educational and Intellectual Functioning in Young Autistic Children," *Journal of Consulting and Clinical Psychology*, vol. 55, no. 1 (1987): 9. Costs are estimated in 1987 American dollars.

33   *Auton v. British Columbia*, 2004, SCC 78, at paragraph 4.

34   Centers for Disease Control and Prevention, "Autism Spectrum Disorder (ASD): Data & Statistics," *CDC* website (March 24, 2014). www.cdc.gov/ncbddd/autism/data.html; see also Lorri Unumb, "Applied Behavior Analysis Benefit for NC State Health Plan" (*Autism speaks* presentation to North Carolina State Health Plan, North Carolina, November 21, 2013). www.shpnc.org/library/pdf/board-materials/November-2013/autism-behavior.pdf.

35   Lavelle et al, "Economic Burden of Childhood Autism Spectrum Disorders," *Pediatrics* vol. 133, no. 3 (March 2014): e520–e529. Costs are calculated in 2011 American dollars.

36   Lavelle et al, "Economic Burden of Childhood Autism Spectrum Disorders," *Pediatrics*, vol. 133, no. 3 (March 2014): e525.

37   John W. Jacobson, James A. Mulick & Gina Green, "Cost-Benefit Estimates for Early Intensive Behavioral Invention for Young Children with Autism — General Model and Single State Case," *Behavioral Interventions*, 13 (1998): 201–226. www.hca. wa.gov/hta/meetingmaterials/supplemental_information_submitted_cited_evidence_ articles_draft_findings_decision_091611.pdf. The projections start with costs in 1996 American dollars and assume 3 per cent annual inflation in the cost of the relevant services.

38   Motiwala et al, "The Cost-Effectiveness of Expanding Intensive Behavioural Intervention to All Autistic Children in Ontario," *Healthc Policy*, vol. 1, no. 2 (January 2006), 135–151. Costs are calculated in 2003 Canadian dollars.

39   Ibid, 144.

40   Canadian Institutes for Health Research, "Harper Government Announces New Research Chair Dedicated to Autism Treatment and Care: Autism Fact Sheet," *Government of Canada Press Release*, Toronto (November 5, 2012). www.cihr-irsc. gc.ca/e/46010.html.

41   Shirlee Engle, "*Agony of Autism*," *Global News* video, 3:20, October 7, 2013. globalnews. ca/news/887710/autism-treatment-means-months-on-wait-lists-relocation-for-some- canadian-families/

42   Ibid. See also CBC News, "Survey Finds Parents Upset with Province over Autism Therapy Wait Times," April 3, 2013. www.cbc.ca/news/canada/ottawa/survey-finds- parents-upset-with-province-over-autism-therapy-wait-times-1.1340534.

43   Shirlee Engle, "Agony of Autism," *Global News* video, 3:20, October 7, 2013. globalnews.ca/news/887710/autism-treatment-means-months-on-wait-lists- relocation-for-some-canadian-families/

44   Bonnie Lysyk, "Children Waiting Too Long for Access to Autism Programs, Auditor General Says," Office of the Auditor General of Ontario press release, Toronto, December 10, 2013. www.auditor.on.ca/en/news_en/13_newsreleases/2013news_3.01a utism.pdf

45   *Montreal Gazette*, "Editorial: Children with autism need better services," July 17, 2014, A12.

46   For more information, see Specialisterne, "Welcome to Specialisterne Canada," *Specialisterne Canada* website (2013). ca.specialisterne.com/about-specialisterne/

47   Shirley S. Wang, "How Autism Can Help You Land a Job," *Wall Street Journal*, March 27, 2014. online.wsj.com/news/articles/SB10001424052702304418404579465561364868556

48   "Factum of the Intervener, Michelle Dawson," *Auton v. British Columbia* (2004), SCC 78.

49   "Factum of the Intervener, Michelle Dawson," *Auton v. British Columbia* (2004), SCC 78, at paragraph 27.

50   Andrew Solomon, *Far From the Tree*, New York: Scribner (2012), 248.

51   James Coplan, "Behaviorism, Part 3: O. Ivar Lovaas and ABA," *Psychology Today Blog*, September 26, 2010. www.psychologytoday.com/blog/making-sense-autistic- spectrum-disorders/201009/023-behaviorism-part-3-o-ivar-lovaas-and-aba.

52   George A. Rekers and O. Ivar Lovaas, "Behavioral Treatment of Deviant Sex-Role Behaviors in a Male Child," *Journal of Applied Behavior Analysis*, vol. 7, no. 2 (Summer 1974): 173–190.

53   Scott Bronstein and Jesse Joseph, "Therapy to Change 'Feminine' Boy Created a
     Troubled Man, Family Says," CNN, June 10, 2011. www.cnn.com/2011/US/06/07/sissy.
     boy.experiment/index.html

CHAPTER 5: MORE PEACEFUL SCHOOLS

1   Canadian Institutes for Health Research, "Canadian Bullying Statistics," *CIHR* website
     (September 28, 2012). www.cihr-irsc.gc.ca/e/45838.html.

2   Canadian Council on Learning, "Bullying in Canada: How intimidation
     affects learning," *Lessons in Learning* (March 20, 2008), 3. www.ccl-cca.ca/pdfs/
     LessonsInLearning/Mar-20-08-Bullying-in-Canad.pdf.

3   Reported in Library of Parliament Research Publications, *Current Issues in Mental
     Health in Canada: Child and Youth Mental Health*, Martha Butler, Melissa Pang,
     Legal and Social Affairs Division (March 5, 2014). www.parl.gc.ca/Content/LOP/
     ResearchPublications/2014-13-e.htm.

4   The Council of Ministers of Education, Canada, "Education in Canada: an Overview,"
     CMEC website: www.cmec.ca/299/Education-in-Canada-An-Overview/index.
     html#01.

5   Canadian Council on Learning, "Bullying in Canada: How intimidation
     affects learning," *Lessons in Learning* (March 20, 2008), 3. www.ccl-cca.ca/pdfs/
     LessonsInLearning/Mar-20-08-Bullying-in-Canad.pdf.

6   Ibid.

7   Ibid.

8   Preamble to Bill 13, *An Act to Amend the Education Act with Respect to Bullying and
     Other Matters*, 1st sess., 40th Legislature, 2012, SO. ontla.on.ca/web/bills/bills_detail.
     do?locale=en&BillID=2549.

9   See "From Safety Net to Springboard" UK Equality and Human Rights Commission,
     2009. www.equalityhumanrights.com/sites/default/files/documents/safetynet_
     springboard.pdf

10   UNICEF Canada, "Stuck in the Middle: Canadian Companion," *Child Well-Being in
     Rich Countries: A comparative overview* (2013), 15. www.unicef.ca/sites/default/files/
     imce_uploads/DISCOVER/OUR%20WORK/ADVOCACY/DOMESTIC/POLICY%20
     ADVOCACY/DOCS/unicef_rc_11_canadian_companion.pdf.

11   Ibid.

12   Manjit Virk, *Reena: A Father's Story*, Victoria: Heritage House (2008).

13   Times Colonist, "The Killing of Reena Virk, 10 Years Later," *CanWest*, November 15,
     2007. www.canada.com/story.html?id=8db62748-78ed-4109-a6f1-04fdc94774f3.

14   *R v. Ellard*, 2009, SCC 27. Available at: scc.lexum.org/decisia-scc-csc/scc-csc/scc-csc/
     en/item/7798/index.do.

15   Manjit Virk, *Reena: A Father's Story*, Victoria: Heritage House (2008).

16   Bullying Canada, "What is Bullying?" *Bullying Canada* website. bullyingcanada.ca/
     content/239900. [Article no longer available online]

17   See, for example, Schaubman, A.; Stetson, E.; Plog, A. 2011. "Reducing teacher stress
     by implementing collaborative problem solving in a school setting," *School Social
     Work Journal*, 35(2): 72–93; Geving, A.M. "Identifying the types of student and
     teacher behaviors associated with teacher stress," *Teaching and Teacher Education*, 23
     (2007): 624–640 (cited in *Issue Brief: Social and Emotional Learning in Canada*, Guyn
     Cooper Research Associates (August 2013).) www.maxbell.org/sites/default/files/
     SELIssueBrief.pdf).

18   Canadian Safe School Network, "About," *Canadian Safe School Network* website. canadiansafeschools.com/about.

19   Emily Dugan, "More than a million British youngsters being bullied online every day," *The Independent*, October 2, 2013.

20   Ibid.

21   Amanda Lenhart, "Cyberbullying: what the research is telling us." (Presentation for National Center for Missing and Exploited Children's Youth Online Safety Working Group, Washington, DC, May 6, 2010). www.pewinternet.org/2010/05/06/ cyberbullying-2010-what-the-research-tells-us.

22   See Canadian Red Cross, "Facts on Bullying and Harassment" (2014). www.redcross. ca/what-we-do/violence-bullying-and-abuse-prevention/educators/bullying-and-harassment-prevention/facts-on-bullying-and-harassment.

23   The incident was widely reported in local, national, and international news coverage. See, for example, Selena Ross, "Who failed Rehtaeh Parsons?" *Halifax Chronicle Herald*, April 9, 2013. thechronicleherald.ca/metro/1122345-who-failed-rehtaeh-parsons.

24   Jane Taber and Caroline Alphonso, "Report on Rehtaeh Parsons' Suicide Says her Absence from School was a Missed Red Flag," *The Globe and Mail*, June 14, 2013. www.theglobeandmail.com/news/national/report-into-rehtaeh-parsons-suicide-calls-for-review-of-halifax-hospital/article12559456.

25   Ibid.

26   Guyn Cooper Research Associates, *Issue Brief: Social and Emotional Learning in Canada*, commissioned by Carthy Foundation and Max Bell Foundation (August 2013). www.maxbell.org/sites/default/files/SELIssueBrief.pdf.

27   Durlak et al, "The Impact of Enhancing Students' Social and Emotional Learning: A Meta-Analysis of School-Based Universal Interventions," *Child Development*, vol. 82, no. 1 (January/February 2011): 474–501.

28   Ibid, 474.

29   P. L. Benson, *All kids are our kids: What communities must do to raise caring and responsible children and adolescents*, 2nd edn. San Francisco: Jossey-Bass (2006); A. M. Klem, & J.P. Connell, "Relationships matter: Linking teacher support to student engagement and achievement." *Journal of School Health*, 74 (2004): 262–273. Cited in Durlak, note 27.

30   Benson, 475.

31   Ibid, 486.

32   Mary Gordon, *Roots of Empathy: Changing the World Child by Child*, Toronto: Thomas Allen (2005), xiii.

33   Ashoka Canada, "Fellows: Mary Gordon," *Ashoka Canada* website (2002). canada. ashoka.org/fellow/mary-gordon.

34   Ibid.

35   Elizabeth Renzetti, "Mary Gordon on Teaching Empathy: Start Young and Start With a Baby," *The Globe and Mail*, May 5, 2013. www.theglobeandmail.com/life/ parenting/mary-gordon-on-teaching-empathy-start-young-and-start-with-a-baby/ article11715642.

36   Maria Yau, *Parenting and Family Literacy Centres: Making a Difference beyond Early School Readiness*, Toronto: Toronto District School Board (October 2009), 7.

37   Mary Gordon, *Roots of Empathy: Changing the World Child by Child*, Toronto: Thomas Allen (2005), 15.

38   Santos et al, "Effectiveness of School Based Violence Prevention for Children and Youth," *Healthcare Quarterly*, vol. 14, Special Issue (April 2011): 80–90.

39   Ibid, 86.

40   Reported in Mary Gordon, *Roots of Empathy: Changing the World Child by Child*, Toronto: Thomas Allen (2005), 6.

41   See also Schonert-Reichl et al, "Promoting Children's Prosocial Behaviors in School: Impact of the 'Roots of Empathy' Program on the Social and Emotional Competence of School-Aged Children," *School Mental Health*, 4 (2012): 1–21. cemh.lbpsb.qc.ca/professionals/RootsofEmpathy.pdf.

42   Roots of Empathy, *Report on Research 2009*, Toronto (2009).

43   David Bornstein, "Fighting Bullying with Babies," *New York Times Opinionator* blog, November 8, 2010. opinionator.blogs.nytimes.com/2010/11/08/fighting-bullying-with-babies/?_r=0.

44   Santos et al, "Effectiveness of School Based Violence Prevention for Children and Youth," *Healthcare Quarterly*, vol. 14, Special Issue (April 2011): 88.

45   See Dennis D. Embry, "Behavioral Vaccines and Evidence Based Kernels: Non-Pharmaceutical Approaches for the Prevention of Mental, Emotional and Behavioral Disorders," *Psychiatric Clinics of North America*, vol. 34, no. 1 (March 2011): 1–34. www.ncbi.nlm.nih.gov/pmc/articles/PMC3064963.

46   Santos et al, "Effectiveness of School Based Violence Prevention for Children and Youth," *Healthcare Quarterly*, vol. 14, Special Issue (April 2011), 88.

47   Caledon Institute, "Roots of Empathy," *Community Stories*, Ottawa: Caledon Institute for Social Policy (June 1999), 1.

48   Rick Phillips, "The Financial Costs of Bullying, Violence, and Vandalism," *National Association of Secondary School Principals* website (April 2010). www.nassp.org/Content.aspx?topic=The_Financial_Costs_of_Bullying_Violence_and_Vandalism.

49   Community Matters, "Suspension Loss and Cost Calculator," *Community Matters* website. community-matters.org/programs-and-services/calculator.

50   S. Scott, M. Knapp, J. Henderson, B, Maughan. 2001. "Financial Cost of Social Exclusion: Follow Up Study of Antisocial Children into Adulthood ", *British Medical Journal* 323: 191-195; cited in Santos et al.

51   Carol Sanders, "Baby Steps Toward Empathy," *Winnipeg Free* Press, May 23, 2013. www.winnipegfreepress.com/local/baby-steps-toward-empathy-208618751.html. See also Highmark Foundation, *The Cost Benefit of Bullying Prevention: A First Time Analysis of Savings*. www.highmarkfoundation.org/publications/HMK_Bullying%20Report_final.pdf.

CHAPTER 6: HEALTHIER HEALTH CARE

1   Jeffrey Simpson, *Chronic Condition: Why Canada's Health-care System Needs to be Dragged into the 21ˢᵗ Century*, Toronto: Penguin (2012), 1.

2   Natasha MacDonald-Dupuis, "The Problem with Canada's Unsustainable Health System," *Huffington Post*, February 11, 2014. www.huffingtonpost.ca/natasha-macdonalddupuis/the-future-of-canadian-healthcare_b_4429892.html.

3   David A. Dodge, "Chronic Healthcare Spending Disease: A Macro Diagnosis and Prognosis," *The Health Papers*, no. 327, Toronto: C. D. Howe Institute (April 2011): 11. www.cdhowe.org/pdf/Commentary_327.pdf.

4   Canadian Institute for Health Information, *National Health Expenditure Trends 1975 to 2012*, Ottawa: CIHI (2012), 24. secure.cihi.ca/free_products/NHEXTrendsReport2012EN.pdf.

5   Jeffrey Simpson, *Chronic Condition*, Allen Lane (2012), 22.

6   With respect to health outcomes, Canada scores very poorly in the effectiveness of its health-care spending, ranking near the bottom on comparative value for money against other developed countries. See: Amin Mawani, "Can We Get Better for Less: Value for Money in Canadian Health Care," *CGA In Focus* (May 2011). www.cga-canada.org/en-ca/ResearchReports/ca_rep_2011-04_healthcare.pdf.

7   Maureen Bilerman, "Connect the Dots" video, 15:02, March 25, 2011. www.youtube.com/watch?v=FkESo1U1Rao.

8   Maureen Bilerman, speech to the second Annual Mental Health Symposium, Bernice MacNaughton High School, Moncton, New Brunswick, May 8, 2012.

9   Maureen estimated the two-year cost for "treating" Sarah to be $250,000 to the New Brunswick tax system. Personal communication with the author, August 13, 2014.

10   Canadian Nurses Association, "Mental Health," *Nurseone* website (2013). www.nurseone.ca/Default.aspx?portlet=StaticHtmlViewerPortlet&stmd=False&plang=1&ptdi=492.

11   Mary Ellen Turpel-Lafond, *Still Waiting: First-Hand Experiences with Youth Mental Health Services in B.C.*, Victoria: Representative for Children and Youth (April, 2013), 4. www.rcybc.ca/sites/default/files/documents/pdf/reports_publications/still_waiting.pdf.

12   Mental Health Commission of Canada, *Making the Case for Investing in Mental Health in Canada* (2011), 26. www.mentalhealthcommission.ca/English/system/files/private/document/Investing_in_Mental_Health_FINAL_Version_ENG.pdf.

13   Centre for Addition and Mental Health (CAMH), "Statistics on Mental Illness and Addictions," *CAMH* website (2012). www.camh.ca/en/hospital/about_camh/newsroom/for_reporters/Pages/addictionmentalhealthstatistics.aspx.

14   Michael Kirby, "We are Failing Young Canadians on Mental Health," *Toronto Star*, October 7, 2013. www.thestar.com/opinion/commentary/2013/10/07/we_are_failing_young_canadians_on_mental_health.html.

15   Mary Ellen Turpel-Lafond, *Still Waiting: First-Hand Experiences with Youth Mental Health Services in B.C.*, Victoria: Representative for Children and Youth (April, 2013), 34.

16   Jacobs et al, *The Cost of Mental Health and Substance Abuse Services in Canada: A Report to the Mental Health Commission of Canada*, Edmonton: Institute of Health Economics (June 2010), 15. www.ihe.ca/documents/Cost%20of%20Mental%20Health%20Services%20in%20Canada%20Report%20June%202010.pdf. See also: Yaldaz Sadakova, "Employers Worry About Healthcare Costs, Mental Health," Benefits Canada (September 10, 2013). www.benefitscanada.com/benefits/health-benefits/employers-worry-about-healthcare-costs-and-mental-health-43818.

17   Mental Health Commission of Canada, *Making the Case for Investing in Mental Health in Canada* (2011), 26. www.mentalhealthcommission.ca/English/system/files/private/document/Investing_in_Mental_Health_FINAL_Version_ENG.pdf.

18   Patrick McGorry, "Leadership workshop" video, 36:26, master class for the TRIP Fellowship, Government of Australia, National Health and Medical Research Council, Melbourne (September 9, 2012). www.youtube.com/watch?v=Mi29vrYaLzw.

19   McGorry, Killackey and Yung, "Early Intervention in Psychosis: Concepts, Evidence and Future Directions," *World Psychiatry*, vol. 7, no. 3 (October 2008): 148. www.ncbi.nlm.nih.gov/pmc/articles/PMC2559918.

20   McGorry, Yung and Edwards, "Early Psychosis Services at Orygen Youth Health." www.wpanet.org/uploads/Examplary_Experiences/WPAEarlyPsychosisMasterFinal.pdf.

21   McGorry et al, "EPPIC: an Evolving System of Early Detection and Optimal

Management," *Schizophrenia Bulletin*, vol.22, no. 2 (1996): 305–326. www.ncbi.nlm.
nih.gov/pubmed/8782288.

22   Swaran Singh, "Outcome Measures in Early Psychosis: Relevance of Duration of
Untreated Psychosis," *British Journal of Psychiatry*, 191 (2007): s58–s63. bjp.rcpsych.
org/content/191/50/s58.full. See also Norman, R.M.G. & Malla, A.K., "Duration
of untreated psychosis: a critical examination of the concept and its importance,"
Psychological Medicine, 31 (2001): 381–400.

23   For more information regarding EPPIC, see: Early Psychosis Prevention and
Intervention Centre, "About Us," *EPPIC* website: eppic.org.au/about-us.

24   For examples, see: Canadian Consortium for Early Intervention in Psychosis, "Who
We Are": epicanada.org.

25   Parliament of Australia, "Health and Ageing," Budget 2011–2012, Canberra:
Government of Australia (May 10, 2011), 230.

26   McGorry, Yung and Edwards, "Early Psychosis Services at Orygen Youth Health."
www.wpanet.org/uploads/Examplary_Experiences/WPAEarlyPsychosisMasterFinal.
pdf.

27   Nordentoft et al, "From Research to Practice: How OPUS Treatment was Accepted
and Implemented throughout Denmark," *Early Intervention in Psychiatry* (December
2013): 2. onlinelibrary.wiley.com/doi/10.1111/eip.12108/pdf.

28   Ibid., 5.

29   McCrone et al, "Cost-effectiveness of an Early Intervention Service for People with
Psychosis," *British Journal of Psychiatry*, 196 (2010): 377–382. www.ncbi.nlm.nih.gov/
pubmed/20435964.

30   Hastrup et al, "Cost-effectiveness of an Early Intervention in First-episode Psychosis:
Economic Evaluation of a Randomised Control Trial (the OPUS study)," *British
Journal of Psychiatry*, 202 (2013): 39. www.ncbi.nlm.nih.gov/pubmed/23174515.

31   Wait Time Alliance, *Canadians Still Waiting Too Long for Health Care: Report Card on
Wait Times in Canada*, WTA/ATA (June 2013): 7. www.gov.nl.ca/HaveYouHeard/wta.
pdf.

32   PEPP Montreal, "Prevention and Early-Intervention Program for Psychosis (PEPP—
Montreal)," *Douglas* website (April 24, 2013). www.douglas.qc.ca/section/pepp-
montreal-165?locale=en.

33   Rahul Manchanda and Ross Norman, "PEPP: Prevention and Early Intervention
Program for Psychosis," *PEPP* website. www.pepp.ca/. See also Ashok Malla, Ross
Norman, Terry McLean, Derek Scholten, and Laurel Townsend, "A Canadian
Programme for Early Intervention in Non-Affective Psychotic Disorders," *Aust N Z J
Psychiatry*, vol. 37, 4 (August 2003): 407–413.

34   Mental Health Commission of Canada, *Changing Directions, Changing Lives:
The Mental Health Strategy for Canada*, Calgary: MHCC (2012), 47. strategy.
mentalhealthcommission.ca/pdf/strategy-text-en.pdf.

35   Iyer, Srividya et al, "Early intervention for psychosis, a Canadian perspective," *Journal
of Nervous and Mental Disease* (May 2015).

36   Hayes and Carroll, "Early Intervention Care in the Acute Stroke Patient," *Archives of
Physical Medicine and Rehabilitation*, vol. 67, no. 5 (1986): 319–321. europepmc.org/
abstract/MED/3707317/reload=1;jsessionid=qPik0FI7HRh7abDSJH5o.2. See also:
Rachel Tilley, "Immediate, Aggressive Stroke Intervention Reduces Recurrent Stroke
Risk," *DG News*, June 4, 2007. www.docguide.com/immediate-aggressive-stroke-
intervention-reduces-recurrent-stroke-risk-presented-esc.

37   Anjail Sharrief, "Stroke Symptoms, Prevention, and Background," *University of Texas*,

Department of Neurology website (2014). neurology.uth.tmc.edu/specialty-programs/ut-stroke/knowledge/brain-attack.html.

38 Netcare Union Hospital, "Early Intervention Can Save Stroke Victim," *Health 24* (September 22, 2010). www.health24.com/Medical/Stroke/About-stroke/Early-intervention-::can-save-stroke-victim-20120721.

39 For Dr. Bolte Taylor's story, see: Bolte Taylor, "My Stroke of Insight" video, 18:19, Ted Talk (February 2008). www.ted.com/talks/jill_bolte_taylor_s_powerful_stroke_of_insight?language=en.

40 Power to End Stroke, *Stroke Warning Signs.* powertoendstroke.org/pdf/stroke-warning-signs.pdf.

41 National Institute for Health and Care Excellence, "NICE guidelines [CG68]," *Stroke: Diagnosis and Initial Management of Acute stroke and Transient Ischaemic Attack (TIA)*, London (July 2008), 14.

42 Heart and Stroke Foundation, "Statistics," *Heart and Stroke Foundation* website (2014). www.heartandstroke.com/site/?c=ikIQLcMWJtE&b=3483991#references.

43 Public Health Agency of Canada, *Tracking Heart Disease and Stroke in Canada*, Ottawa (2011), 3. www.phac-aspc.gc.ca/cd-mc/cvd-mcv/sh-fs-2011/pdf/StrokeHighlights_EN.pdf.

44 Nova Scotia Health, "Stroke Care in Canada – How Are We Doing?," *Cardiovascular Health Nova Scotia Bulletin*, vol. 6, no. 2 (Fall 2011).

45 Heart and Stroke Foundation press release, October 6, 2014.

46 Ibid.

47 Canadian Stroke Network, *The Quality of Stroke Care in Canada* (2011), 53. www.canadianstrokenetwork.ca/wp-content/uploads/2011/06/QoSC-EN1.pdf.

48 Deloitte Access Economics, *The Economic Impact of Stroke in Australia, a report prepared for the National Stroke Foundation*, Sydney: Doloitte (2013). www.deloitteacceseconomics.com.au/uploads/File/Stroke%20Report%2014%20Mar%2013.pdf.

49 Luengo-Fernandez, Gray and Rothwell, "Effect of Urgent Treatment for Transient Ischaemic Attack and Minor Stroke on Disability and Hospital Costs (EXPRESS study): A Prospective Population-based Sequential Comparison," *Lancet, Neurology*, vol. 8, no. 3 (March 2009): 235-24. www.ncbi.nlm.nih.gov/pubmed/19200786.

50 Liz Moench and Claude Wischik, "A New Era in Alzheimer's Research," *Journal for Clinical Studies*, vol. 4, no. 6 (2012): 24.

51 Alzheimer Society of Canada, *Rising Tide: The Impact of Dementia on Canadian Society*, Toronto: Alzheimer Society (2010), 17. www.alzheimer.ca/~/media/Files/national/Advocacy/ASC_Rising_Tide_Full_Report_e.pdf.

52 Ibid, 27.

53 Ibid, 37.

54 Chris I. Ardern and Michael Rotundi, "The Role of Physical Activity in the Prevention and Management of Alzheimer's Disease —Implications for Ontario," *Knowledge Synthesis Report*, prepared for the Ontario Brain Institute (February, 2013): 2. www.alzheimer.ca/on/~/media/Files/on/Media%20Releases/2013/OBI%20Report%20March%208%202013.ashx.

55 Rolland, van Kan and Vallas, "Physical Activity and Alzheimer's Disease: From Prevention to Therapeutic Perspectives," *JAMDA* (July 2008): 390–405. www.udel.edu/PT/PT%20Clinical%20Services/journalclub/noajc/08_09/Nov08/Physical%20Activity%20and%20Alzheimer's%20disease.pdf.

56 Alzheimer Society of Canada, *Rising Tide: The Impact of Dementia on Canadian Society*, Toronto: Alzheimer Society (2010), 29. www.alzheimer.ca/~/media/Files/national/Advocacy/ASC_Rising_Tide_Full_Report_e.pdf.

57 Alzheimer's Association, *How is Alzheimer's Disease Diagnosed?* www.alz.org/texascapital/documents/How_is_AD_Diagnosed.pdf.

58 Ibid.

59 Maribeth Bersani, "Why Fall Prevention Could Save Our Health-Care System," *Senior Living* (November/December 2012): 54–56. www.alfapublications.org/alfapublications/20121112#pg56.

60 Scott, Wagar and Elliott, *Falls & Related Injuries Among Older Canadians: Fall-Related Hospitalizations & Prevention Initiatives*, prepared on behalf of the Public Health Agency of Canada, Division of Aging and Seniors, Victoria: Victoria Scott Consulting (2010): 4. www.hiphealth.ca/media/research_cemfia_phac_epi_and_inventor_20100610.pdf

61 Isabel Teotonio, "Why Falling is a Downward Spiral to Death," *Toronto Star*, November 18, 2011. www.thestar.com/life/2011/11/18/why_falling_is_a_downward_spiral_to_death.html.

62 Ibid.

63 Tom Slear, "6 Simple Ways to Prevent a Hip Fracture," *AARP The Magazine* (November 2011). www.aarp.org/health/conditions-treatments/info-10-2011/prevent-hip-fracture.html (language of six titles slightly adapted for context).

64 Kaiser Permanente, "Elderly Women Who Break a Hip at Increased Risk of Dying Within a Year," *Kaiser Permanente* press release, Portland, Oregon (September 26, 2011). share.kaiserpermanente.org/article/elderly-women-who-break-a-hip-at-increased-risk-of-dying-within-a-year.

65 The Economic Burden of Injury in Ontario, SMARTRISK, For Ministry of Health Long-Term Care in partnership with Ministry of Health Promotion (Ontario), 2006 (Toronto), page 47. www.parachutecanada.org/downloads/research/reports/EBI2006-Ont-Final.pdf.

66 Division of Aging and Seniors, *Report on seniors' falls in Canada*. Public Health Agency of Canada, Ottawa (2005). publications.gc.ca/collections/Collection/HP25-1-2005E.pdf.

67 Jeffrey Simpson, *Chronic Condition: Why Canada's Health-care System Needs to be Dragged into the 21st Century*, Toronto: Penguin (2012).

68 Ibid, 261.

CHAPTER 7: PROACTIVE POVERTY REDUCTION

1 Statistics Canada, "Low income cut-offs," *Statistics Canada Catalogue no. 13-551-XIB*, Ottawa (December 1999). www5.statcan.gc.ca/bsolc/olc-cel/olc-cel?catno=13-551-xib&lang=eng.

2 Statistics Canada, "Low Income Lines, 2010-2011," *Income Research Paper Series, Statistics Canada Catalogue no. 75F0002M–no.002*, Ottawa (June 2012). www.statcan.gc.ca/pub/75f0002m/75f0002m2012002-eng.pdf.

3 See, for example, Christopher Sarlo, *Poverty: Where do we draw the line?*, Fraser Institute (November 2013).

4 Ibid, 10.

5 Statistics Canada, "Persons in Low Income After Tax," *Statistics Canada Catalogue no. 75-202-X, CANSIM table 202–0802*, Ottawa (June 27, 2013). www.statcan.gc.ca/tables-tableaux/sum-som/l01/cst01/famil19e-eng.htm.

6   James Struthers, "The Great Depression," *The Canadian Encyclopedia*, ed. Davida Aronovitch, Toronto: Historica (October 2013). www.thecanadianencyclopedia.com/en/article/great-depression.

7   Ibid.

8   Citizens for Public Justice, *Poverty Trends Scorecard: Canada 2012*. www.cpj.ca/files/docs/poverty-trends-scorecard.pdf. See also: Richard Shillington, "Poverty – A Short History," Tristat Resources. www.shillington.ca/poverty/Poverty_a_short_history.pdf.

9   Attributed to Ronald Reagan, 1980 Presidential Campaign.

10   Newfoundland's two-parent, two-child category rose slightly above LICO in 2012. See: Anne Tweddle, Ken Battle and Sherri Torjman, *Welfare in Canada 2012*, Ottawa: Caledon Institute for Social Policy (December, 2013), 47. www.caledoninst.org/Publications/PDF/1031ENG.pdf.

11   Ibid, 46.

12   Ibid, 50.

13   Quebec, "Table 5.7: Clientele de l'aide sociale, 2005–2009," *Comparaisons Interprovinciales*, Quebec: Institut de la Statistique du Quebec (October 26, 2010), reproduced in Gilles Seguin, "Welfare Dependency in Canada: National Statistics," *Canadian Social Research Links*. www.canadiansocialresearch.net/stats.htm#welfare.

14   This estimate is based on the following calculation: In 2009, the average Canadian family size was three people. See Statistics Canada, "Census families, number and average size," Statistics Canada Catalogue no. 91-213-X, Ottawa), September 19, 2007. www.statcan.gc.ca/tables-tableaux/sum-som/l01/cst01/famil40-eng.htm. There were 16.8 million working people in Canada in 2009 (see: www.statcan.gc.ca/pub/75-001-x/75-001-x2010104-eng.pdf). If, conservatively, one-quarter of the 1.2 million working poor families were children, the percentage of working adults who are poor is the quotient obtained by dividing 900,000 by 16.8 million, or 5 per cent. See also Employment and Social Development Canada Financial Security: *Low Income Incidence* report at www4.hrsdc.gc.ca/.3ndic.1t.4r@-eng.jsp?iid=23#M_8. (Last modified August 18, 2014.).

15   An extensive study by Helene Breton on New Brunswick social assistance data in 2013 found that the average applicant for welfare had already been on assistance more than twice in a seven-year period: correspondence between the author and the Department of Social Development, March 24, 2014.

16   Sheena Starky, "Scaling the Welfare Wall: Earned Income Tax Credits in Brief," *Parliamentary Information and Reserve Service, PRB 05-98E*, Ottawa: Library of Parliament (March 31, 2006): 1. www.parl.gc.ca/Content/LOP/researchpublications/prb0598-e.html.

17   New Brunswick, "The New Brunswick Economic and Social Inclusion Corporation," *Overcoming Poverty Together*, Fredericton, New Brunswick (2009).

18   Anne Tweddle, Ken Battle & Sherri Torjman, "Welfare in Canada 2012," Ottawa: Caledon Institute for Social Policy (December, 2013), 57. www.caledoninst.org/Publications/PDF/1031ENG.pdf.

19   Douglas Clement, "Interview with James Heckman," *Banking and Policy Issues Magazine: The Region* (June 2005).

20   Douglas Clement, "Interview with James Heckman," *Banking and Policy Issues Magazine: The Region* (June 2005).

21   Ibid.

22   Ibid.

23   Ramey et al., "Persistent Effects of Early Childhood Education on High-Risk Children and Their Mothers," *Applied Developmental Science*, vol. 4, no. 1 (2000): 11.

24   Douglas Clement, "Interview with James Heckman," *Banking and Policy Issues Magazine: The Region* (June 2005).

25   James Heckman, "The Heckman Equation," *Heckman* website: www.heckmanequation.org/heckman-equation.

26   James Heckman and Dimitriy V. Masterov, "The Productivity Argument for Investing in Young Children," *Invest in Kids Working Group Committee for Economic Development* (October 4, 2004), 8. jenni.uchicago.edu/Invest/FILES/dugger_2004-12-02_dvm.pdf. The dollar return has been calculated by others up to $13 for every dollar spent. See: Leslie J. Calman and Linda Tarr-Whelan, *Early Childhood Education for All: A Wise Investment* in recommendations arising from The Economic Impacts of Child Care and Early Education: Financing Solutions for the Future, a conference sponsored by Legal Momentum's Family Initiative and the MIT Workplace Center (2005): 2. web.mit.edu/workplacecenter/docs/Full%20Report.pdf.

27   See Dylan Matthews, "James Heckman: In Early Childhood Education, 'Quality Really Matters,'" *Washington Post Wonkblog*, February 14, 2013. www.washingtonpost.com/blogs/wonkblog/wp/2013/02/14/james-heckman-in-early-childhood-education-quality-really-matters.

28   Brendan Greely, "The Heckman Equation: Early childhood Education Benefits All," *Bloomberg Businessweek*, January 16, 2014. www.businessweek.com/articles/2014-01-16/the-heckman-equation-early-childhood-education-benefits-all.

29   Quebec, Lucien Bouchard, "Government of Québec Communiqué, January 23, 1997," translation by Jocelyne Tougas. www.famille-enfance.gouv.qc.ca/5_communique/19_communique.html. Cited in Jocelyne Tougas, *Reforming Québec's early childhood care and education: The first five years*, Occasional Paper 17 for Childcare Resource & Research Unit, Toronto: Centre for Urban & Community Studies (March 2002), 1. www.childcarecanada.org/sites/default/files/op17ENG.pdf.

30   Ibid.

31   Fortin, Godbout and St-Cerny, "Impact of Quebec's Universal Low Fee Childcare Program on Female Labour Force Participation, Domestic Income and Government Budgets," Chaire de recherche en fiscalité et finances publiques Working Paper 2012/02, University of Sherbrooke (May 2012): 1.

32   In November 2014, the new Quebec Liberal government announced a reform of the child-care program to modulate the price of a child-care space based on family income. See, for example, *Metro* news, "Fees set to rise for Quebec's cherished $7 daycare program," November 20, 2014. metronews.ca/news/canada/1218806/fees-set-to-rise-for-quebecs-cherished-7-daycare-program.

33   For number of spaces, see: Quebec, Director General of Educational Childcare Services, "Creation de places en service de garde," *Ministry of the Family* website: www.mfa.gouv.qc.ca/fr/services-de-garde/portrait/places/Pages/. And to compare with Quebec demographics, see: Institut de la Statistique du Quebec, *Le bilan demographique du Qubec*, 2013 ed., Quebec (December 2013), 21. www.stat.gouv.qc.ca/statistiques/population-demographie/bilan2013.pdf#page=21.

34   New Brunswick's 2009 poverty reduction plan, Overcoming Poverty Together, set 50 per cent of children aged two to five years as the provincial child-care target. See: New Brunswick, *Overcoming Poverty Together: The New Brunswick Economic and Social Inclusion Plan*, Fredericton (November 2009).

35   Christa Japel, "Early Childhood Education Programs in Quebec: How Can We Raise the Bar?," Presentation for the Atkinson Centre for Society and Childhood Development, University of Toronto, Toronto (May 3, 2010). www.oise.utoronto.ca/atkinson/UserFiles/File/Events/2010-05-03%20-%20Measuring%20Quality/MeasuringQuality_Japel.pdf.

36   Fortin, Godbout and St-Cerny, "Impact of Quebec's Universal Low Fee Childcare
      Program on Female Labour Force Participation, Domestic Income and Government
      Budgets," Chaire de recherche en fiscalité et finances publiques Working Paper
      2012/02, University of Sherbrooke (May 2012), 6.

37   Ibid, 14.

38   Ibid, 7–8.

39   Haeck, Lefebvre and Merrigan, "Quebec's Universal Childcare: The Long-term
      Impacts on Parental Labour Supply and Child Development," *Département des sciences
      économiques, UQÀM* (September, 2012): 19. www.er.uqam.ca/nobel/r15504/pdf/
      ChidcareV55.pdf. By contrast, Fortin, suggests that by 2008 there was no difference in
      net benefit between mothers with differing levels of education. See Fortin, Godbout &
      St-Cerny, 13.

40   Fortin, Godbout and St-Cerny, "Impact of Quebec's Universal Low Fee
      Childcare Program on Female Labour Force Participation, Domestic Income
      and Government Budgets," Chaire de recherche en fiscalité et finances publiques
      Working Paper 2012/02, University of Sherbrooke (May 2012), 27. (Provincial
      government only.).

41   For more on the long-term returns of investing in early childhood education, see also
      Craig Alexander & Dina Ignjatovic, "Early Childhood Education Has Widespread and
      Long-lasting Benefits," *Special Report*, TD Economics (November 27, 2012). www.
      td.com/document/PDF/economics/special/di1112_EarlyChildhoodEducation.pdf.

42   See the *You Bet I Care!* report, which shows that steady increases in the wages and
      benefits of early learning staff are slowing driving up quality measures in the early
      learning sector in Quebec. Doherty et al, *You Bet I Care! A Canada-Wide Study on
      Wages, Working Conditions and Practices in Child Care Centres*, Guelph, Ontario:
      Centre for Families, Work and Well-being, University of Guelph (2000).

43   James Heckman and Dimitriy V. Masterov, "The Productivity Argument for
      Investing in Young Children," *Invest in Kids Working Group Committee for
      Economic Development* (October 4, 2004): 4. jenni.uchicago.edu/Invest/FILES/
      dugger_2004-12-02_dvm.pdf.

44   New Brunswick, *Overcoming Poverty Together: The New Brunswick Economic and
      Social Inclusion Plan*, Fredericton (November 2009). www2.gnb.ca/content/dam/gnb/
      Departments/esic/pdf/Plan-e.pdf.

45   "Poverty Reduction Strategies with Targets and Timelines Matter," *Daily Bread Food
      Bank* blog, August 9, 2013. www.dailybread.ca/poverty-reduction-strategies-with-
      targets-and-timelines.

CHAPTER 8: HOMES FOR HOMELESS PEOPLE

1   For detailed explanations of the rise of homelessness, see: Forchuck et al., "From
      Psychiatric Wards to the Streets and Shelters," *Journal of Psychiatric and Mental Health
      Nursing*, vol. 13, no. 3 (2006): 301–308; and Gordon Laird, *Shelter — Homelessness
      in a growth economy: Canada's 21st century paradox*, Calgary: Sheldon Chumir
      Foundation for Ethics in Leadership (2007), 6. www.chumirethicsfoundation.ca/files/
      pdf/SHELTER.pdf.

2   City of Toronto, *Taking Responsibility for Homelessness: An Action Plan for Toronto*,
      Report of the Mayor's Homelessness Action Task Force (Toronto, 1999), 14. www.
      toronto.ca/pdf/homeless_action.pdf. (Also known as the "Golden Report.").

3   City of Calgary, *Results of the 2006 Count of Homeless Persons in Calgary*, Calgary:
      Community & Neighbourhood Services, Policy & Planning Division (May 10, 2006),
      45. intraspec.ca/2006_calgary_homeless_count.pdf.

4   Hwang et al., "Mortality Among Residents of Shelters, Rooming Houses, and Hotels in Canada: 11-year Follow-up Study," *BMJ*, 339 (October 26, 2009): b4036. www.bmj.com/content/339/bmj.b4036.

5   See: Stephen W. Hwang, "Mortality Among Men Using Homeless Shelters in Toronto, Ontario," *JAMA*, vol. 283, no. 16 (April 26, 2000): 2152–2157; and Angela M. Cheung & Stephen W. Hwang, "Risk of Death Among Homeless Women: A Cohort Study and Review of the Literature," *CMAJ*, vol. 170, no. 8 (April 13, 2004): 1243–1247. For a quick reference on homelessness health facts, see: Centre for Research on Inner City Health, "Homelessness & Health," *CRICH Inner City Health Primer Series*, St. Michael's Hospital website: www.stmichaelshospital.com/pdf/crich/homelessness-health.pdf.

6   Employment and Social Development Canada, "Housing — Homeless Shelters and Beds," *HRSDC* website: www4.hrsdc.gc.ca/.3ndic.1t.4r@-eng.jsp?iid=44.

7   Jesse Thistle, *Homelessness is Only One Piece of My Puzzle: Implications for Policy and Practice*, Toronto: The Homeless Hub Press (2014).

8   See the website of the Canadian Observatory on Homelessness: www.homelesshub.ca/CanadianObservatoryOnHomelessness.

9   Ibid, 7.

10 Malcolm Gladwell, "Million-Dollar Murray," *The New Yorker*, February 13, 2006, 96–107. Also available at gladwell.com/million-dollar-murray.

11 Ibid.

12 Interview of Dr. Sam Tsemberis by the author, December 2, 2013.

13 Tsemberis and Stefancic, "The role of an espiritista in the treatment of a homeless, mentally ill Hispanic man," *Psychiatric Services*, vol. 51, no. 12 (2000): 1572–74.

14 Interview of Dr. Sam Tsemberis by the author, December 2, 2013.

15 Tsemberis, Gulcar, and Nakae, "Housing First, Consumer Choice, and Harm Reduction for Homeless Individuals with a Dual Diagnosis." *American Journal of Public Health*, vol. 94, no. 4 (April 2004), 651–656.

16 Tsemberis, Kent and Respress, "Housing Stability and Recovery Among chronically Homeless Persons with Co-Occurring Disorders in Washington, DC," *American Journal of Public Health*, vol. 102, no. 1 (January 2012): 13–16. pathwaystohousing.org/wp-content/uploads/2013/03/Housing-Stability-and-Recovery-Among-Chronically-Homeless-Persons-with-Co-Occuring-Disorders-in-Washington-DC.pdf.

17 Ibid, 15.

18 Latimer et al. *At Home/Chez Soi Project: Montreal Site Final Report*, Calgary: Mental Health Commission of Canada (2014), 16. www.mentalhealthcommission.ca/English/document/32101/montreal-final-report-homechez-soi-project.

19 Goering et al. *National At Home/Chez Soi Final Report*, Calgary: Mental Health Commission of Canada (2014), 17. www.mentalhealthcommission.ca/English/system/files/private/document/mhcc_at_home_report_national_cross-site_eng_2.pdf.

20 Ibid, 23.

21 Ibid, 22.

22 Fiona Scott, "Nikihk Housing First/Homeward Trust," *Housing First Case Studies*, Edmonton: Housing First in Canada (2013), 1. www.homelesshub.ca/ResourceFiles/Documents/Edmonton_HFCaseStudyFinal.pdf.

23 Edmonton Homeless Commission, "A Chance to Live Again: Charles' Story," *Homeless Hub* website, video, 3:25, Edmonton (2011). www.homelesshub.ca/resource/chance-live-again-charles-story.

24   Sam Tsemberis, *Housing First: The Pathways Model to End Homelessness for People with Mental Illness and Addiction.* Hazelden: Center City, MN.
25   Charlie Fidelman, "'Housing First' Approach to Homelessness in Jeopardy as Program Ends," *Montreal Gazette*, March 17, 2014. www.montrealgazette.com/news/Housing+first+approach+homelessness+jeopardy+program+ends/9238156/story.html.

CHAPTER 9: A BETTER SOCIAL SAFETY NET FOR CANADA

1   *YouTube* video: www.youtube.com/watch?v=Ij1yDpfZI8Q.
2   James Hughes, "Why We Can't Afford Poverty," *Literary Review of Canada* (April 2012). reviewcanada.ca/magazine/2012/04/why-we-cant-afford-poverty.
3   National Institutes of Health, *Fogarty International Center* website. www.fic.nih.gov/News/Events/implementation-science/Pages/faqs.aspx.
4   CBC Manitoba, January 30, 2013. *CBC News* website. www.cbc.ca/manitoba/features/phoenixsinclair.
5   Paul Meier, "The Biggest Public Health Experiment Ever: The 1954 Field Trial of the Salk Poliomyelitis Vaccine," in *Statistics: A Guide to the Biological and Health Sciences,* ed. Tanur et al, San Francisco: Holden-Day (1977), 89.
6   Rohini Busur, "Immunization," *Ontario Ministry of Health and Long-Term Care* website (April 9, 2014). www.health.gov.on.ca/en/pro/programs/ecfa/action/primary/prev_immunize.aspx.
7   Rutty et al., "Conquering the Crippler: Canada and the Eradication of Polio," *Canadian Journal of Public Health,* special insert (2005), I–17. www.healthheritageresearch.com/ConqueringtheCrippler_e.pdf.
8   Thompson and Tebbens, "Retrospective Cost-Effectiveness Analyses for Polio Vaccination in the United States," *Risk Analysis,* vol. 26, no. 6 (December 2006), 1423–1440. www.ncbi.nlm.nih.gov/pubmed/17184390.
9   This somewhat contrarian idea of a crisis having potentially long-terms benefits was summed up ably by Tim Brodhead, former President of Canada's leading philanthropic foundation, The J.W. McConnell Family Foundation, in the title of a short book he penned in 2010 entitled *On Not Letting a Crisis Go to Waste: An Innovation Agenda for Canada's Community Sector,* Toronto: The J.W. McConnell Family Foundation (February 2010). www.mcconnellfoundation.ca/kh/resources/publication/on-not-letting-a-crisis-go-to-waste-an-innovation-agenda-for-can.
10   Edmonton Committee to End Homelessness, *A Place to Call Home: Edmonton's 10 Year Plan to End Homelessness* (January 2009). homelesscommission.org/index.php/overview.
11   See: Monique Bégin, "A country of perpetual pilot projects," *CMAJ,* vol. 180, no. 12 (June 2009): 1185.
12   The Conference Board of Canada, "Innovation," *The Conference Board of Canada* website (2014). www.conferenceboard.ca/hcp/details/innovation.aspx.
13   James Hughes, "A Bipartisan Approach to Aboriginal Affairs," *Policy Options* (June 2013). policyoptions.irpp.org/issues/nudge/a-bipartisan-approach-to-aboriginal-affairs.
14   Ibid.
15   Amy Dockser Marcus, "Lessons From AIDS/HIV Advocacy Efforts," *The Wall Street Journal* (June 16, 2011). blogs.wsj.com/health/2011/06/16/lessons-from-aidshiv-advocacy-efforts.
16   Loren Grush, "'Dallas Buyers Club' highlights patient advocacy's role during HIV/AIDS epidemic," *Fox News* website (November 19, 2013). www.foxnews.com/health/2013/11/19/dallas-buyers-club-highlights-patient-advocacys-role-during-hivaids-epidemic.

17   Road Safety Canada Consulting, *Road Safety in Canada*, Ottawa: PHAC (March 2011), 6. www.tc.gc.ca/eng/motorvehiclesafety/tp-tp15145-1201.htm.

18   Ibid.

19   Canadian Paediatric Society, "Bicycle helmet use in Canada: The need for legislation to reduce the risk of head injury," in Paediatrics & Child Health, 18(9) (2013): 475–8. www.cps.ca/documents/position/bike-helmets-to-reduce-risk-of-head-injury.

20   Ibid.

21   Jeffrey Brubacher et al., "Reduction in Fatalities, Ambulance Calls, and Hospital Admissions for Road Trauma After Implementation of New Traffic Laws," *American Journal of Public Health* (October 2014). www.ncbi.nlm.nih.gov/pmc/articles/PMC4167084.

22   See Ontario's Asset Management plan called Building Together: www.moi.gov.on.ca/pdf/en/Municipal%20Strategy_English_Web.pdf.

23   *The Institute of Asset Management* website. theiam.org/what-asset-management.

24   See, for example, Wildlife-Vehicle Collisions in Canada: A Review of the Literature and a Compendium of Existing Data Sources, Traffic Injury Research Foundation (April 2012). tirf.ca/publications/PDF_publications/WildlifeVehicle_Collision_Deliverable1_Eng_6.pdf.

25   Colin Carrie, Parliamentary Secretary to the Minister of the Environment (December 9, 2014). openparliament.ca/debates/2014/12/9/colin-carrie-3/only.

26   Canada is not the only jurisdiction improving its road-safety outcomes through early intervention. The Catalonia region in Spain has seen a remarkable amelioration in its results. A recent report said this on the topic: "During the 10 years from 2001 to 2010, there were 26 063 fewer road traffic collisions with victims than expected, 2909 fewer deaths (i.e. a 57% reduction), 25 444 fewer hospitalizations, 1 141 727 fewer days of temporary sick leave and 69 321 fewer working years of permanent sick leave. The estimated cost savings for all cost categories are shown in Table 3. The total cost savings were 17 967 396 369: 97% of this figure comprised indirect costs, including the cost of productivity lost due to institutionalization, sick leave for the injured and their careers and death. Overall, 63% of the direct cost savings comprised specialized health-care costs, 15% comprised the cost of adapting to disability and 8.1%, hospital care costs." See: Anna García-Altés, Josep M. Suelves and Eneko Barbería, "Cost savings associated with 10 years of road safety policies in Catalonia, Spain," *World Health Organization Bulletin* (December 7, 2012). www.who.int/bulletin/volumes/91/1/12-110072/en.

SELECTED BIBLIOGRAPHY

CHAPTER 2: THE DEVELOPMENT OF CANADA'S SOCIAL SAFETY NET

Books

Berton, Pierre. *The Great Depression: 1929–1939*. Toronto: Anchor, 1990.

Guest, Dennis. *The Emergence of Social Security in Canada*, 3rd edition. Vancouver: UBC Press, 2003.

Moscovitch, Allan. *The Welfare State in Canada*. Waterloo: Wilfred Laurier University Press, 1983.

Moscovitch, Allan and Glenn Drover. "Social Expenditures and the Welfare State: The Canadian Experience in Historical Perspective." In *The Benevolent State: The Growth of Welfare in Canada*, edited by Moscovitch and Albert. Toronto: Garamond, 1987.

Piven, Frances Fox and Richard A. Cloward. *Regulating the Poor: the Functions of Public Welfare*. New York: Pantheon, 1971.

Raphael, Dennis. *Poverty and Policy in Canada: Implications for Health and Quality of Life*. Toronto: Canadian Scholars, 2007.

Periodicals

Coutts, Jim. "Windows of opportunity: social reform under Lester B. Pearson." *Policy Options*, November 2003. policyoptions.irpp.org/issues/corporate-governance/windows-of-opportunity-social-reform-under-lester-b-pearson.

Hughes, James. "Homelessness: Closing the Gap between Capacity and Performance." *Policy Options*, December 2012. mowatcentre.ca/wp-content/uploads/publications/56_homelessness.pdf.

Maioni, Antonia. "New century, new risks: the Marsh Report and the post-war welfare state in Canada." *Policy Options*, August 2004. policyoptions.irpp.org/issues/social-policy-in-the-21st-century/new-century-new-risks-the-marsh-report-and-the-post-war-welfare-state-in-canada.

Government Reports

Canada. Department of Finance. "Putting Transfers on a Long-Term, Sustainable Growth Track." Canada's Economic Action Plan. actionplan.gc.ca/en/initiative/putting-transfers-long-term-sustainable-growth.

Canada. Office of the Parliamentary Budget Officer. *Renewing the Canada Health Transfer: Implications for Federal and Provincial Territorial Sustainability*. Ottawa, January 12, 2012.

"Restoring Fiscal Balance in Canada: Focusing on Priorities. Canada's New Government Turning a New Leaf." *Budget 2006*. Ottawa: Public Works and Government Services Canada, 2006. www.fin.gc.ca/budget06/pdf/fp2006e.pdf.

Quebec. Loi sur l'aide aux personnes et aux familles, LRQ 2005 c. A-13.1.1, ss. 74–78.

Statistics Canada. "Population, urban and rural, by province and territory (Canada)." *2011 Census of Population*. Ottawa, February 4, 2011. www.statcan.gc.ca/tables-tableaux/sum-som/l01/cst01/demo62a-eng.htm.

CHAPTER 3: SAFER CHILD PROTECTION
Books

Doolan, Mike. "The Family Group Conference: Changing the Face of Child Welfare." In *Diversity and Community Development: An intercultural approach,* ed. Clarijs, Guidikova and Malmberg, 57-68. Amsterdam: SWP, 2011. www.coe.int/t/dg4/cultureheritage/culture/Cities/Publication/BookCoE08-MikeDoolan.pdf.

Graff, Linda. *Better Safe . . . Risk management in Volunteer Programs and Community Service.* Hamilton: Linda Graff and Associates, 2003.

Maurice, Catherine. *Let Me Hear Your Voice: A Family's Triumph Over Autism.* New York: Fawcett, 1993.

McRae, Allan and Howard Zehr. *The Little Book of Family Group Conferences New Zealand Style.* Intercourse, PA: Good Books, 2004.

Periodicals

Anda, Robert F. and Vincent J. Felitti. "Origins and Essence of the Study," *ACE Reporter,* vol. 1, no. 1 (April, 2003):1-4. acestudy.org/yahoo_site_admin/assets/docs/ARV1N1.127150541.pdf.

Blatchford, Christie. "Allegation of 'altered' report in Phoenix Sinclair fiasco only a tiny part of CFS bureaucracy's sheer ineptitude." *National Post,* December 10, 2012. fullcomment.nationalpost.com/2012/12/10/christie-blatchford-allegation-of-altered-report-in-phoenix-sinclair-fiasco-only-a-tiny-part-of-cfs-bureaucracys-sheer-ineptitude.

CBC News Manitoba, "Phoenix Sinclair's Death 'Unimaginable,' Says RCMP Officer." April 18, 2013. www.cbc.ca/news/canada/manitoba/story/2013/04/18/mb-phoenix-sinclair-inquiry-rcmp-investigator.html.

Clewett, Slowley and Glover. *Making plans: Using Family Group Conferencing to reduce the impact of caring on young people.* Barkingside, Essex, UK: Barnardos, 2010. www.barnardos.org.uk/making_plans_12634.pdf.

Doyle, Joseph J. "Child Protection and Child Outcomes: Measuring the Effects of Foster Care." *The American Economic Review,* vol. 97, no. 5 (December 2007): 1583–1610. www.mit.edu/~jjdoyle/fostercare_aer.pdf.

Huntsman, Leone. *Family group conferencing in a child welfare context — A review of the literature.* Ashfield, NSW, Australia: Centre for Parenting & Research, July 2006. www.community.nsw.gov.au/docswr/_assets/main/documents/research_family_conferencing.pdf.

King, Colin B., Alan W. Leschied, Paul C. Whitehead, Debbie Chiodo and Dermot Hurley. *Child Protection Legislation in Ontario: Past, Present and Future?* London: Western, 2003. www.edu.uwo.ca/cas/pdf/child%20welfare%20legislation%20aug%20technical%20report.pdf.

Mandell, Sullivan and Meredith. *Family Group Conferencing Final Evaluation Report.* Toronto: Etobicoke Family Group Conferencing Project, 2001.

Nelson, Charles A., Charles H. Zeanah, Nathan A. Fox, Peter J. Marshall, Anna T. Smyke and Donald Guthrie. "Cognitive Recovery in Socially Deprived Young Children: The Bucharest Early Intervention Project." *Science,* vol. 318, no. 5858 (December 21, 2007): 1937–1940. www.sciencemag.org/content/318/5858/1937.short.

OACAS. Child Welfare Report 2012. Toronto: Ontario Association of Children's Aid Societies, 2012. www.oacas.org/newsroom/releases/12childwelfarereport.pdf.

Turner, James. "CFS response in Phoenix Sinclair case 'deeply disturbing': Inquiry told." *Toronto Sun,* January 16, 2013. www.torontosun.com/2013/01/16/cfs-response-in-phoenix-sinclair-case-deeply-disturbing-inquiry-told.

Wolfe, David A., Betty Edwards, Ian Manion and Caherine Koverola. "Early intervention for parents at risk of child abuse and neglect: A preliminary investigation." *Journal of Consulting and Clinical Psychology,* vol. 56, no. 1 (February 1988): 40–47. psycnet.apa.org/journals/ccp/56/1/40.

Wulczyn, Hislop and Goerge. *Foster Care Dynamics 1983–1998.* Chicago: Chapin Hall Centre for Children, 2000. www.chapinhall.org/sites/default/files/old_reports/75.pdf.

Government Reports

Australian Institute of Health and Welfare. "Child protection Australia 2011-2012." *Child Welfare Series,* no. 55, cat. no. CWS 43, Canberra: AIHW, 2013. www.aihw.gov.au/WorkArea/DownloadAsset.aspx?id=60129542752

Hughes, Ted. *The Legacy of Phoenix Sinclair: Achieving the Best for All Our Children,* vol. II. Winnipeg: Commission of Inquiry into the Circumstances Surrounding the Death of Phoenix Sinclair, December 2013.

New Brunswick. Ombudsman and Child & Youth Advocate. *Broken Promises: Juli-Anna's Story.* Fredericton, January 2008. www.gnb.ca/0073/PDF/JASPFinalReport-e.pdf.

Ontario. Commission to Promote Sustainable Child Welfare. *Realizing a Sustainable Child Welfare System in Ontario — Final Report.* Toronto, September 2012. www.children.gov.on.ca/htdocs/English/documents/topics/childrensaid/commission/2012sept-Final_report.pdf.

Public Health Agency of Canada. *Canadian Incidence Study of Reported Child Abuse and Neglect — 2008: Major Findings.* Ottawa, 2008. cwrp.ca/sites/default/files/publications/en/CIS-2008-rprt-eng.pdf.

Richard, Bernard and Shirley Smallwood. *Staying Connected: A Report of the Task Force on a Centre of Excellence for Children and Youth with Complex Needs.* Fredericton: Office of the Ombudsman and Child and Youth Advocate, March 2011. www.gnb.ca/0073/Child-YouthAdvocate/centre_excellence/PDF/staying_connected-e.pdf.

United Kingdom. House of Commons Justice Committee. "Mediation and other mean of preventing cases reaching court." *Sixth Report Operation of the Family Courts,* June 28, 2011. www.frg.org.uk/fgcs-quotes-from-official-documents.

U.S. Department of Health & Human Services, Administration for Children and Families, Administration on Children, Youth and Families, Children's Bureau. *Child Maltreatment 2012.* Washington, 2013. www.acf.hhs.gov/programs/cb/research-data-technology/statistics-research/child-maltreatment.

Websites

Centers for Disease Control. "Injury Prevention & Control: Adverse Childhood Experiences (ACE) Study Major Findings." CDC website, May 13, 2014. www.cdc.gov/ace/findings.htm.

Doolan, Mike and Marie Connolly. "Care and protection: Capturing the essence of our practice." *New Zealand Child, Youth and Family.* www.practicecentre.cyf.govt.nz/

practice-vision/care-and-protection/capturing-the-essence-of-our-practice/care-and-protection-capturing-the-essence-of-our-practice.html.

CHAPTER 4: ADDRESSING AUTISM
Books
American Psychiatric Association. "Autism Spectrum Disorder Factsheet." *Diagnostic and Statistics Manual 5*. Arlington, VA: American Psychiatric Publishing, 2013. www.dsm5.org/Documents/Autism%20Spectrum%20Disorder%20Fact%20Sheet.pdf.

Grandin, Temple. *Thinking in Pictures*. New York: Vintage, 1995.

   The Autistic Brain. New York: Mariner Books, 2013.

Lee, Linda. *Autism Physician Handbook,* Canadian Edition. Bothwell, ON: Autism Canada Foundation, 2011. www.autismcanada.org.

Solomon, Andrew. *Far From the Tree*. New York: Scribner, 2012.

Periodicals
Bronstein, Scott & Jesse Joseph. "Therapy to Change 'Feminine' Boy Created a Troubled Man, Family Says." *CNN*, June 10, 2011. www.cnn.com/2011/US/06/07/sissy.boy.experiment/index.html.

Dawson, Rogers, Munson, Smith, winter, Greenson, Donaldson and Varley. "Randomized, Controlled Trial of an Intervention for Toddlers with Autism: The Early Start Denver Model." *Pediatrics* 125 (2010): e17–e23. www.ncbi.nlm.nih.gov/pubmed/19948568.

Fox, Margalit. "O. Ivar Lovaas, Pioneer in Developing Therapies for Autism, Dies at 83." *New York Times,* August 22, 2010. www.nytimes.com/2010/08/23/health/23lovaas.html.

Gay, Peter. "Per Ardua: review of *The Empty Fortress* by Bruno Bettelheim." *New Yorker,* May 18, 1968, 160–172. Cited in Mary Beth Walsh. "Top 10 Reasons Children with Autism Deserve ABA." *Behavior Analysis in Practice,* 4(1) (Summer 2011): 72–79.

Grant, Allan. "Screams, Slaps and Love: A surprising, shocking treatment helps far-gone mental cripples." *Life Magazine,* vol. 58, no. 18 (May 7, 1965): 90A-105.

Jacobson, John W., James A. Mulick & Gina Green. "Cost-Benefit Estimates for Early Intensive Behavioral Invention for Young Children with Autism — General Model and Single State Case." *Behavioral Interventions,* 13 (1998): 201–226. www.hca.wa.gov/hta/meetingmaterials/supplemental_information_submitted_cited_evidence_articles_draft_findings_decision_091611.pdf.

Kanner, Leo. "Problems of Nosology and Psychodynamics of Early Infantile Autism." *American Journal of Orthopsychiatry* 19 (1949): 416–426.

Lavelle, Tara A., Milton C. Weinstein, Joseph P. Newhouse, Kerim Munir, Karen A. Kuhlthau and Lisa A Prosser. "Economic Burden of Childhood Autism Spectrum Disorders." *Pediatrics,* vol. 133, no. 3 (March 2014): e520–e529.

Lovaas, O. Ivar. "Behavioral Treatment and Normal Educational and Intellectual Functioning in Young Autistic Children." *Journal of Consulting and Clinical Psychology,* vol. 55, no. 1 (1987): 3–9.

Montreal Gazette. "Editorial: Children with autism need better services." July 17, 2014, A12.

Motiwala, Sanober, Shamali Gupta, Meredith B. Lilly, Wendy J. Unger and Peter C. Coyte.

"The Cost-Effectiveness of Expanding Intensive Behavioural Intervention to All Autistic Children in Ontario." *Health Policy*, vol. 1, no. 2 (January 2006): 135–151.

Rekers, George A. and O. Ivar Lovaas. "Behavioral Treatment of Deviant Sex-Role Behaviors in a Male Child." *Journal of Applied Behavior Analysis*, vol. 7, no. 2 (Summer 1974): 173–190.

Sea, Scott. "Planet Autism." Salon, September 27, 2003. www.salon.com/2003/09/27/autism_8.

Sinclair, Jim. "Don't Mourn for Us." *Our Voice*, vol. 1, no.3 (1993).

Smith, Tristram and Svein Eikeseth. "O. Ivar Lovaas: Pioneer of Applied Behavior Analysis and Intervention for Children with Autism." *Journal of Autism and Developmental Disorders*, 41 (2011): 375-378. www.ncbi.nlm.nih.gov/pubmed/21153872.

Wang, Shirley S. "How Autism Can Help You Land a Job." *Wall Street Journal*, March 27, 2014. online.wsj.com/news/articles/SB10001424052702304418404579465561364868556.

Warren, McPheeters, Sathe, Foss-Feig, Glasser and Veenstra-Vanderweele. "A systematic Review of Early Intensive Intervention for Autism Spectrum Disorders." *Pediatrics* 127 (2011): e1303–1311. www.ncbi.nlm.nih.gov/pubmed/21464190.

Government Reports

Auton v. British Columbia, 2004, SCC 78.

Canadian Institutes for Health Research. "Harper Government Announces New Research Chair Dedicated to Autism Treatment and Care." *Government of Canada Press Release.* Toronto, November 5, 2012. www.cihr-irsc.gc.ca/e/46009.html.

Lysyk, Bonnie. "Children Waiting Too Long for Access to Autism Programs, Auditor General Says." Office of the Auditor General of Ontario press release. Toronto, December 10, 2013. www.auditor.on.ca/en/news_en/13_newsreleases/2013news_3.01autism.pdf

Ontario. Ministry of Child and Youth Services. *The Autism Parent Resource Kit.* Toronto, 2014. www.children.gov.on.ca/htdocs/English/documents/topics/specialneeds/autism/aprk/Autism_Parent_Resource_Kit.pdf.

Websites

Buckmann, Steve. "Lovaas Revisited: Should We Have Ever Left?" *BBB Autism Support Network* website, May 9, 2002. www.bbbautism.com/pdf/article_40_Lovaas_revisited.pdf.

Centers for Disease Control and Prevention, "Autism Spectrum Disorder (ASD): Data & Statistics." *CDC* website (March 24, 2014). www.cdc.gov/ncbddd/autism/data.html.

Coplan, James. "Behaviorism, Part 3: O. Ivar Lovaas and ABA." *Psychology Today Blog,* September 26, 2010. www.psychologytoday.com/blog/making-sense-autistic-spectrum-disorders/201009/023-behaviorism-part-3-o-ivar-lovaas-and-aba.

Engle, Shirlee. "*Agony of Autism*." *Global News* video, 3:20, October 7, 2013. globalnews.ca/news/887710/autism-treatment-means-months-on-wait-lists-relocation-for-some-canadian-families.

Rzucidlo, Susan F. "Welcome to Beirut" *BBB Autism Support Network* website. www.bbbautism.com/beginners_beirut.htm.

CHAPTER 5: MORE PEACEFUL SCHOOLS

Books

Gordon, Mary. *Roots of Empathy: Changing the World Child by Child.* Toronto: Thomas Allen, 2005.

Virk, Manjit. *Reena: A Father's Story.* Victoria: Heritage House, 2008.

Periodicals

Caledon Institute. "Roots of Empathy." *Community Stories.* Ottawa: Caledon Institute for Social Policy, June 1999.

Canadian Council on Learning. "Bullying in Canada: How intimidation affects learning." *Lessons in Learning,* March 20, 2008. www.ccl-cca.ca/pdfs/LessonsInLearning/Mar-20-08-Bullying-in-Canad.pdf.

Dugan, Emily. "More than a million British youngsters being bullied online every day." *Independent,* October 2, 2013. www.independent.co.uk/news/uk/home-news/more-than-a-million-british-youngsters-being-bullied-online-every-day-8852097.html.

Durlak, Weissberg, Dymnicki, Taylor and Schellinger. "The Impact of Enhancing Students' Social and Emotional Learning: A Meta-Analysis of School-Based Universal Interventions." *Child Development,* vol. 82, no. 1 (January/February 2011): 405–432.

Embry, Dennis D. "Behavioral Vaccines and Evidence Based Kernels: Non-Pharmaceutical Approaches for the Prevention of Mental, Emotional and Behavioral Disorders." *Psychiatric Clinics of North America,* vol. 34, no. 1 (March 2011): 1–34. www.ncbi.nlm.nih.gov/pmc/articles/PMC3064963.

Guyn Cooper Research Associates. *Issue Brief: Social and Emotional Learning in Canada,* commissioned by Carthy Foundation and Max Bell Foundation, August 2013. www.maxbell.org/sites/default/files/SELIssueBrief.pdf

Renzetti, Elizabeth. "Mary Gordon on Teaching Empathy: Start Young and Start With a Baby." *Globe and Mail,* May 5, 2013. www.theglobeandmail.com/life/parenting/mary-gordon-on-teaching-empathy-start-young-and-start-with-a-baby/article11715642.

Sanders, Carol. "Baby Steps Toward Empathy." *Winnipeg Free Press,* May 23, 2013. www.winnipegfreepress.com/local/baby-steps-toward-empathy-208618751.html.

Santos, Robert G., Mariette J. Chartier, Jeanne C. Whalen, Dan Chateau and Leanne Boyd. "Effectiveness of School Based Violence Prevention for Children and Youth." *Healthcare Quarterly,* vol. 14, Special Issue (April 2011): 80–90.

Taber, Jane & Caroline Alphonso. "Report on Rehtaeh Parsons' Suicide Says her Absence from School was a Missed Red Flag." *Globe and Mail,* June 14, 2013. www.theglobeandmail.com/news/national/report-into-rehtaeh-parsons-suicide-calls-for-review-of-halifax-hospital/article12559456.

Times Colonist. "The Killing of Reena Virk, 10 Years Later." *CanWest,* November 15, 2007. www.canada.com/story.html?id=8db62748-78ed-4109-a6f1-04fdc94774f3.

UNICEF. "Stuck in the Middle: Canadian Companion." *Child Well-Being in Rich Countries: A comparative overview,* 2013. www.unicef.ca/sites/default/files/imce_uploads/DISCOVER/OUR%20WORK/ADVOCACY/DOMESTIC/POLICY%20ADVOCACY/DOCS/unicef_rc_11_canadian_companion.pdf

Government Reports

Butler, Martha and Melissa Pang. *Current Issues in Mental Health in Canada: Child and Youth Mental Health*. Library of Parliament Research Publications, Legal and Social Affairs Division, March 5, 2014. www.parl.gc.ca/Content/LOP/ResearchPublications/2014-13-e.htm.

Preamble to Bill 13, An Act to Amend the Education Act with Respect to Bullying and Other Matters, 1st sess., 40th Legislature, 2012, SO. ontla.on.ca/web/bills/bills_detail.do?locale=en&BillID=2549.

R v. Ellard, 2009, SCC 27.

Yau, Maria. *Parenting and Family Literacy Centres: Making a Difference beyond Early School Readiness*. Toronto: Toronto District School Board, October 2009.

Websites

Ashoka Canada. "Fellows: Mary Gordon" Ashoka Canada website, 2002. canada.ashoka.org/fellow/mary-gordon.

Bornstein, David. "Fighting Bullying with Babies" *New York Times* Opinionator blog, November 8, 2010. opinionator.blogs.nytimes.com/2010/11/08/fighting-bullying-with-babies/?_r=0.

Canadian Institutes for Health Research. "Canadian Bullying Statistics." CIHR website, September 28, 2012. www.cihr-irsc.gc.ca/e/45838.html.

Community Matters. "Suspension Loss and Cost Calculator." Community Matters website. community-matters.org/programs-and-services/calculator.

The Council of Ministers of Education Canada. "Education in Canada: an Overview." CMEC website: www.cmec.ca/299/Education-in-Canada-An-Overview/index.html#01.

Phillips, Rick. "The Financial Costs of Bullying, Violence, and Vandalism." National Association of Secondary School Principals website, April 2010. www.nassp.org/Content.aspx?topic=The_Financial_Costs_of_Bullying_Violence_and_Vandalism. Healthier Health Care

CHAPTER 6: HEALTHIER HEALTH CARE

Books

Simpson, Jeffrey. *Chronic Condition: Why Canada's Health-care System Needs to be Dragged into the 21st Century*. Toronto: Penguin, 2012.

Periodicals

Alzheimer Society of Canada. *Rising Tide: The Impact of Dementia on Canadian Society*. Toronto: Alzheimer Society, 2010. www.alzheimer.ca/~/media/Files/national/Advocacy/ASC_Rising_Tide_Full_Report_e.pdf.

Ardern, Chris I. and Michael Rotundi. "The Role of Physical Activity in the Prevention and Management of Alzheimer's Disease —Implications for Ontario." *Knowledge Synthesis Report*, prepared for the Ontario Brain Institute, February, 2013. www.alzheimer.ca/on/~/media/Files/on/Media%20Releases/2013/OBI%20Report%20March%208%20 2013.ashx.

Bersani, Maribeth. "Why Fall Prevention Could Save Our Health-Care System."

Senior Living (November/December 2012): 54–56. www.alfapublications.org/alfapublications/20121112#pg56.

Canadian Institute for Health Information. *National Health Expenditure Trends 1975 to 2012*. Ottawa: CIHI, 2012. https://secure.cihi.ca/free_products/NHEXTrendsReport2012EN.pdf.

Canadian Stroke Network, *The Quality of Stroke Care in Canada*, 2011. www.canadianstrokenetwork.ca/wp-content/uploads/2011/06/QoSC-EN1.pdf.

Deloitte Access Economics. *The Economic Impact of Stroke in Australia*. A report prepared for the National Stroke Foundation, Sydney: Deloitte, 2013. www.deloitteaccesseconomics.com.au/uploads/File/Stroke%20Report%2014%20Mar%2013.pdf.

Dodge, David A. "Chronic Healthcare Spending Disease: A Macro Diagnosis and Prognosis." *The Health Papers* no. 327, Toronto: C. D. Howe Institute, April 2011. www.cdhowe.org/pdf/Commentary_327.pdf.

Hastrup, Kronborg, Bertelsen, Jeppesen, Jorgensen, Petersen, Thorup, Simonsen and Nordentoft. "Cost-effectiveness of an Early Intervention in First-episode Psychosis: Economic Evaluation of a Randomised Control Trial (the OPUS study)." *British Journal of Psychiatry*, 202 (2013): 35-41. www.ncbi.nlm.nih.gov/pubmed/23174515.

Hayes and Carroll. "Early Intervention Care in the Acute Stroke Patient." *Archives of Physical Medicine and Rehabilitation*, vol. 67, no. 5 (1986): 319–321. europepmc.org/abstract/MED/3707317/reload=1;jsessionid=qPik0FI7HRh7abDSJH5o.2.

Luengo-Fernandez, Gray and Rothwell. "Effect of Urgent Treatment for Transient Ischaemic Attack and Minor Stroke on Disability and Hospital Costs (EXPRESS study): A Prospective Population-based Sequential Comparison." *Lancet*, Neurology, vol. 8, no. 3 (March 2009): 235-243. www.ncbi.nlm.nih.gov/pubmed/19200786.

MacDonald-Dupuis, Natasha. "The Problem with Canada's Unsustainable Health System." *Huffington Post*, February 11, 2014. www.huffingtonpost.ca/natasha-macdonalddupuis/the-future-of-canadian-healthcare_b_4429892.html.

McCrone, Craig, Power and Garety. "Cost-effectiveness of an Early Intervention Service for People with Psychosis." *British Journal of Psychiatry*, 196 (2010): 377–382. www.ncbi.nlm.nih.gov/pubmed/20435964.

McGorry, Edwards, Mihalopoulos, Harrigan and Jackson. "EPPIC: an Evolving System of Early Detection and Optimal Management." *Schizophrenia Bulletin*, vol.22, no. 2 (1996): 305–326. www.ncbi.nlm.nih.gov/pubmed/8782288.

McGorry, Killackey and Yung. "Early Intervention in Psychosis: Concepts, Evidence and Future Directions." *World Psychiatry*, vol. 7, no. 3 (October 2008): 148-156. www.ncbi.nlm.nih.gov/pmc/articles/PMC2559918.

Moench, Liz and Claude Wischik. "A New Era in Alzheimer's Research." *Journal for Clinical Studies*, vol. 4, no. 6 (2012).

National Institute for Health and Care Excellence. "NICE guidelines [CG68]." *Stroke: Diagnosis and Initial Management of Acute stroke and Transient Ischaemic Attack (TIA)*, London, July 2008.

Nordentoft, Merete, Marianne Melau, Tina Iversen, Lone Petersen, Pia Jeppesen, Anne Thorup, Mette Bertelsen, Carsten Rygaard Hjorthoj, Lene Halling Hastrup and Per Jorgensen. "From research to Practice: How OPUS Treatment was Accepted and

Implemented throughout Denmark." *Early Intervention in Psychiatry* (December 2013): 1-7. onlinelibrary.wiley.com/doi/10.1111/eip.12108/pdf.

Nova Scotia Health. "Stroke Care in Canada – How Are We Doing?" *Cardiovascular Health Nova Scotia Bulletin* vol. 6, no. 2 (Fall 2011).

Rolland, van Kan and Vallas. "Physical Activity and Alzheimer's Disease: From Prevention to Therapeutic Perspectives." *JAMDA* (July 2008): 390–405. www.udel.edu/PT/PT%20 Clinical%20Services/journalclub/noajc/08_09/Nov08/Physical%20Activity%20and%20 Alzheimer's%20disease.pdf.

Scott, Wagar and Elliott. *Falls & Related Injuries Among Older Canadians: Fall-Related Hospitalizations & Prevention Initiatives.* Prepared on behalf of the Public Health Agency of Canada, Division of Aging and Seniors Victoria: Victoria Scott Consulting, 2010. www.hiphealth.ca/media/research_cemfia_phac_epi_and_inventor_20100610. pdf.

Singh, Swaran. "Outcome Measures in Early Psychosis: Relevance of Duration of Untreated Psychosis." *British Journal of Psychiatry*, 191 (2007): s58–s63. bjp.rcpsych.org/ content/191/50/s58.full.

Slear, Tom. "6 Simple Ways to Prevent a Hip Fracture." *AARP The Magazine*, November 2011. www.aarp.org/health/conditions-treatments/info-10-2011/prevent-hip-fracture. html.

Teotonio, Isabel. "Why Falling is a Downward Spiral to Death." *Toronto Star*, November 18, 2011. www.thestar.com/life/2011/11/18/why_falling_is_a_downward_spiral_to_death. html.

Wait Time Alliance. *Canadians Still Waiting Too Long for Health Care: Report Card on Wait Times in Canada.* WTA/ATA, June 2013. www.gov.nl.ca/HaveYouHeard/wta.pdf.

Government Reports

Division of Aging and Seniors. *Report on seniors' falls in Canada.* Public Health Agency of Canada. Ottawa, 2005. Publications.gc.ca/collections/Collection/HP25-1-2005E.pdf

Jacobs, Dewa, Lesage, Vasiliadis, Escober, Mulvale and Yim. *The Cost of Mental Health and Substance Abuse Services in Canada: A Report to the Mental Health Commission of Canada.* Edmonton: Institute of Health Economics, June 2010. www.ihe.ca/documents/ Cost%20of%20Mental%20Health%20Services%20in%20Canada%20Report%20 June%202010.pdf.

Mental Health Commission of Canada, *Changing Directions, Changing Lives: The Mental Health Strategy for Canada.* Calgary: MHCC, 2012. strategy.mentalhealthcommission. ca/pdf/strategy-text-en.pdf.

Making the Case for Investing in Mental Health in Canada. 2011. www. mentalhealthcommission.ca/English/system/files/private/document/Investing_in_ Mental_Health_FINAL_Version_ENG.pdf.

Ontario. *Program Policy Framework for Early Intervention in Psychosis.* Toronto: Queen's Printer for Ontario, December, 2004. www.health.gov.on.ca/en/common/ministry/ publications/reports/mentalhealth/psychosis.pdf

Parliament of Australia. "Health and Ageing." *Budget 2011–2012.* Canberra: Government of Australia, May 10, 2011.

Public Health Agency of Canada. *Tracking Heart Disease and Stroke in Canada.* Ottawa, 2011. www.phac-aspc.gc.ca/cd-mc/cvd-mcv/sh-fs-2011/pdf/StrokeHighlights_EN.pdf.

Turpel-Lafond, Mary Ellen. *Still Waiting: First-Hand Experiences with Youth Mental Health Services in BC.* Victoria: Representative for Children and Youth, April, 2013. www.rcybc.ca/sites/default/files/documents/pdf/reports_publications/still_waiting.pdf

Websites
Alzheimer's Association. *How is Alzheimer's Disease Diagnosed?* www.alz.org/texascapital/documents/How_is_AD_Diagnosed.pdf.

Bilerman, Maureen. "Connect the Dots." video, 15:02, March 25, 2011. www.youtube.com/watch?v=FkESo1U1Rao.

Canadian Nurses Association. "Mental Health," *Nurseone* website, 2013. www.nurseone.ca/Default.aspx?portlet=StaticHtmlViewerPortlet&stmd=False&plang=1&ptdi=492.

Centre for Addition and Mental Health. "Statistics on Mental Illness and Addictions." *CAMH* website, 2012. www.camh.ca/en/hospital/about_camh/newsroom/for_reporters/Pages/addictionmentalhealthstatistics.aspx.

CHAPTER 7: PROACTIVE POVERTY REDUCTION
Periodicals
Citizens for Public Justice. *Poverty Trends Scorecard: Canada 2012.* www.cpj.ca/files/docs/poverty-trends-scorecard.pdf.

Clement, Douglas. "Interview with James Heckman." *Banking and Policy Issues Magazine: The Region,* June 2005.

Fortin, Godbout and St-Cerny. "Impact of Quebec's Universal Low Fee Childcare Program on Female Labour Force Participation, Domestic Income and Government Budgets." Chaire de recherche en fiscalité et finances publiques Working Paper 2012/02, University of Sherbrooke, May 2012.

Haeck, Lefebvre and Merrigan. "Quebec's Universal Childcare: The Long-term Impacts on Parental Labour Supply and Child Development." *Université de Quebec à Montreal,* September, 2012. www.er.uqam.ca/nobel/r15504/pdf/ChidcareV55.pdf.

Heckman, James and Dimitriy V. Masterov. "The Productivity Argument for Investing in Young Children." *Invest in Kids Working Group Committee for Economic Development,* October 4, 2004. jenni.uchicago.edu/Invest/FILES/dugger_2004-12-02_dvm.pdf.

Greely, Brendan. "The Heckman Equation: Early childhood Education Benefits All." *Bloomberg Businessweek,* January 16, 2014. www.businessweek.com/articles/2014-01-16/the-heckman-equation-early-childhood-education-benefits-all.

Ramey, Campbell, Burchinal, Skinner, Gardner and Ramey. "Persistent Effects of Early Childhood Education on High-Risk Children and Their Mothers." *Applied Developmental Science,* vol. 4, no. 1 (2000): 2-14.

Sarlo, Christopher. *Poverty: Where do we draw the line?* Fraser Institute, November 2013.

Tougas, Jocelyne. *Reforming Québec's early childhood care and education: The first five years.* Occasional Paper 17 for Childcare Resource & Research Unit, Toronto: Centre for Urban & Community Studies, March 2002. www.childcarecanada.org/sites/default/files/op17ENG.pdf.

Tweddle, Anne, Ken Battle and Sherri Torjman. *Welfare in Canada 2012.* Ottawa: Caledon Institute for Social Policy, December 2013. www.caledoninst.org/Publications/PDF/1031ENG.pdf.

Government Reports

New Brunswick. "The New Brunswick Economic and Social Inclusion Corporation." *Overcoming Poverty Together*. Fredericton, New Brunswick, 2009.

Quebec. "Table 5.7: Clientele de l'aide sociale, 2005–2009." *Comparaisons Interprovinciales*. Quebec: Institut de la Statistique du Quebec, October 26, 2010.

Starky, Sheena. "Scaling the Welfare Wall: Earned Income Tax Credits in Brief." *Parliamentary Information and Reserve Service, PRB 05-98E*. Ottawa: Library of Parliament, March 31, 2006. www.parl.gc.ca/Content/LOP/researchpublications/prb0598-e.html.

Statistics Canada. "Low income cut-offs." *Statistics Canada Catalogue no. 13-551-XIB*. Ottawa, December 1999. www5.statcan.gc.ca/bsolc/olc-cel/olc-cel?catno=13-551-xib&lang=eng

"Low Income Lines, 2010-2011." *Income Research Paper Series, Statistics Canada Catalogue no. 75F0002M–no.002*. Ottawa, June 2012. www.statcan.gc.ca/pub/75f0002m/75f0002m2012002-eng.pdf.

"Persons in Low Income After Tax." *Statistics Canada Catalogue no. 75-202-X, CANSIM table 202–0802*. Ottawa, June 27, 2013. www.statcan.gc.ca/tables-tableaux/sum-som/l01/cst01/famil19e-eng.htm.

Websites

Daily Bread. "Poverty Reduction Strategies with Targets and Timelines Matter." Daily Bread Food Bank blog, August 9, 2013. www.dailybread.ca/poverty-reduction-strategies-with-targets-and-timelines.

Heckman, James. "The Heckman Equation." Heckman website. www.heckmanequation.org/heckman-equation.

Struthers, James. "The Great Depression." *The Canadian Encyclopedia*, ed. Davida Aronovitch. Toronto: Historica, October 2013. www.thecanadianencyclopedia.com/en/article/great-depression.

CHAPTER 8: HOMES FOR HOMELESS PEOPLE

Books

Tsemberis, Sam. *Housing First: The Pathways Model to End Homelessness for People with Mental Illness and Addiction*. Center City, MN: Hazelden, 2010.

Periodicals

Fidelman, Charlie. "'Housing First' Approach to Homelessness in Jeopardy as Program Ends." *Montreal Gazette*, March 17, 2014. www.montrealgazette.com/news/Housing+first+approach+homelessness+jeopardy+program+ends/9238156/story.html

Gladwell, Malcolm. "Million-Dollar Murray." *New Yorker*, February 13, 2006, 96–107.

Hwang, Stephen, Russell Wilkins, Michael Tjepkema, Patricia J. O'Campo and James R. Dunn. "Mortality Among Residents of Shelters, Rooming Houses, and Hotels in Canada: 11-year Follow-up Study." *BMJ*, 339 (October 26, 2009). www.bmj.com/content/339/bmj.b4036.

Scott, Fiona. "Nikihk Housing First/Homeward Trust." *Housing First Case Studies*, Edmonton: Housing First in Canada, 2013. www.homelesshub.ca/ResourceFiles/Documents/Edmonton_HFCaseStudyFinal.pdf.

Thistle, Jesse. *Homelessness is Only One Piece of My Puzzle: Implications for Policy and Practice.* Toronto: The Homeless Hub Press, 2014.

Tsemberis, Sam, Douglas Kent and Christy Respress. "Housing Stability and Recovery Among chronically Homeless Persons with Co-Occurring Disorders in Washington, DC." *American Journal of Public Health,* vol. 102, no. 1 (January 2012): 13–16. pathwaystohousing.org/wp-content/uploads/2013/03/Housing-Stability-and-Recovery-Among-Chronically-Homeless-Persons-with-Co-Occuring-Disorders-in-Washington-DC.pdf.

Government Reports

City of Calgary. *Results of the 2006 Count of Homeless Persons in Calgary.* Calgary: Community & Neighbourhood Services, Policy & Planning Division, May 10, 2006. intraspec.ca/2006_calgary_homeless_count.pdf.

City of Toronto. *Taking Responsibility for Homelessness: An Action Plan for Toronto.* Report of the Mayor's Homelessness Action Task Force, Toronto, 1999. www.toronto.ca/pdf/homeless_action.pdf.

Goering, Paula, Scott Veldhulzen, Aimee Watson, Carol Adair, Brianna Kopp, Eric Latimer, Tim Aubry, Geoff Nelson, Eric MacNaughton, David Steiner, Daniel Rabouin, Angela Ly and Guido Powell. *National At Home/Chez Soi Final Report.* Calgary: Mental Health Commission of Canada, 2014. www.mentalhealthcommission.ca/English/system/files/private/document/mhcc_at_home_report_national_cross-site_eng_2.pdf.

Latimer, Eric, Daniel Rabouin, Christian Methot, Christopher McAll, Angela Ly, Henri Dorvil, Anne Crocker, Laurence Roy, Daniel Poremski, Jean-Pierre Bonin, Marie-Josee Fleury and Erika Braithwaite. *At Home/Chez Soi Project: Montreal Site Final Report.* Calgary: Mental Health Commission of Canada, 2014. www.mentalhealthcommission. ca/English/document/32101/montreal-final-report-homechez-soi-project.

Websites

Edmonton Homeless Commission. "A Chance to Live Again: Charles' Story." *Homeless Hub* website, video, 3:25, Edmonton, 2011. www.homelesshub.ca/resource/chance-live-again-charles-story.

Employment and Social Development Canada. "Housing — Homeless Shelters and Beds." *HRSDC* website. www4.hrsdc.gc.ca/.3ndic.1t.4r@-eng.jsp?iid=44.

INDEX